Microcosms

Also by Claudio Magris in English translation

DANUBE

A DIFFERENT SEA

Claudio Magris

Microcosms

Translated from the Italian by
Iain Halliday

THE HARVILL PRESS
LONDON

First published with the title *Microcosmi* in 1997 by
Garzanti editore, Milan

First published in Great Britain in 1999
by The Harvill Press,
2 Aztec Row,
Berners Road,
London N1 0PW

www.harvill-press.com

1 3 5 7 9 8 6 4 2

Copyright © Garzanti editore s.p.a., 1997

Translation copyright © Iain Halliday, 1999

Claudio Magris asserts the moral right to be
identified as the author of this work

A CIP catalogue record for this book
is available from the British Library

ISBN 1 86046 618 4

Designed and typeset in Galliard at
Libanus Press, Marlborough, Wiltshire

Printed and bound in Great Britain by Butler & Tanner Ltd
at Selwood Printing, Burgess Hill

To Marisa

Even though all the World by now is known, many being the books brought before us which furnish general descriptions of it, when dealing with a single Province a dutiful description is not easily found . . .

AMEDEO GROSSI,
Architect, Geometer, and Surveyor, 1791

A man determines upon the task of portraying the world. As the years pass he peoples a space with pictures of provinces, kingdoms, mountains, bays, ships, islands, fishes, dwellings, instruments, stars, horses and people. Shortly before he dies he discovers that the patient labyrinth of lines traces the image of his own face.

JORGE LUIS BORGES

TABLE OF CONTENTS

Microcosms

Caffè San Marco

The masks are up on high, above the black inlaid wood counter that comes from the renowned Cante workshop – at least it was renowned once. But prestigious signs and fame last a bit longer at the Caffè San Marco, even the fame of those whose only qualification for being remembered is the simple, but not inconsiderable, fact of having spent years at those little marble tables with their cast-iron legs that flow into a pedestal sitting on lion's paws, and of having given forth every now and then on the correct pressure of the beer and on the universe.

The San Marco is a Noah's Ark, where there's room for everyone – no one takes precedence, no one is excluded – for every couple seeking shelter in a downpour and even for the partnerless. By the way, I've never understood that story about the Flood, observed Mr Schönhut, *shammes* at the Israelite Temple next door, so someone recalls. The rain was beating against the window-panes and in the Public Garden at the end of Via Battisti, immediately to the left as one leaves the café, the big trees were crashing, soaked heavy in the wind under an iron sky. If it was for the sins of the world, said Mr Schönhut, He might as well have finished it off for once and all, why destroy and then start again? It's not as if things have gone better since; in fact there's been no end to blood and cruelty, and yet never another Flood . . . nay, there was even the promise not to eradicate life on earth.

Why so much pity for the murderers who came after and none for those before, all drowned like rats? He should have known that together with every being – man or beast – evil entered the Ark. Those He felt compassion for carried within themselves the germs of every epidemic of hatred and pain that was destined to break out right up to the end of time. And Mr Schönhut drank his beer, confident that the thing went no further, because he could say whatever he liked about the God of Israel, he could really let rip, because it all remained in the family. But for others to say these things would have been indelicate and even, at certain times, strictly below the belt.

Your hair's a mess, go to the washroom and sort yourself out, that's what the old lady said to him, severely, on that occasion. To reach the washroom whoever is in the room where the bar is has to pass under the masks, beneath those eyes that peep out avid and frightened. The background behind those faces is black, a darkness in which Carnival lights up scarlet lips and cheeks; a nose projects lewd and curving, the very hook for grabbing someone standing below and dragging him or her into that dark party. It seems that those faces, or some of them, are the work of Pietro Lucano – the attribution is uncertain, despite the work of scholars who devote as much patience to the San Marco as to an ancient temple. In the church of the Sacred Heart – not too far from the café, just across the Public Garden or back up Via Marconi which runs alongside the park – this painter was responsible for the two angels in the apse that hold up two circles of fire: two acrobats of eternity whose skirts the artist was obliged by the Jesuit fathers to lengthen almost to their ankles, so as not to leave their androgynous legs in view.

There are those who maintain that some of the masks are by Timmel, who was perhaps responsible for a mask (female) in another room. The

hypothesis barely holds up: undoubtedly at that time, towards the
end of the Thirties, this "favourite of the road", as the roving painter
loved to define himself – he was born in Vienna and came to Trieste to
achieve his self-destruction – undoubtedly contrived some bearable
evenings in the cafés to provide himself an hour or two's distraction
from the impossibility of living. He would make a gift of some little
masterpiece to one or other of the rich Trieste merchants, patrons for
whom an artist was a dancing bear and could be tripped up, in exchange
for generous drinking sessions that allowed him to get through an
evening and which gradually sent him to the bottom altogether.

Timmel reinvented his own childhood. The meningitis he'd had as
a child, he recounted, was a base lie invented by his parents out of
their hatred for him, and while his mind and his memory were unravel-
ling he was writing the *Magic Notebook*, a mixture of striking lyrical
epiphanies and verbal sob-stuff verging on aphasia and rendered crazed
by amnesia, which he called nostalgia – the desire to cancel out all
the names and signs that enmesh the individual in the world. The
wayfaring rebel, fated to end his days in the madhouse, was trying
even before reaching that utmost refuge, to escape from the tentacles
of reality by closeting himself in an empty, dizzy inertia, "sitting to
one side idle and uninterested", arms crossed, immobile and content
just to feel himself rotating together with the planet in its vacuum. He
sought passivity and welcomed Fascism, which liberated him from the
weight of responsibility and spared him the frustration of pursuing
liberty without being able to find it, rather it thrust him back into
the submission of infancy: "To achieve beatitude requires absolute
dependence."

The route through the café and its L-shaped structure, even if only
to satisfy what Principal Lunardis could never bring himself to define
as anything other than an impulsion, is not straight. Chessplayers love
the café – it resembles a chessboard and one moves between its tables

like a knight, making a series of right angles and often finding oneself, as in a game of snakes and ladders, back at square one ... back at that table where one had studied for the German literature exam and now, many years later, one wrote or responded to yet another interview about Trieste, its *Mitteleuropa* culture and its decline, while not far away one son is correcting his degree dissertation and another, in the end-room, is playing cards.

People come and go from the café and behind them the doors continue to swing; a slight breath of air makes the stagnant smoke waver. The swinging loses some of its strength each time, a shorter heartbeat. Strips of luminous dust float in the smoke, serpentine coils that unroll slowly, feeble garlands round the necks of the shipwrecked holding on to their tables. The smoke envelops things in a soft and opaque blanket, a cocoon in which the chrysalis would like to shut itself up indefinitely, sparing itself the pain of being a butterfly. But the scribbling pen bursts the cocoon and frees the butterfly, which flutters its wings in fear.

Above the French windows the fruit bowls and the bottles of champagne gleam. A red marbled lampshade is an iridescent jellyfish. Up high the chandeliers glow and sway like moons in water. History states that the San Marco opened on 3 January, 1914 – despite resistance put up by a consortium of Trieste café-owners, who in an attempt to obstruct it turned in vain to the Royal Imperial authorities – and immediately it became a meeting place for irredentist youth and a workshop for the production of false passports for anti-Austrian patriots who wanted to escape to Italy. "Those youngsters had an easy time," grumbled Mr Pichler, ex-Oberleutnant on the Galicia front during the 1916 massacres. "They had great fun with that traffic in cutting and pasting photographs, it was like taking down one of those masks and putting it on, without thinking that those masks can pull you into the darkness and make you disappear, as then happened to many of them and us, in Galicia or on the Carso. . . . and don't let's exaggerate with the famous destruction of the café on 23 May, 1915 by the Austrian pigs . . . yes, the pigs, that's the right name for those desk officers and the scum that came after them – of course it was a terrible business, such a beautiful café all smashed up and broken . . . but Austria, on the whole, was a civilized country. De Frieskene, the governor, even apologised during the war to an irredentist like Silvio Benco for having to keep him under special surveillance, on orders from above. If the Empire existed today everything would still be the same, the world would still be a Caffè San Marco, and don't you think that's something, if you take a look out there?"

The San Marco is a real café – the outskirts of History stamped with the conservative loyalty and the liberal pluralism of its patrons. Those places where just one tribe sets up camp are pseudocafés – never mind whether they are frequented by respectable people, youth most-likely-to, alternative lifestyles or à la page intellectuals. All endogamies are suffocating; colleges too, and university campuses, exclusive clubs, master classes, political meetings and cultural symposia, they are all a negation of life, which is a sea port.

Variety triumphs, vital and florid, at the San Marco. Old long-haul captains, students revising for exams and planning amorous manoeu-vres, chessplayers oblivious to what goes on around them, German tourists curious about the small plaques commemorating small and large literary triumphs whose begetters used to frequent those tables, silent newspaper readers, joyous groups predisposed towards Bavarian beer or *verduzzo* wine, spirited old men inveighing against the iniquity of the times, know-it-all commentators, misunderstood geniuses, the odd imbecile yuppie, corks that pop like a military salute, especially when Doctor Bradaschia, already under suspicion because of miscel-laneous vaunted credits – including his degree – and in trouble with the law, brazenly offers drinks to all within reach, peremptorily instructing the waiter to put it on his account.

"Basically, I was in love with her, but I didn't like her, while she liked me, but she wasn't in love with me," says Mr Palich, born in Lussino, summing up a tormented marital romance. The café is a buzz of voices, a disconnected and uniform choir, apart from a few exclamations at a table of chessplayers, or, in the evening, Mr Plinio's piano – sometimes rock, more often popular music from the years between the wars, *Love is the sweetest thing* ... fate advances stepping to a danceable kitsch.

But what do you mean "for the money"? As if someone like old Weber would let himself be ripped off. In fact she was the one with the money, not he and she knew well enough that he had almost nothing to leave her. For the likes of you and me maybe a little apartment in New York would be a fortune, but for someone like her it wouldn't even register. He wanted to marry her – his cousin Ettore said so too. They hadn't been speaking for almost fifty years because of that business over the family tomb in Gorizia, and anyway when Ettore heard that the old man, who in fact was two years younger than him, had only a few months left to live, he got on the plane and went to see him in New York. Almost before inviting Ettore to sit down he told him there was big news, that he was getting married the following week – yes, because, he said, he'd done almost everything in life except get married, and he didn't want to make his exit without having tried marriage as well. He emphasized marriage, a proper marriage, it was impossible to die without having been married; everyone's capable of living together, even you, which is saying a lot, he added, giving his cousin a glass of Luxardo maraschino. And so, explained Ettore, having crossed the ocean I had to sample that maraschino which used to turn my stomach when I was a young man, in Zara. Anyway, he died peacefully – now that I've filled in the last box in the questionnaire, as he put it – and I have to admit that he wasn't a trial to anybody, not even during the last days, and here was a man who had always been a royal pain ... marriage evidently did him good.

Voices rise, they blend, they fade, one hears them at one's shoulder, moving down to the end of the room, the noise of the undertow. The sound waves drift away like circles of smoke, but somewhere continue in existence. They are always there, the world is full of voices, a new Marconi might be able to invent a device capable of picking them all up, an infinite chatter over which death has no dominion; immortal and immaterial souls are stray ultrasounds in the universe. That's according to Juan Octavio Prenz, who listened to the murmuring at those tables and turned it into a novel in his *Fable of Innocent Honest, the Beheaded*, a grotesque and surreal story that is ravelled and unravelled by voices that are crossed, are superimposed, are separated and are lost.

Prenz was born in Buenos Aires but his roots were in the hinterland of Croatian Istria. He taught in Italian and wrote in Spanish. He taught and wandered in the most diverse countries this side and that side of the ocean. Perhaps he settled in Trieste because the city reminded him of the cemetery of boats and figureheads at Ensenada de Barragán, between Buenos Aires and La Plata, which only lives on now in a slender volume of his poems. He sits in the Caffè San Marco still feeling the gaze of the figureheads on him – worn by wind and water, and dumbstruck at the approach of catastrophes that no one else can see yet. He leafs through the translation of one of his collections. There is a poem dedicated to Diana Teruggi, who was his assistant at the University of Buenos Aires. One day, in the time of the generals, the girl disappeared for ever. Once again poetry speaks of absence, of something or someone who is not here any more. It's not much, a poem. A little card left in an empty place. Poets know this and don't give it too much weight, but they give even less weight to the world that celebrates or ignores them. Prenz pulls his pipe from a pocket, smiles at his two daughters sitting at another table, chats with a Senegalese who's going round the tables selling junk, buys a cigarette lighter from him. Chatting is better than writing. The Senegalese moves on, Prenz sucks on his pipe and makes a start.

It's not bad, filling up sheets of paper under the sniggering masks and amidst the indifference of the people sitting around. That good-natured indifference balances the latent delirium of omnipotence that exists in writing – purporting to sort out the world with a few pieces of paper and to hold forth on life and death. Thus the pen is dipped, willingly or otherwise, into ink diluted with humility and irony. The café is a place for writing. One is alone, with paper and pen and at most two or three books, hanging onto the table like a shipwreck survivor tossed by the waves. A few centimetres of wood separate the sailor from the abyss that might swallow him up, the tiniest flaw and the huge black waters break ruinously, pulling him down. The pen is a lance that wounds and heals; it pierces the floating wood and leaves it to the mercy of the waves, but it also plugs the wood and renders it capable of sailing once again and keeping to a course.

Keep a hold on the wood, fear not – a shipwreck can also be salvation. How does the old story go? Fear knocks at the door, faith opens; there's no one there. But who teaches you to go and open? For some time you've done nothing but close doors, it's become a habit; for a while you hold your breath, but then anxiety grabs your heart again and the instinct is to bolt everything, even the windows, without realizing that this way there's no air and as you suffocate, the migraine batters your temples; eventually all you hear is the sound of your own headache.

Scribble, free the demons, bridle them, often simply presume to ape them. In the San Marco the demons have been relegated up on high, overturning the traditional scenario, because the café, with its floral decor and its Viennese Secessionist style reminds us that it can be alright down here: a waiting room in which it's pleasant to wait, to put off leaving. The manager, Mr Gino, and the waiters, who come to the table with one glass after another – sometimes off their own bat offering, but not to everyone, salmon canapés with a special *prosecco* – are angels of a lower order, but they are trustworthy, enough at any rate to keep an eye on things so that these exiles from the earthly paradise feel at home in this clandestine Eden and no snake tries to tempt them away with false promises.

The café is a Platonic academy, said Hermann Bahr at the beginning of the century – the man who also said that he liked being in Trieste because here he had the impression of being nowhere. Nothing is taught in this academy, but sociability and how to break spells are learned. One may chat, tell stories, but preaching, making political speeches, giving lessons are against the rules. All, at their respective tables, are close to and distant from the person next to them. Love your neighbour as you love yourself, or bear your neighbour's mania for biting his nails just as he endures some habit of yours that is even more unpleasant. At these tables it is not possible to found a school, draw up ranks, mobilize followers and emulators, recruit disciples. In this the place of disenchantment – in which how the show ends is common knowledge but where no one tires of watching nor chafes at the actors' blunders – there is no room for false prophets who seduce those vaguely anxious for a facile and instant redemption, misleading them with empty promises.

Out there, the false Messiahs have an easy time of it, as they drag their followers blinded by mirages of salvation down roads they cannot travel and thus setting them off towards destruction. The prophets of drugs, men who can control their own habit without being overborne by it, seduce helpless disciples into following them on the road along which they will destroy themselves. Someone, in a drawing room, proclaims that revolutions are made with rifles, knowing well that this is an innocuous metaphor while leaving other simple souls to take them literally and end up having to pay the penalty. Among the newspapers on their long sticks an illustrated magazine displays the face of Edie Sedgwick, the beautiful and vulnerable American model who believed in the testament of disorder preached with order and method by that tribal guru Andy Warhol. She let herself be convinced to seek not pleasure, but an indefinable sense of life in those feverish sexual transgressions, those ingenuous group rites and those drugs that led her, with painful banality, to unhappiness and death.

In the San Marco no one has any illusions that the original sin was never committed and that life is virginal and innocent; for this reason it's difficult to pass off anything phoney on its patrons, any ticket to the Promised Land. To write is to know that one is not in the Promised Land and that one will never reach it, but it also means continuing doggedly in that direction, through the wilderness. Sitting in the café, you're on a journey; as in a train, a hotel, on the road, you've got very little with you and you cannot in your vanity grace that nothing with your personal mark, you are nobody. In that familiar anonymity you can dissimulate, rid yourself of the ego as if it were a shell. The world is a cavity of uncertainty into which writing penetrates in obstinate bewilderment. To write, take a break, chat, play at cards; laughter at the next table, a woman's profile, as incontrovertible as Fate, the wine in the glass, time the colour of gold. The hours flow . . . amiable, carefree, almost happy.

The owners and the ex-owners of the café – almost a list of the sovereigns of ancient dynasties. Marco Lovrinovich of Fontane d'Orsera near Parenzo, who started restaurants and wine houses much as others write poems or paint landscapes, opened the café on 3 January, 1914 on the site where The Trifolium Central Dairy had once stood, complete with cowshed. Officially Lovrinovich said he had named it San Marco in his own honour, but he took every opportunity to repeat the image of the Venetian lion, the irredentist Italian symbol even in the decoration on the chairs. Perhaps he was convinced, deep down, that the winged lion was indeed a tribute to his Christian name. You don't reach the age of ninety-four, as he did, without being intimately convinced that the world revolves around you.

And yet some died young and alone among his tables, devastated by the imbalance between their spirit and the world, which was definitely not tailor-made for them: for example that youngster who was always a bit sweaty, the one who went round like a hunted animal; his eyes forever spoke his awareness of being already caught between the tiger's jaws. He used to come every afternoon with so many sheets of paper which he filled one after another and always carried with him, until one day he came no more; he'd thrown himself into the courtyard the previous evening.

The cafés are also a sort of hospice for those whose hearts suffer need and café-owners like Lovrinovich are benefactors too, offering a temporary refuge from the elements, like the founders of shelters for the homeless. And why shouldn't they earn something on the side, even patriotic glory as Lovrinovich did following the devastation of the San Marco and his detention in the Austrian punishment camp in Liebenau, near Graz, where the Austrians sent him because he'd infected both eyes with trachoma to avoid being sent to fight against Italy.

Among the various owners the Stock sisters stand out, minute and relentless. And then there are also memories of a seasoned barwoman with lank blonde hair; they still talk about the occasion when an enormous drunk, to whom she'd denied one final whisky, threatened her with a little demonstration, lifting up the coffee machine – a massive weight – from the bar as if it were a twig, then dropping it with an almighty clang. Meanwhile the nearest regulars, among them one intently writing at his usual table, alas all too close to the bar, looked around in fright, hoping that someone else might nobly step forward to prevent the slaughter of the woman. Finally the enraged giant lunged at her just as she pulled a hatchet from a drawer and jumped at him, ready to plant the thing in his neck and the dutiful customer, who had stood up from his paper-strewn table and had been moving as slowly as possible towards the furious colossus, was only too glad to tackle the barwoman, firmly seizing and twisting the wrist that brandished the hatchet, and thus saving the impulsive youngster's life.

It might be one of the few places in Trieste where there are plenty of young people to be seen, but the San Marco suggests a rejuvenated existence, it seems to imprint on the faces of its habitués the same seasoned and decorous robustness that a little restoration periodically confers on the decor. The Triestine Mephistopheles is a prudent, bourgeois demon; his rejuvenation of the friezes when they are about to crumble away and of the walls cracked like a wrinkled face, provides a noble, vigorous middle age – not the tempestuous and improvident youth of a Faust that spells Marguerite's ruin, but the charm of the teacher who in bed concludes the seduction of the pupil begun austerely in the classroom, a little misunderstanding soon to be dissipated.

So far as the structure is concerned, the rejuvenative function tends to be carried out by the Generali insurance company, which restores to the cafés and public buildings of Trieste the ordered and mysterious beauty of the florid bourgeois city it once was. The portrait of the writer who spends much of his life at the San Marco, receiving mail and visitors who ask him about that flourishing, lost city that once was – a city which he only knows about second-hand, through other people's gossip and nostalgia – the portrait, by Valerio Cugia, hangs on the lefthand wall as one enters, in front of the board with the plaques dedicated to the illustrious patrons. The portrait could justifiably be replaced by the old nineteenth-century portrait of Masino Levi, insurance director, which hangs in the foyer of the Politeama Rossetti theatre, next to the Public Garden: waistcoat, paper in one hand, goose quill in the other, a discreet and elusive Jewish smile on his lips.

A Mephistopheles insurer of lives and guarantor, with a policy to boot, of a healthy middle age for which it's worth signing and handing over one's soul.

Indeed that middle age – or post-middle age – offers good possibilities for success, delayed yet sweet. On certain evenings the sun lights up the broad, gilded coffee leaves that surround the medallions on the walls; the light as it moves sinks the mirror behind the table into a lake of shadow enclosed by shining borders, the last rays of a distant sun that gleams and sets over the sea. A nostalgia for marine clarity reflects on the half-submerged faces in the dark waters of the mirror, the insidious call of real life. But one is quick to shut it up, if it is too insistent. When, in a certain period, assiduous regulars who also attend the adjacent synagogue stop coming and disappear one after another from their usual tables, then almost no one, not even those who up until recently loved to chat with the people who came out of the Temple and into the café for refreshment, almost no one asks indiscreet questions about their absence.

In the café the air is veiled, a protection against remoteness; no gust blows the horizon open and the red of the evening is the wine in one's glass. Mr Crepaz, for example, certainly does not regret his youth; in fact just now he's busy touching it up, like an unsuccessful painting that's not beyond repair. As a young man things never went well for him with women. Oh, nothing dramatic – simply nothing happened, or very little, ever since he was a youngster, since the time when they all used to meet up at the summer cinema in the Public Garden, just a few hundred metres from the San Marco. The girls were kind, pleased if he was there too, but when the dark white-capped sea of the *Bounty* appeared on the screen, bright spray and black waves, a black as deep as the night so that it seemed blue, and there was freshness and darkness around them and noises among the leaves, the girls' eyes shone and tender laughter in the shadow was the promise of happiness, and he felt that none of this was for him. He felt it in the awkwardness of his body which was a barrier between himself and those tanned arms that, all right, they were flung about his neck at the moment of going home, but it was nothing to compare to what happened with the others, even just the clasp of a hand in the dark.

It had been more or less always that way, at any rate often; those beauties opened up like flowers in water, and in vain he'd passed them by, the art of placing a hand on another's had remained an unknown initiation. Until once, many years later, he had seen Laura again – beautiful in her ageing, which was already clear in the lines in her face and the abundance of her breasts; suddenly she had looked at him differently and everything had loosened up, it had become so easy. "You were so immature," Clara said to him months later, in bed. They used to sit together at school and then, as now, she would throw her black hair into his face like a wave, although now it had the odd streak of white.

And so his life had changed. Not that he'd become a womanizer, anything but. He was faithful, he was only interested in the women he'd desired in vain in his youth, he wanted to square things up. He was methodical in his research; the girls had left him behind, but he had caught up on more than one of them. Slowly things reverted to a new order, a new balance. He was making up for that day of useless heartbreak at the seaside with Maria, the unbridgeable distance he'd felt then as he gave her his hand to help her up on to the rock. He made revisions to that lunch when Luisa, with that sidelong, teasing glance of hers, had eyes only for Giorgio, while now her soft, plump fingers, so practised in awakening desire, were only for him.

Little by little he retraced his path backwards, back to that little girl in the white socks in the cycling area in the Public Garden, the one who'd ordered him sulkily to sort her wheel our for her and then had shot off without so much as a glance. But now, she was an odalisque, a woman with avid, imperious lips who would have inspired envy in the fine daughter she'd had all those years ago by one of the lucky ones, a rival who in the meantime had been removed from the scene with a divorce.

And then there were the ladies he'd pined for in an even more distant time, his mother's friends and his friends' mothers, elegant and perfumed women who always picked up and cuddled the other children, kissing and stroking them on the cheek or putting a chocolate in their mouths, even pushing it through their lips with a finger, the nail varnished. Indeed there was even a rumour – but it's easy to exaggerate in the café – that he recently had gone to bed with Mrs Tauber, perhaps the doyenne of her line, who some fifty years previously had been a real beauty; even now she still had the pert little nose that was his by rights. Anyway, gentleman as he was, he said nothing because they all knew her and she sometimes still came to the café with the few surviving friends of her own sex.

Giorgio Voghera has for years sat at a table on the bottom right, as one comes in. He is an acknowledged leader and purported author of *Secret*, a distasteful and charming masterpiece, its subject, renunciation seen in its heartless geometry, a book written against life that serves to highlight all of life's seductive qualities. Next to Voghera sit mild-mannered ladies, cousins who are also writers of some merit, undemanding friends, aspiring writers who cling to past literary glory, journalists who every two or three months come up with the same questions on Trieste, students looking for dissertation topics, the odd scholar from far away perhaps sniffing out a future banquet of unpublished works. Piero Kern, expert in oral literature and a protected specimen of the grand Triestine cosmopolitan bourgeoisie now in danger of extinction, if it ever existed, tells of a robbery in a Rio de Janeiro travel agency; he is highly critical of the robbers' lack of professionalism, but even more so of the unseemly behaviour of a fat American, a fellow victim.

Voghera listens good-humouredly, patient and distrait, letting his own words and others' slide into the great indifference of the universe. Those watery sky-blue eyes have seen the other side of life, its underside, and their glance roves meekly among the tables. "Basically, I'm optimistic," he loves to repeat, "because things always end up working out worse than my gloomy predictions." He's been through historic catastrophes and personal hells, skirted abysses into which he cannot have found it easy to avoid being swallowed, especially as a young man.

It's not easy being in the desert, outside of and far away from the Promised Land. It's not just the big sand storms in the desert, the strong wind that stuns and sweeps one away; there are even more venomous dangers – the grains that stick everywhere and take the air away from one's skin, the dryness that desiccates the body and dries up the soul's sap. Perhaps as a young man, before he reached this state of indulgence for his own and others' shortcomings, Voghera must have been fairly unbearable – an irritable teacher who found life slapdash and in need of correction and failed it. But his syntax is clear and smooth, doggedly honest, like Ariadne's Thread running through the labyrinth without getting tangled and implacably weaving the image of a random, painful, grotesque reality.

In this prose Voghera writes out his kaleidoscope, celebrating the useless virtues of a white-collar universe – methodical precision and assiduous effort dedicated to nothing. He describes the process of ethical reverse selection that inevitably brings the worst onto the bridge of society and history. He reviews the sciences that venture into the meanders of the soul, those like psychoanalysis that reveal tortuous truths that soon become banalities, cruel misunderstandings in the comedy of existence. He re-evokes the years of exile and the war in Palestine, a war that for him was above all a solemn labour of patience. He gazes with disenchantment and compassion on the world, as though viewing it from another planet; the contemplation of chaos does away with trust and illusion but not with good manners, a pure style and that melancholy nineteenth-century respect that is one manifestation of goodness.

"I know, I know that everyone has so much to do in this world," Voghera murmurs, as though he himself does not belong to it. Often, despite the aches and pains and the years, and there are many of them by now, he goes to visit a venerable and despotic authoress, forgotten by everyone; she keeps him for hours, hassling him and tearing him apart because he's the only victim she has left. "Well, what am I to say?" he explains, almost apologetically, "I know what loneliness is, to be alone and forgotten . . . and then she was kind to my parents, once, although in truth . . . well, it doesn't matter. But above all it's because if I don't call on her she phones me up and bends my ear relentlessly, which is much more tiring." Every now and then, at night, in the Jewish rest home where he lives, an addled old woman from a neighbouring room makes a mistake, comes in and sits on his bed, for hours sometimes. "Even if it had happened fifty years ago," he says, "it wouldn't have made any difference . . . "

God continues to inflict sores on Job and Voghera keeps the record. *Our Lady Death*, a questionable but unforgettable book, is the diary of the bereavements he's been through: his father, his mother, Aunt Letizia, Uncle Giuseppe, Aunt Olga, his friend Paolo, his cousin Cecilia. Jewish Trieste, to which he bears witness and of which he is perhaps the last chronicler, exits from the stage. One by one the bit players disappear, in the final hours of his many characters, whose agony also includes the bureaucratic processes to be gone through, the emergency hospital admissions, the vesical haemorrhages, the smells of old age and illness, the red tape for hospital in-patients, the arteriosclerosis, the tyrannical manias of the ill and the egoism of their carers, the wiles, the pains and the great detachment of those who suffer and die.

The archivist of the end neglects no detail of the disintegration, nor of the squalor that accompanies it – the vomit choking the breath, and the rude arrogance of the switchboard operator at the emergency unit. He's like a beast of burden, beneath his pack and the blows – he absorbs it all, patient and helpless, but he lifts his eyes and repeats: "Now mind, because I'm noting it all down." Those hospital admissions and those deaths pursuing one another from chapter to chapter produce in the end an involuntarily comic result, just like any exaggerated sequence of tragedies that initially awakes compassion but then, beyond a certain point, provokes hilarity in the observer. This irresistible comic quality of tribulations brings out the extreme weakness of the human condition, which under an overload of misery is robbed even of its decorum, exposed to ridicule and reduced to waste and refuse.

In a certain sense Voghera rewrites the Book of Job, but with himself taking the part of Job's first sons and daughters, who, during their father's trials, perish in the ruins of the house, decimated like the flocks by the wind in the desert, and in the happy ending they are replaced just like the flocks and the camels, so that their memory will not disturb Job's late and happy years. Job is protagonist of a terrible story, but one which is set in motion in order to make him stand out; from his point of view, from the perspective of a man to whom the Lord and his Opponent dedicate much attention, it is easier to acknowledge that life, despite its tragedies, has a sense. Nobody wonders, even, whether and how Job's first children, crushed under the rubble, accepted their fate as mere extras brought in to glorify Job. If one identifies with them, with their nameless destiny, it's more difficult to praise the order of things.

Voghera adopts the point of view of those creatures who have been devastated, overlooked, the viewpoint of the stone which the builders rejected, mindful and perhaps mistrustful of the Lord's promise to use it as the cornerstone of His house. His objective and fastidious prose is a great memorial to the vanquished. But something blocks and dilutes, the watery gaze clouds over, the goodness darkens, perhaps becomes polluted. Whether or not he is the author of the splendid *Secret*, it anyway couldn't have been easy to be its protagonist, the bitter hero of a mania and an inhibition, which in stories are transformed into magic, into love's abandonment, but in real life leave scars that rarely heal – all the more so if the author of that great book was (as he maintains without letting anyone know what it is he really wants us to believe) his father, Guido Voghera, in an improper, almost incestuous profanation of the deep and heartbreaking unhappiness of his son.

His crystalline style and his preferred topics – love's enchantment, life's failure – sometimes seem to come from a page of *Secret*, but often they are weakened and watered down in mere fastidious verbiage; straightforward, charming simplicity slides away into banality, and humility dissolves into a questionable submissiveness. Perhaps anyway Voghera is a plaster saint, a man who had to master the lessons of life's meanness and perhaps did not mind doing so. When his writing is praised he retires shyly and blushes, saying that the true writers in his family are his father, his uncle and his cousin. But in the myopic eyes as they look past his interlocutor, there is perhaps a glint of malice, if he gets the impression you might just end up believing him.

Doctor Velicogna sits near the counter where the newspapers are; he's not interested in reading them because they all say the same things, but he likes to hold them, the stick in his left hand while he leafs through with his right. The world is there, in his hands, threatening disasters with enormous black headlines, but one has the sense of keeping it at bay. Doctor Velicogna has a theory, founded on personal experience, about the best ways of saving a marriage: mine, for example, he blethers in front of his beer – draught, naturally, bottled beer's not for him because pressure and temperature are crucial and the head has to be just right, not that stuff that comes out when you take the cap off, which looks like a syrup shaken before use – mine was saved thanks to that stunt of spending the whole night out, a couple of times; that way I opened my eyes and I understood. Even the most irreproachable can find himself, without quite knowing how, caught up in some little affair and to begin with it's not even unpleasant. But often, almost from the start, she asks you to stay over at her place for the night and, who knows, maybe it seems more decorous and besides, despite all the complications and the manoeuvres to be set in motion, how do you say no? I at all events always felt surprised and grateful if a woman was attracted to me and it seemed all wrong not to be kind.

It's true that kindness and courtesy pay, continues Doctor Velicogna, still holding the newspaper stick. Thanks to that kindness the whole show soon came apart; soon enough, anyway, before anyone got hurt. Because after a while, in bed, what are you supposed to do? It's not your woman, the one who goes with you through all the business and the strife of living – she's the one you never tire of, never tire of simply being close to her and doing nothing, just feeling her shoulder and her breath.

Now when you're with another woman – she might even be a better woman and warrant all the respect in the world – after a while you're lying there and you don't even have the courage to get up and go and read a book – all right, you can go to the bathroom and stay in there a while, but only once, at the most twice. You can sleep a bit, but even falling asleep too quickly doesn't do, it's not polite. And so I used to lie in bed, hoping she'd fall asleep. When I heard the first trams I was relieved and the Municipal Transport Authority shot up in my esteem as their pre-dawn heralds announced the imminent end of my embarrassment. A couple more hours and leaving would no longer be a discourtesy, indeed it was a duty, a delicate gesture given that they, too, had to go out to work.

That's how I understood that sleeping together – not just sleeping, but being close together in the dark, living even, and I don't mean anything special but just chatting, sharing a few laughs, a few anxieties, going to the cinema or to the sea for the last swim at the end of October, on the rocks between Barcola and Miramare – you can only do that with the woman of your life. And I understood all that because I stayed over and slept with another woman and the next morning it was all over without a word spoken. Otherwise I would have carried on for who knows how long and with who knows what complications, songs and dances, mix-ups and upsets for everyone. I'll have to tell all this to Father Guido, he might come today as well, he likes his beer and the Sacred Heart church is just down the road. He might be able to work it up into a fine topic for a sermon on marriage. On the supremacy of marriage, I mean. And perhaps he could spare a thought for those fine girls – one or two at most, for someone like me that's more than enough – who lead us back onto the straight and narrow and to the knowledge of ourselves. For them, too, it was a good thing not to have me hanging around any more.

At the table of Voghera and cousins, the memoirs of his uncle, Giuseppe Fano, are doing the rounds in typescript. He'd started writing them just before he died, in 1972, at the age of ninety-one. He could have recounted an active, colourful life in this work: already a merchant before the Great War, he'd then taken on the leadership of an Italian committee for aid to Jewish emigrants and in this role he had carried out an epic job, with imperturbable calm and stolid fidelity to his daily habits, chartering ships for voyages to Palestine, collecting donations with persistent tenacity and organizing services, helping refugees from all over the world, doing all he could for others and trying, whenever possible, to stay in bed with his skullcap on his head in order to save his strength and reach old age.

The memoirs carry barely more than an echo of these risky and charitable deeds; what chiefly comes across is the worry about punctiliously recovering the energy so generously expended in the doing of them. The protagonists of the memoirs are colds and draughts, which bothered Fano more than any other disaster, to the point where he wore, even in summer, several pullovers one on top of another, and Saba used to tell him that it took an iron constitution like his to bear the measures he took to protect it, measures that would have given anyone else pneumonia. So as not to abandon those who needed him, he'd stayed in Trieste even during the German occupation, despite the risk of being deported; one September or October day while going round the Nazi-controlled city in a fur greatcoat that made him look as though he'd just come out of a Polish ghetto, he observed with relief, in German, that luckily the cold of the past few days had relented. The entire Third Reich was completely powerless to make him budge from his habits; Hitler could make him risk death, but not a cold.

With his Central European discretion, Fano almost never speaks of himself, in his memoirs, but of others; he, the narrative I, is simply the connecting thread. He does not permit himself to alter nor to colour events unduly and neither does he evaluate them subjectively, but depicts the world as it is, with God's eye, which sees everything and its opposite. He does not select things, neither does he eliminate incoherent data, because he claims no right to establish hierarchies of importance or the authority of the demiurge who sets reality aside or corrects it. He admires, venerates Saba and recounts how in Milan in 1914 the poet begged him, when he had to return to Trieste, "To take the fate of his mother and his aunt to heart, and to make sure that his aunt's will was in his favour, thus avoiding the loss of the little nest-egg she had. Back in Trieste I kept the promise scrupulously and visited the dear old ladies if not every day, at least three times a week. . . . I took the aunt to the solicitor and she, willingly, happily, made out her will in favour of her nephew."

In Fano's testimony there is no trace of derision, no debunking. The comedy, never provoked, never repressed, is born out of faithfulness to reality, which brings out the foolishness, the incoherence but also the picaresque adventure of life, the family epic lived day by day with loved ones. The details, entertaining or embarrassing, are recorded with an entomologist's precision. During his adolescence when his father suggested cold showers for quenching the fires of puberty, Fano naturally heeded the advice: "I got up warm from my bed, and went into the freezing kitchen. To the water tap I applied a rubber hose that terminated in a coneshaped funnel with holes (like a rose on a watering can) . . . This treatment was useless for my neurosis, but it strengthened my lungs and protected me from colds."

The size of his family is suggested indirectly by some marginalia: "I can't remember which newborn it was, but Mother was exhausted and Father . . . " Order is defended punctiliously: a distant relative is one of the first young women to receive educational qualifications in nineteenth-century Trieste; when she turns to an aunt who was most involved with numerous charity committees and specialized in aid for prostitutes and their rehabilitation in society, hoping that this aunt, thanks to her contacts, might find her a job, the latter regretfully replies that she would be only too pleased to but she cannot, "because we only help whores", and if one starts mixing things up there's no telling how it all might end.

The nineteenth-century positivist intelligence is too honest to attempt any synthesis of the random multiplicity of what is real – this would be too presumptuous. "Compromise as much as you like, but for God's sake no syntheses!" warned Guido Voghera, presumed anonymous author of *Secret*. Objects exist and they demand loyalty, even at the cost of ridiculousness. For Fano there are no data to be removed because they are incoherent or contradictory in relation to the picture one wants to offer or because they are at variance with an image – even one's own – that is now accepted. Fano does not even worry about the coherence of his memoirs, which he dictated from his bed, sometimes renarrating entire episodes that he had forgotten he had already recounted; he would repeat them once more in his pages because, when the typist told him she had already set them down, he told her not to give it a thought, since it was none of her business, and to keep going.

Every life, like Fano's pages, repeats itself many times, in its passions, in its acts and in its whims. His autobiography has the coherence of its fragmentary nature, there is no pretence at a conclusion and it interrupts itself in homage to reality, which remains unfinished and inconclusive. So be it even for the pen that means to recount it all and snaps in two while it attends to this heroic-comic task. Whatever happens, respect for others, even for things, remains paramount. "May I have your revered telephone number?" Fano would ask if he thought he might need to call someone.

In the medallions on the walls – accredited to illustrious artists but not always confirmed, certainly to Napoleone Cozzi (climber, decorator, writer and irredentist), possibly to Ugo Flumiani, painter of foam-flecked waters – the nudes represent the rivers which "from the Italian peninsula, from Friuli, from Istria and from Dalmatia flow into the Adriatic, into the sea of Saint Mark". That apotheosis of Mare Nostrum, of Our Sea, which was supposed to be Italic on both shores, is toned down in the amber glaze of the decor, an evening of gold verging on russet. The estuary looks like a highly decorated exit leading into a larger room. In the aisle near Via Battisti, the characters in the *Offerers* by Giuseppe Barison – who also painted the allegories of

Electricity and Geography in the railway station café – parade with gifts in their arms, to propitiate unknown gods; a red glow illuminates the greys, the ochre, the brown of the figures. Flumiani's seascapes and lagoon paintings, in the wing nearest the synagogue, are bright; sails and water, sand and mud, too, gleam in the sparkle of the midday sun. Oh to leave the ark, to plunge and disappear into that water gilded by the sunset; even just to paddle in the lagoon, to squeeze and splatter the mud that glitters with nuggets.

"Your hair's a mess, go to the washroom and sort yourself out." With the authority that normally derives from a physical intimacy, the old lady that time brooked no nonsense. Since then, whenever he goes to the washroom, he feels as though he's obeying that injunction, the conclusion of their vapid dialogue. "Well done, what a worker . . . bravo!" she had said to him when once she was left sitting alone at the table next to his. Perhaps the compliments were a peace offering after her tirade against modern times and the youth of today, which had developed out of her chat with her friend and now, seeing that he had stopped writing and was looking around vacantly, she wanted to repair the damage. "Bravo! . . . what a worker!" He sketched an embarrassed smile. "And what's your area of interest?" "Well . . . let's see . . . German literature." "Splendid . . . the most beautiful literature, most interesting, most spiritual . . . bravo!" With each reply his smile became progressively more inane. "But you're already wearing a wedding ring, and you being so young . . . how old are you? Really, I'd never have guessed. You look much younger . . . well done, you've done the right thing, marriage is the most important thing. No children yet though, I imagine. Yes? Congratulations! That's really important. One? Oh . . . two! You really are very lucky . . . the right number. Boy and a girl? Oh . . . two boys. The best thing. You'll see what it means to them, in life, to have a brother. . . . Glad you married so young?"

The affirmative response to this last question, that involuntary final touch to the portrait of perfection – husband, father, worker and what's more young and replete – was followed by a long silence, which he had turned to account by starting to write again until, after a few minutes, she leaned over him and, crossing that distance between two faces and two bodies that is only ever crossed under special circumstances, whispered angrily because of the single blemish on the general perfection: "Your hair's a mess, go to the washroom and sort yourself out!"

Such an authoritative tone, which usually comes from a bed, demands to be obeyed. The washroom is at the end on the right. On the walls a Siamese dancer closes her unfathomable eyes, the sinuous art nouveau lines curve the cruel eyebrows and shameless legs of female figures, a wave finishes in the vortex of the void like Mr Plinio's waltz, music for a backstage exit. The coffee leaf is repeated in a vegetal proliferation, and the grimace on a Harlequin's face bespeaks a raw, nameless pain.

Some paintings have been recovered after being painted over for decency's sake, so say the scholars of restoration. But it's difficult, for all one might try, to find anything indecent in them. Anyway it doesn't hurt to repaint, to cover, to close the hatches. Perhaps writing is covering up too, an accomplished coat of paint applied to one's own life, so that it assumes a mantle of magnanimity thanks to the skilful display of faults under a pretence of hiding them in a tone of candid self-accusation that makes them seem big-hearted, while the real filth remains below. All saints, that's what writers are; yes ... daredevils, prodigal sons, full of lusty sins shown off with meretricious shame, but still large, beautiful souls. Is it possible that among us there is not a single pig, no truly shabby, mean-spirited swine?

The washroom is cramped, a reddish trickle runs under the urinals, it clots in lumps, glass from a shattered bottle on the beach. Now and then a jet of clear water comes down. Get washed, a change of underwear. In the face at the mirror something comes undone, as though whatever it was that had held it together up to that moment has started to work loose. The hair is dirty, tangled serpents on a Gorgon's head that emerges from the depths of Hades. There's someone smiling on a scrap of newspaper. The washroom is the antechamber before Judgment, an indefinite wait, eternity is the dribble that runs along the urinals. Back to the café, kill time, read the newspapers. A quick rinse has made the face presentable, but the hair's all sweaty. Go to the washroom and sort oneself out. To plunge into the sea, even just to wash one's hands in the shallow, tepid water of the lagoon, to put one's face into the drinking fountain in the nearby Public Garden, as one used to do back then after having run, or in the snow that was so white it seemed blue, and in the small spring in that clearing in the wood where the deer used to go to drink, or in the holy-water stoup in the Sacred Heart church, in Via del Ronco – so fresh. Indeed, it is all so close by, little more than a stone's throw. For those who want to stretch their legs and take a little tour of the world, the San Marco is in an excellent position. Central, an estate agent would say. To reach the church in Via del Ronco, going through the Garden and all the other necessary places, takes only a few minutes.

Valcellina

The *fusina* always takes place on the last Saturday in August. In Malnisio that's the name given to the festival of the first corn cobs, grilled in a grassy open space at the foot of Mount Sarodinis and eaten with *sorc*, a bread made with corn flour. People walk up from the village and come by car from Udine, from Trieste, from even farther away, bringing cheese and wine; people who left these places young, or children and grandchildren of those who left long ago, together with some who have remained. Every journey is above all a return, even if the return, almost always, lasts very little and it's soon time to leave. In these harsh valleys, once among the poorest of the poor Friuli foothills, the men would emigrate, they would go to dig mines or to build roads and railways in France or in Siberia, and the women, with panniers on their backs full of wooden spoons and ladles, would walk from one village to the next selling their wares from door to door, sleeping in ditches and in haystacks. But the journey's end, for all of them, always, was the brief return.

Great-grandmother's uncle, or great-uncle, an extremely young grenadier in Napoleon's army, also returned on foot from the Russian campaign after some years as a prisoner and a wanderer, and when he first arrived in Malnisio the villagers did not recognize him. They say that some decades later, during the third war of independence in 1866, when he was very old and very tough-skinned, he recruited a battalion of irregulars to support the Italian army as partisans against the Austrians; but that he'd also had a flag made up with the motto "Become Italian to become French". The *Empereur* for whom he had lost his youth in the Russian snows, the hardships and the battles, had left him with a nostalgia for something grand, for revolutionary change in the world. Perhaps this far-off echo is the reason why, despite everything, his grandchildren would always choose the *Marseillaise* over the Radetzky March.

Nobody knows the name of that great-great-uncle, the parish registers at Malnisio only go as far back as the generation after his. For many the *fusina* is also a return. Luciano Daboni, who organizes the event with authority and method, is known for his mathematical studies and his scholarly contribution to probability theory, which gives formal definition to the unpredictability and the randomness of life. Dario Magris, too, Daboni's worthy deputy, has learned from the Hippocratic art that life and above all death, which he knows how to keep at bay, do not allow for programmes and don't respect deadlines. But even for these two men of science this Saturday at the end of August is an exception to the chaos that otherwise dominates the universe, an exception to the indeterminate and treacherous nature of things. And it is a certainty beyond debate, an anniversary that obeys a firm necessity, around which time winds and rotates like the earth on its axis.

It's not unpleasant to obey the law that prescribes the return to this village, from which grandfather Sebastiano, during the final decades of the last century, left at the age of thirteen for Trieste to initiate a modest bourgeois ascent. His brother, Barba Valentin, stayed in Malnisio until the age of ninety-two to till the fields, and in the evenings – in the stable in winter – to read and reread *Les Misérables, The Betrothed, The*

Wretch Guerino, The French Monarchs and a universal encyclopaedia in two volumes.

Malnisio has a thousand or so inhabitants who share not many surnames, to which nicknames are often added in order to tell the various families apart; otherwise it would all be confused in an indistinct mass, like curdled milk, out of which – according to Menocchio, the sixteenth-century heretic dairyman from nearby Montereale who was burned at the stake for his metaphors – the universe, man and God Himself were born. Behind Malnisio, towards Aviano and Pordenone, the valley descends and opens out, broad and airy; on the other side, beyond Montereale, the real Valcellina begins, a rugged place carved from the rock. Up until the beginning of the century it was cut off from the world, except for a muletrack along the Croce pass. It took ten hours on foot to carry essential provisions from Maniago to Erto, the last village in the valley.

Malnisio is set among the fields of maize; in late summer the corn cobs are trophies of barbarian gold, but the village, having almost forgotten a recent century-long poverty, is relaxed and prospering; the ancient curse of tilling the soil has forged solid folk who have overcome it. The countryside may begin just a few metres away, but in fact it is remote – peasant misery has been cleared away like cow dung from the roads. Now it is sight, the noble sense, that captures the reality of the village in the decor of the houses, whereas once it was distinguished in sounds, smells and tastes: a thicket of canes in a lane that used to bend with a swish louder than elsewhere, a road more trampled than others by the animals returning from the pastures, a great heap of cut grass that spread a sharper smell, the hot pulp of the corn cob as it melts in the mouth, the fragrance of the *Clinton* wine and the slightly harsher taste of the *Fragola* cut with *Bacò*, the grapes picked and pressed just behind the house.

From the square, the centre of the village, and in the direction of

Mount Sarodinis, runs the Calle Grande, today's Via Risorgimento, known in days gone by as "vial major" or "the road above the cortina". This last was a ditch and a fence behind which the villagers hid whenever there were threats or invasions in the air. The small holdings of the old families of the village – house, stable, a few fields – were grouped around that road.

The church, in the square, is dedicated to Saint John the Baptist and has several centuries' history of alterations and restorations. Hirsute and clad in the skins of wild beasts, the intractable prophet of the desert does not evoke seraphic, conciliatory feelings; not for nothing was he the Bulgarian Bogomils' messenger of darkness, while for the Mandaeans, also at odds with the material world in the hands of evil, he was the supreme master, harshly superior to Christ. The church in Malnisio has also seen more of bitterness than of peace; already at the end of the sixteenth century, the cohabitation of Malnisio's parishioners with those of nearby Grizzo, although equally satisfied at having been freed from the parish of Santa Maria di Montereale, gave rise to resentful fights, and the feast of the irascible patron saint, although lightened by the German zither played by Menocchio and the cakes sold on the streets for the sweet-toothed, could easily degenerate into bloody riots. On 24 June, 1584, for example, the parish priest Odorico, who lived in Grizzo, offended the Malnisians, pronouncing them "cuckolds in word and deed", and had to defend himself with a dagger and dodge blows from axes and spears. Two centuries later, the *procurator fabricario*, the administrator Sebastiano Magris, who kept the parish books, complained of the damage caused by the louts who chased one another up onto the roof, breaking the tiles so that the rain came into the nave.

Inside, the *Christ on the Cross*, by an anonymous eighteenth-century woodcarver, the very wood suggesting a rugged, painful pity, gives a sudden authority to the dubious idea that every primitive church, in its wretchedness and its abasement, is a refuge for those travelling towards new lands and new skies. Certainly one is curious to know what was wrong with the *Resurrection of Christ* painted above the right-hand lateral door, to the point where in 1903 the Bishop of Concordia, Francesco Isola, found it "indecent" and had it removed and replaced by today's *San Domenico Guzman Preaching*.

Below the organ loft, two confessionals hark back to models from the Counter-Reformation,with a space designed next to the priest's cubicle to contain the list of the *Casus Reservati*, an aide mémoire of the sins that none but the Bishop or even the Pope could absolve. In that confessional, many years ago now, there used to be a mild reception for one's own run-of-the-mill sins. The priest was a drinker who struggled as he could against that demon. Some of the villagers enjoyed buying him drinks, getting him drunk after midnight and thus causing him to commit sacrilege by celebrating Mass the next day. In the end the battle between him and the wine went the wine's way and he came to a sticky end. Life often finds a way of beating us, with the means befitting our weaknesses – wine, drugs, ambition, fear, success.

Of that priest, thus brought low, one remembers with gratitude the words he used to say in the confessional, no less intelligent than many others heard from illustrious pulpits and platforms; and the goodness in his voice comes back. A man enters the empty church; when asked where the parish office is, he doesn't answer but looks sideways through two bright, sharp slits; he skips towards the first rows of pews, leans over and sniffs one of them meticulously, then out he goes into the square and runs off to disappear behind the houses.

At Malnisio the Cellina, which just a few kilometres away cuts into the valley in Dantesque circles, is channelled into the large pipes of the old hydroelectric power station dating back to 1903, and now being turned into a museum. Not far away, at Montereale, excavations have brought to light a considerable historic past – the ancient Caelina recalled by Pliny, bronze swords thrown into the water centuries and centuries ago in homage to the gods of the rivers and the fords. But even Industry is of a respectable age and displays, as in this power-station-cum-museum, its own archaeology with gigantic turbines and manometers and solemn photographs of the bearded engineers who tamed the waters; Technology, guarantor of Peace and Progress, is an angel sculpted on a sarcophagus.

Paolo Bozzi recalls that his uncle was one of those engineers – Francesco Harrauer, specialized in the pressurized ducts that led the waters through the infernal meanders of the valley. He had married a Mreule, a relative of Enrico, the fugitive who had sought real life, true persuasion in solitude and in self-denial. She was a woman with splendid gentian-coloured eyes, which with the years were absorbed by her ever fatter face; while her husband was ever more taken with his pressurized ducts, old age and obesity isolated her from the prolixity of existence. Engineer Harrauer spoke all day about his ducts to his sister and she, a seamstress by trade, divided her interest between these last and her own work, which included the underwear that she stitched charitably for the friars in a nearby monastery, the door of which displayed the Latin motto, *àbstine sùstine*, and who were indeed abstemious, eating only as much as was necessary to sustain themselves. But in their motto what she read was *abstìne sustìne*, with a change of stress that rendered this last homonymous word the local dialect term for a stud-type button.

Baudelaire and Montale are not the only ones who can capture a plurality of meanings in a few condensed, Delphic lines to the delight of the literary interpreters. Engineer Harrauer's sister managed to concentrate the totality of her existence in a quatrain worthy of structuralist exegesis – absorbed by her brother's hydraulic obsession, her own cutting and sewing and the contact with the convent, she loved to recite the lines as she worked, forcing them out through her closed lips that held on tightly to needles and pins: *Abstìne sustìne / mudande del frate / condotte forzate / orate per me* . . . "Abstain sustain / the friar's drawers / pressurized ducts / *orate* for me" . . . and that final *orate* probably was not a verb at all, but was an Italian plural noun – sea-bream in English . . . fine fish to pray for in any language.

The few surnames in Malnisio – Muran, Borghese, Magris, Ongaro, Favetta – multiply and mingle, each splintering into a wealth of ramifications indicated by differing nicknames; Sior, Brusulata, Del Grillo, Miu, Palazzo, they seem to indicate so many and nobody. And the more one recovers in terms of names, traces and dates, the more one loses in terms of tenderness, insignificance, mysterious origins, memory. Great-grandmother Santina, who looked after her grandchildren when they were orphaned as teenagers, rather lost her marbles when she had passed ninety and completely forgot her husband, the Herculean Favetta the Red, who specialized in taming mad bulls; she'd lived with him for half a century and borne his children, but to her grandchildren she spoke only of her first love, who died in the 1848 war as an Austrian soldier. There are many debatable interpretations of the matter – some more materialistic, others more psychological and less flattering for Great-grandfather Favetta. And yet this illiterate great-grandmother had been endowed with an excellent memory for more than eighteen lustrums and had conveyed to her grandchildren the only episode of history she knew of – the Empress Maria Theresa seeking refuge among the Hungarian nobility, who swear allegiance to her and, in this version, offer her a throne. *"Non mi sento* . . . I don't feel like it," replied Maria Theresa according to Great-grandmother Santina, but since in dialect *sento* can mean either "I sit" or "I feel", she added, "And we'll never know whether she didn't feel like it or whether she simply didn't sit on it."

*

A very elderly woman says, "When I saw you on television I knew you were Duilio's son. When we were kids we used to go to throw stones at the Grizzo lot – I carried them and he threw them." In war, too, it is taken for granted that women are given auxiliary, subaltern tasks. That son, who never misses the *fusina*, can compete with his father's culture, even if his father read Latin and especially Greek much better than he does, but the son does not have his father's stone-throwing ability that perhaps left him more relaxed in confronting life as well as the political battles in the bitter moments of the Resistance and the years immediately after the war.

Grizzo is the neighbouring village, and as far back as 1784 a parish priest complained about its youth's "bullying" activities. The invisible border runs just beyond the small church of the *Salute* and the loves that transgressed it resulted in unleashed rivalries, variations on Romeo and Juliet. Every identity is also a horror, because it owes its existence to tracing a border and rebuffing whatever is on the other side. Only a greater hatred transcends the smaller hatreds, which come back to life once the common enemy is no longer there. Just before the church there is the cemetery of Malnisio. Of Walter, cousin three times removed, there is only a photograph because, unlike that great-great-uncle, he never came back from Russia. He was last heard of, reported missing, in 1942. Ruben, his father, never tired of searching for him and never gave up; for years, whenever he heard of someone who had come back from Russia, he went to visit him in the hope of news.

Ruben travelled round these valleys with his cart, pulled by an old donkey, Morro, a wise and fleet-footed beast; whoever spent any length of time with Morro sooner or later realized that they owed him a small part of their vision of the world. Ruben was a peacable, extremely strong man. Once, at the inn, during a heated political discussion,

someone said it served him right that he'd lost a son in Russia; Ruben
picked the man up by the neck and, since the window was just a metre
from the ground, threw him out in the road across the sill, and the
next day he went to his house to make up.

Giulio Trasanna gathered many youngsters around the telescope in
Grizzo, attracted there by his personality. Friulian by choice, having
found himself in the homeless homeland of the emigrants, Trasanna is
a good writer. The precise brushstrokes of his bone-hard, rapid prose
capture the changing colours of life, the tragedy of war and the pain of
a generation or an evening. He is not unlike his adopted land Friuli,
destined to slip by, unobserved, on the margins of history. His legend
is alive in the memory of the writers and the artists who met him, but
his fragments, flashes and epiphanies do not carry those obvious and
facile handles that literary society needs to hold onto in order to ratify
the glory of a name; he never wrote any book that – like a successful
slogan – constituted a claim to fame. Fame of course is concerned less
with the value of a page than with its suitability for being turned into
an object of intellectual consumption, an easily digestible formula.

There is an Italy of the provinces that has no truck with partisan
hatreds and is full of life and intelligence, often more so than the so-
called metropolitan centres, which think of themselves as première
cinemas when sometimes they are nothing but old studios that have
had their day. Menocchio also lends his name to the cultural circle in
Montereale Valcellina – little more than two thousand inhabitants,
some six thousand including all its hamlets – led by Aldo Colonnello.
There are those who know how to respect the values of a place while
remaining immune to that municipal gut feeling that today often
makes the rediscovery of ethnicities and identities throughout present-
day Italy, indeed throughout Europe, so obtuse and reactionary. Friuli,
too, is often suffocated by "Friulianity", Trieste by "Triesteness".

Friuli, especially following the Second World War, has a considerable tradition in poetry – Pasolini and Turaldo are not isolated peaks – and Montereale, too, is a centre for poets, discreetly tucked away in their little world. For them the Friulian dialect (or rather its several dialects – they vary from valley to valley) is not a mere piece of local colour, it is a source language, at once archaic and contemporary, collective and individually reinvented; a language that finds its level in an alluvial bed of present existence and past history. *Te vardi tài óe te bùsse i zinóe*, "I look in your eyes I kiss your knees," sings Beno Fignon, melding the spoken tongues of Montereale and Andreis into a piping music of the valley, and touching on an immemorial, an epic cosmos. *A plòuf la vita ta l'erba dei ans* goes a line from Rosanna Paroni Bertoja – "Life sinks into the grass of the years." For the region's uprooted heirs, the emigrants who don't know how to speak the language, Friulian is a sort of pre-language, a prenatal murmur that sinks into that which cannot be spoken, as an infant's face sinks into a large breast. These mountains are breasts that have been squeezed dry, they are milkless, unlike the udders of mother earth in primordial myth. Centuries of poverty have hardened them, but have also rendered them strong: a firm body like the one praised in a colourful local saying about the women of Friuli and which Jacopo da Porcìa celebrated in the women of Montereale in particular.

Domenico Scandella, Menocchio, was also a poet in his own way. Perhaps his cosmogonic hypotheses were "twaddle", as some of his townsfolk told him, but certainly no more so than others patented with guaranteed metaphysical or scientific brands. In contrast to his perse-cutor Odorico, the quarrelsome parish priest who was custodian of orthodoxy and tempter of his daughter, Menocchio knew love, love for his children, the lynchpin of his existence, and for his wife. "She was my helm," he said, in despair, when she died – words that deserve to be included in a poetic anthology of conjugal love and shared life – an anthology that is so poor and unsubstantial compared to the relevance of its theme, further proof that poetry so often fails to measure up to real life.

The family no longer owns the fine big house with the huge courtyard, reached from the square by passing under a portico, although it had belonged to them for generations. It was sold many years, indeed many decades ago in order to purchase an extravagant dowry destined to rot and be eaten away by the moths. It was for Aunt Esperia, made ready for her impending marriage with the General, a wedding planned and postponed for years. Perhaps it was all prepared just to gain time and to distract her from the torment of her wait.

Those who know Esperia from childhood, with her nervous loquacity, remember her as an excitable and submissive child and describe her assiduous diligence at school, her friendship – respectful even in the games she played – with the daughter of the headmaster, her elated and scrupulous adolescence, her constant preoccupation with sin, despite the encouragement of her confessors who invited her to say her morning prayers and to then let herself go, carefree and confident as to whatever the rest of the day would bring.

As a girl and a young woman Esperia was punctiliously devoted to religion and also to the equally punctilious cultivation of every superstitious practice condemned by the Church. She was for ever washing her hands, she hesitated before posting a letter for fear that she might have unwittingly made some mistake or written some obscenity and, once she'd posted it she worried that perhaps she had not done so, perhaps she'd thrown it away instead. She was a haunted creature; she had not been granted that saving oblivion thanks to which one forgets that death is never far from one's heels and, that before it catches up, there are other catastrophes.

With her obsessions, her phobias and her rituals, Esperia had organized a labyrinthine defence, to escape the anxiety that crept in everywhere. She had also decided, and managed to convince herself of it right up to the penultimate stratum of her brittle psyche, that the world was a good place, populated and above all governed by good people. In this way she sought to live without fears, entrusting herself to general goodness and allowing her heart to love those around her – because she really did love them, she was born to love the world, human beings and even animals, despite the fact that not merely insects, but even cats and dogs disgusted her – and she struggled darkly to prevent this fear from suffocating the tenderness that was in her. When her faith in the goodness of life and of people began to waver, deep down, in the depths of her person, she buried the anxiety that came welling up in her throat in a torrent of verbosity; she would talk non-stop about everything and with everyone.

Towards the end of the Thirties she met, on a train, an officer from Emilia – the man who was to become, for her and for everybody else, the General. Esperia was tall, her hair copper blonde and the officer, inexorably assigned to that particular compartment by the iron chain of circumstance, got talking to her. Respect was important in those days and the officer, an honourable man who would never have set out to delude let alone cheat a woman, would never have thought that such an innocent acquaintance, for which the noun flirtation would have been almost excessive, could ever have been misunderstood. It was almost nothing, but for Esperia it was immediately everything; her fervour bestowed on it a visceral absoluteness, she made it the single, boundless, vital substance of her life. The wretched officer had no intention of marrying her, neither had he done anything that might lead a reasonable person to attribute those intentions to him, but he realised that if he told her so, it would be a tragedy for her. He therefore decided not to decide, to do neither the one thing nor the other, to prolong indefinitely this sort of pre-engagement, which became all the more indissoluble the more it was dragged out.

Thus began a vague and enervating period of waiting that was to last for years; for him it was a conscious trial, ever more deeply enmeshed as he was in that unbearable situation, but for her it was all unconscious excitement. She did not want to discover the truth and she was increasingly overcome by feverish obsessions, by all-consuming fixations that possessed her actions, making her see nauseating insects in her plate and prolonging her increasingly interminable conversations with relatives and neighbours. The king's permission was required for career officers who wished to get married, but it simply never came through. He was transferred from one unit to another and the two met briefly between departures, often in railway stations, the perfect setting for that desolation and that nostalgia.

The cautious temper of the times and Esperia's own naivety made additional rendezvous unimaginable, fortunately for both of them. In his exasperation, he tormented himself, he confided in Esperia's brothers, and they understood and supported him; together with them he studied plans of retreat that proved to be ever more unfeasible. She tore herself apart, like a tortured, seething Medea, and savaged her involuntary seduced seducer as well, persecuting him with her pain, which afflicted his conscience. In the meantime to the family she read aloud the letters that came from her General – she always called him so, never used his name – believing that their increasing vagueness was the acme of love, and papering the walls of her room with large photographs of him in uniform. These portrayed a large, mild man, whose uniform and decorations conferred on him an authority and dignity without in any way diminishing his good nature. In the meantime her dowry grew with the addition of new elements, and in the end this had required the sale of that family house in Malnisio, much to the chagrin of her brothers, who were sorry for her but above all dreaded the unimaginable consequences were they to refuse to sell; sheets, counterpane and rugs that were stored in trunks and chests of drawers, furniture piled up in the cellar, even a pianoforte.

To the General's relief, after years of grey fury came the Second World War and with it the African campaign, the distance, a wound to a lung; the probability that he would die and the fact of being so far from home rendered Esperia's letters less painful and the possibility that he might not return at all made them almost a comfort, something to cherish. It was their happy, or at least their bearable time, because the collective tragedy of the war and the material impossibility of meeting transformed the torture of delay into a lofty sacrifice. This merciful pause seemed to have finished with the end of the war, but when the General had just come back to Italy and had returned to his small estate in Emilia, before he was able to see Esperia, who had remained in Trieste, he was picked up one night by some armed men – in that chaos and in those places where the Resistance had become corrupted into private and social vendettas – and was shot dead.

This shed over Esperia the grand, beneficent liberation of a noble grief. From that moment on she was no longer a bride-never-to-be, she was a widow, a woman who had suffered but lived, who had lost her man in a cruel tragedy, but who had possessed him. The General's many relatives were shocked by his death and welcomed her as though she really were his widow, and so began Esperia's years of happiness. Freed of all reticence, she went to visit the relatives of the spouse who had passed on to a better world, she visited them in the various cities where they lived; she spent time with brothers- and sisters-in-law and looked after nephews and nieces and great-nephews and great-nieces, she took an interest in christenings, confirmations, school progress, weddings. She was always travelling as she used to, but now the world was friendly and attractive, full of colours, of things, of seasons, supported by memories sad and cheerful.

She was replete; her figure became more rounded in a reassuring and moderate plumpness, her skin no longer displayed that soft virginal freshness, but was marked by life's wrinkles with satisfied insouciance. Her obsessions had almost disappeared and when she took her nephews and nieces to the Public Garden she stood out less and less from the other mothers and grandmothers. She even learned, late but very well, to make warm and soft pullovers, for one nephew in particular who was her favourite. She still talked a lot – almost always about the General, who kept her company from many photographs – but with a mellow, relaxed eloquence, free of hysteria.

Esperia's first life of restless torment had lasted thirty-five years; her second life, of untroubled serenity, lasted forty-seven. The third one lasted but a month and a half. At the age of eighty-two, when her legs suddenly developed semi-paralysis and she could no longer look after herself, she was put in a rest home in Trieste. After a week she threw herself from a third-floor window. Despite the height the fractures were not serious, but Esperia never got out of her hospital bed. Clinically she was well enough, but her expression had changed, she was laconic now and allusive, replying with a formal smile to the small talk and the encouragement of her relatives. She spoke in hard, dry monosyllables. The photographs of the General had disappeared from her room; she must have got rid of them before she jumped.

Her nephew went to see her now and then in the hospital, in a rush, as one does. He noticed immediately that she never spoke about the General; throughout that month and a half she never once mentioned him. She must have suddenly opened her eyes to the emptiness of her life, to the lie she had lived, and she had decided to close the account. Six weeks after being admitted she died of one of those vague causes that the medical certificates define as "cardio-vascular failure". In any case her organs were now tired of closing ranks, and her Chief of Staff had ordered her troops to dismiss. After gazing into that void Esperia no longer wanted to live, was no longer capable of doing so. One might term her condition arteriosclerosis, but that's just another way of saying the same thing, just as H2O indicates the fleeting, indifferent poetry of water.

It might also be asked when Esperia was actually alive – in the long years of hunger, in those equally long years of replete self-deception, or in the final revelation of nothing. Her nephew, from his point of view, reflects with mild discomfort on the haste of those few visits to the hospital, and about the warmth the pullovers gave him in winter.

Opposite Ruben's house, near the old Calle Grande, is the one belonging to Vinicio Ongaro; he lives in Trieste but never misses the *fusina* and spends a month in Malnisio in the summer. Ongaro is a doctor; his reassuring calm and his mild and firm precision immediately give a sense of relief to the patients who go to him with their anxieties, the ghosts of their insomnia and panic, their compulsive obsessions, the vacuum of a life that seems to be sucked into the darkness. He is accessible, he listens, takes his time; something in his face and his demeanour recalls Freud's polished rectitude and melancholic goodness, laced with a canny irony. He penetrates into the spirals of anguish with the patient delicacy of a cat; he tests the ground with discreet questions, he suggests a drug without promising miracles, but the feline paw does not let the serpent of anxiety slip past, it makes a grab for it, drags it out and often, with time, the people who were haunted by the demons are capable of living once more.

Between patients Ongaro sits at the typewriter; sometimes, if the time he has left for himself is too little, he dictates into a tape-recorder. Lines of dialogue, isolated images, sketches for plot and character, the epiphany of an instant, the light of an afternoon or a face, the flash of lightning in the rain, the plume from the fire that rises from the *fusina* and disappears in the air. Around these sketches a story gradually condenses, a novel is born. Ongaro is a clandestine narrator; one of the most clandestine because he has published books on the sly with small publishing houses that find it impossible to gain access to the cultural circuit. Thus he has received admiration and appreciation, but fame, and an entrance ticket to the officially recognized club, have eluded him while still losing the tantalizing virginity of the typescript in the drawer.

Ongaro knows nothing of ideological programmes and overt poetics, he simply recounts life, capturing in its opaque flow, as though clouded in an aquarium of thoughts, memories, associations that emerge from the depths and sink back into them once again. He portrays straight-forward daily life, no easy thing to narrate – its actions, objects, instants – and especially the grey area of pre-consciousness where the conscious mind is veiled, affording a glimpse of experience as it were in clots, a veiled consciousness, but never extinguished. The protagonist of his novel *A Poor Tomorrow* is an unforgettable female character, a simple heart à la Flaubert. Who knows if that's enough to win the laurels.

Life, sometimes, hurts; it gives headaches even to those who know how to cure others' headaches. Perhaps for Ongaro life is a migraine, which in his pages becomes a way of being. But there are things there too – offered generously to the senses – the women, the colours of the seasons, the tenderness of affection, the reflection of light in water, those large trees in front of his house in Malnisio. Between writing prescriptions and listening paternally to endless phobias Ongaro writes his stories in pieces and in mouthfuls, fragments with timid irony that gradually resolve themselves into an ordered novel, whose structure and whose sense come to light at the end, as happens in life. Perhaps writing in the shadows is also a form of migraine, but from this one can learn how to understand existence, how to tame it and savour it, benignly independent of the world.

The real Valcellina in its awesomeness and gentleness, begins beyond the Magredo tunnel, which seems to lead, like those wormholes dreamed up by science (fiction), into another time, remote and static. Until the

opening of the road through the Montereale pass in 1903, the isolation
had been centuries old; legend has it that Attila and Napoleon looked
in and turned back, perhaps because their lust for conquest saw
nothing to conquer in that valley, in which nobody could have been
induced to settle were it not for their flight from the Magyars and other
barbarians. Up until 1805 even the cartographic representations of
the area were uncertain and full of errors.

The mountain displays its ridges like the folds in a haggard face,
mottled by the wine-coloured tufts of purple heather; the soil and the
stone are the colour of lead and poverty. In these valleys the people,
whom Sgorlon writes about in his books, have lived submerged in the
detritus of the river of history, which has passed over them. But even
under a sky steeped in mist and rain the Cellina, which runs along the
valley floor, has an unalterable luminous transparency, its water-green
colour is enough to make the valley bright.

Andreis is secluded, off to one side, calmly, indeed majestically indifferent; even its dialect has its own autonomous individuality. There
are those who carve and weave wooden baskets, and those who carve
and weave words. Andreis has two poets who make for an ideal
contrast, almost reflecting the confrontation – indeed the harsh clash –
between the Friulian Philological Society's traditionalism and the
archaic–revolutionary innovation of Pasolini's Academiuta. Federico
Tavan is the *poète maudit*, the innocent transgressor, socially offbeat
and tedious, marked by alienation and inclined, like many authors
of his stamp, to flaunt this quality in his life – this psychological vulner-
ability can also be an effective shield – but he is capable of plumbing
the depths of language and immersing himself in unease. *Anc'jò 'e
ven jù*, "Me too, I'm coming down." Ugo Piazza, ninety years old, is
the feel-good poet of fine words assembled in decorous rhymes. But
when he reads one of his poems about a snowflake falling on a lantern
and is moved as he does so, one realizes that in poetry's house, as in

our Father's, there are many mansions. All this even if "everyone wants to write poetry, but Europe needs something firmer and more real than verse", as Leopardi wrote in 1826, complaining that so many were attracted by "poetry and frivolity".

From Andreis a little side track leads to Poffabro in Val Colvera. The village is virtually deserted, the windows empty eye sockets and here and there wooden doors hang rotting. Searching for a craftsman who carves flowers, a man praised for his skill and for the old stories he tells, we ask about him from the only passer-by in the lanes – an elderly man, his face red and opaque from wine. He replies, with dignity, that he doesn't know and adds that he has lost his memory, placidly dominating just for a moment the void into which he has fallen. Someone, observing the balcony doors inlaid with dark wood, the tidiness of the logs stacked under the stairs, the graceful windows, remarks that the houses are beautiful. "No, they're not beautiful, come and see how ugly they are inside . . . " – a woman leans from a window, her hair ruffled. "They're ugly, come and see just how ugly they are," she repeats several times, her voice stridulant and too loud, even when the imprudent admirers of the village have turned the corner.

Claut, Cimolais, Erto and Casso come after the Barcis *conca*, the basin with its lake; the road climbs towards the Vajont through a ferrous and dusty landscape, the sides of the hill that slid during those tragic minutes of 9 October, 1963 display their lesions and bruises, splintered rock like broken teeth come loose from the gum. "We poor subjects of Your Serene Highness," recite ancient petitions from these villages. Squalor and hardship in hard-pressed Friuli, the desolation of life lost and suffocated by the brutality of survival – Maria Zef, the great and tragic heroine of the great and tragic story by Paola Drigo walks through this mud of history and existence.

The houses in lower Erto and in Casso are empty and falling apart;
they look down onto steep, bottomless slopes. These places carry the
sadness of Purgatory, so much more difficult to represent than Hell's.
The village has its geometric beauty, worthy of an old painting, in
the old houses that face the new ones; the difficulties here, even
the earthquakes are shocks that reawaken vital energy. In the old
lanes the mud and slime have coagulated in the deserted pigsties; the
clay we are made of is not much different, and yet some maintain
that it was worthy of the hands of the Creator who modelled it.

In Erto the hands of Mauro Corona know the magic of creating
life with things. Corona, who at first glance looks like an eccentric
hillsman, is a great sculptor, perhaps not yet fully aware of the fact.
His wooden figures carry incredible power together with the painful
brittleness of life. Women's bodies, absolute faces of old people,
animals, crucifixions, an olive-trunk transformed into a tragic torso,
into a Nike of these valleys, at once age-old and yet bitterly contemporary. When he's not sculpting, Mauro Corona climbs the arduous
faces of various mountains around the world and sells the photographs he takes which publicize sports equipment, for a song almost,
to unscrupulous sponsors. His body is wire-taut and his lightning
intelligence has the simplicity of the dove in the Gospel. It is necessary
to be as sly as a serpent, expert in the evil of the world and aware of just
how much acumen it takes to avoid being destroyed by the world's
malice. Who knows if the head, the heart and the hands that create
those figures can do without the prudence of the serpent.

On the way back, a break at Barcis. The waters of the artificial lake
sparkle emerald green, proving that artifice is no less enchanting than
Nature, or rather that there is nothing artificial because it is always
Nature who produces and puts on the show, even all the things that
seem to contradict her. We ask an old woman, dressed in black, where

the mountain community is. "Where else could it be? In the school
of course. Once there were children, but nobody has them now, and in
the empty schools is where they put all this stuff." Inside the building
it seemed more than legitimate to turn to an assistant and ask whether
there are books in the library on the village and its history, in particular
the works of Giuseppe Malattia della Vallata, the nineteenth-century
rhymester, author of the *Songs from the Valcellina* and of a Hymn
to Matter. "But who do you represent?" asks the assistant in his
turn, unable to conceive of the idea that anyone might want to look
for a book or simply to wander about off their own bat. It's a difficult question and not even Marisa and the others, hanging back
in bewilderment by the door, know what to say. True, there are
many categories that one might legitimately claim to represent:
bipeds, teachers, married people, fathers, children, travellers, mortals,
motorists, but . . . Thus the essence of this journey into the land of
one's forbears is the loss of another little piece of individual autonomy,
of His Majesty the Ego. One will simply have to get used to the idea
of no longer saying, "You don't know who I am," but, "You don't
know whom I represent."

Lagoons

Blackened *burchi*, flat-bottomed lighters, eaten by the water and here and there stripped to their rusty skeleton, lie grounded since Heaven knows when on the shallow bed of the lagoon, next to the island of Pampagnola. Our boat, a flat-bottomed *batela,* draws very little and at moments almost slips across a minimal skin of water covering the ground; it has just left Grado behind and is on its way along the Venetian coastal route, the salt-water road that leads to Venice, well marked with red and black poles to either side and on these, at the watery forks, signs indicate directions with their arrows: Aquileia, Venezia, Trieste. On a *briccola*, a tripod tower of poles, is a white statue of the Madonna, star of the seas and protectress of navigators: on her head sits a seagull, motionless against the large, empty summer brightness.

Immediately after the bridge, the lagoon begins with a cemetery for larger boats. From the side of one an upturned crane protrudes and on deck the capstans are rusted, but the hawsers are still intact and solid. This is a benevolent wreck, the ship rests tired and calm in a shoal after a lifetime of carrying fish and especially sand; and now it awaits its final consummation. Even more devastated is one of the lighters,

of which almost nothing but the rib timbers and the keel remain –
abstract embroidery of long, stark nails. But the rest are still solid; the
wood is hard, the strong bellying form displays all the knowledge of
the hands that shaped it, awareness of winds and tides accumulated
over generations. Red and blue stripes on the hull are fading, but here
and there the colour is still alive and warm.

It will take a long time before the tides, the rain and the wind reduce
those boats to pieces and still longer before those pieces rot and disintegrate. The gradual process of death: the tenacious resistance of form
to extinction. Travelling is also a futile guerrilla war against oblivion,
the rearguard on the march; one stops to observe the figure of a rotten
trunk that is still not quite completely gone, the profile of a dune that
is crumbling away, traces of lives lived in an old house.

The lagoon is a landscape, a seascape appropriate to this slow, aimless
wandering search for signs of metamorphosis, because the mutations,
those of both sea and land, are visible and take place before one's eyes.
The sandbank to the left, which holds back the open sea, is the Banco
d'Orio and it moved several metres during the two years in which Fabio
Zanetti studied it for his degree dissertation, especially towards the
west because of an exceptional Bora, a north-east wind. The movement
is tangible, like the passing of time on a person's face. The winds are
the inspired architects of the landscape: the Sirocco breaks things up,
the Bora sweeps and carries away, the breeze builds and rebuilds.

The *batela* slides through the seaweed between one shoal and another,
and it skirts a *tapo*, one of the countless islets that only just emerge
from the lagoon; little red-headed birds jump among the tufts of
grass which just a few metres away become indistinguishable from
the seaweed in the water. In the feeble wind the *tapo* flowers move,
a lavender-blue colour. *Tapo Flowers* was the title of Marin's first
poetry collection, published in 1912. Together with the shells, those

flowers are the symbol of his poetry and of the essence that pervades it indefatigably, creation born of the clots and sludge of life. Out of the brackish mud protrudes the slender, delicate stem, the slimy mollusc generates the perfect and iridescent spiral of the shell; this was the psalm of the eternal that Marin heard being sung among the canes and the sea lapping on the shore, and that he found again in the choirs singing the liturgy in the shadows of Sant'Eufemia, the venerable basilica at Grado.

The *tapo* is always visible, but the *velma* is land that appears only at low tide and then returns below, one moment familiar and exposed to full view, the next moment sunk in the mystery of the waters, which even half a metre is enough to create. The veiled and apparently immobile mystery of the depths, of the rocks and the shells on the sea-bed, all so strange and remote when one's hand dips in even just a few centimetres to violate their spell – the sorcery of undersea cities such as Vineta or Atlantis, whose charm shines forth in even just a little bit of underwater slime.

The tide enters the lagoon through the channels that cut the sandy coastline and through them the big waters of far away penetrate the salty ponds, the gulleys where the farmed fish spend the winter. The slow tranquillity of the lagoon, which in the bad weather the fog and the soft sludge can transform into a dangerous trap, is another of the sea's faces, its noble indifference. Put on a rock to dry, some shells have a sheen to them – abalones, pink and violet tellins, scallops, bluish limpets.

A cormorant struggles to take to the air, skims the water and, on reaching a deeper channel, dives and disappears; its neck, black as a periscope, re-emerges several metres further on. The island of Ravaiarina is left behind on the right: two boats with black rags hanging from their masts, markers to be left where the lobsterpots are dropped, slip by in silence, suspended between two mirrors. The *casoni*, the big houses, stand out on the islands; this is the centuries-old building type on the lagoon, functioning as a house and a warehouse for the fishing, made of wood and canes, with the door to the west, the floor made of mud, the hearth, *fughèr*, in the centre and the mattress stuffed with dried seaweed. There are still a few left, in fact several; television aerials stick out of some of them, others have been restored or transformed. In Porto Buso, where the Grado lagoon ends, there are none left, perhaps because during the Abyssinian war a Fascist party official who was passing through observed that it was outrageous to be off to civilize Africa and yet to tolerate mud huts at home and so he had them demolished, replacing them with little houses of stone.

Once upon a time the *casoneri* used on occasions to take their fish to Grado; then they would dress up and grease their hair with fried oil, to keep it straight and smooth and when they went to Mass the smell spread throughout the church. Apart from these cosmetic recipes, the lagoon, like all seas, is a great receptacle of water and air that eliminates the usual distinction between clean and dirty. Just a little further away a breath of wind and some currents render it as transparent as an aquamarine, that water-green that is the colour of life, but one's foot gladly sinks into the sludgy marsh. The turbid colour that clouds the gold of the sand with a dense brown is warm and good, a primordial silt; the silt of life, which is neither dirty nor clean, out of which men are made as are the faces that they love and desire and with which men make sandcastles and the images of their gods.

That mud seems to be dirty but instead it is healthy, like mould on a wound; it's pleasant to free oneself of it with a stroke of the arm in the clear, deep water, but on landing on some islet one wallows in that mire with an infantile familiarity, too often lost. The sores, on which that broth acts as a salve, like saliva on a scratch, are also the thorns planted every day, every hour in one's body like darts: the spines that leave their venom in one's flesh, in one's soul by virtue of the commands, the prohibitions, the injunctions, the invitations, the appeals, the pressures, the initiatives, ruining all taste for living and increasing one's anxiety about death.

The lagoon is also peace, slowing down, inertia, lazy and extended abandon, silence in which one slowly learns to distinguish minimal nuances of noise, hours that pass by without purpose or destination like the clouds; therefore it is life, not strangled in the vice of having to do, of having already done and having already lived – barefoot life, the bare feet that gladly feel the heat of the stone that burns and the dampness of the seaweed that rots in the sun. Not even the mosquito bites are annoying; they're almost pleasant, like the acrid taste of the wild garlic or the salty water.

On a *tapo*, among the flowers, there is a cross, commemorating someone. Sitting on board the *batela*, looking at the tufts of tamarisk that hang down over the water like the foam of a wave that breaks over the dune, one is a little less afraid of dying; perhaps one kids oneself that there's still a lot of time ahead, but above all one worries a little less about this reckoning, in the same way that the children who play caked in mud on the shore don't worry about it. The boat passes in front of fishing gulleys, in front of farmhouses, in the vicinity of whose drains a type of crab prospers which, in honour of its gastronomic preferences, is called "shit-eater". It seems that some restaurants serve them up together with *granzo poro*, another, more dignified local crab, in tasty sauces for the tourists, creating a perfect and vital cycle, recycle even.

The water – sea and lagoon – is life and a threat to life; it erodes, submerges, fertilizes, bathes, abolishes. During the first half of the century, between the Primero channel and Punta Sdobba on the estuary of the Isonzo, the shoreline to the east retreated by 196 metres; to the west the island of San Pietro d'Orio was once connected to Grado. The violent storms that overwhelm the earth- or dune-barriers form the lagoons, which proceed, more silently, to eat into terra firma. The chronicles make reference to battles and plagues, but very often – as in the testimony of Fortunato, the energetic and controversial patriarch of Grado in the times of Charlemagne, or the *Chronicon Gradense* of the eleventh and twelfth centuries – they mention the *aqua granda*, the high water that rises and spreads, the sea that enters the church of Saint Agatha to the point of covering the martyrs' tombs, or goes on to break against the palace of the Count, the seat of Venetian authority. Centuries later Nievo observed that "the sea invests the patriarchal basilica more and more closely every year."

Besieged as it is by water, the church is both a hard-pressed vessel calling for assistance and a dam or ark that offers help to those who are in peril of drowning. For the fisherman and the sailor, water is life and death, sustenance and menace; it eats away the wood of the ship just as it does the life of a man who ventures out on the treacherous, bitter sea, putting his trust in the fragile board his foot stands on and which is all that keeps him from the abyss. The ship protects from the storms, but she also turns her bow towards the hurricane and ship-wreck: beyond this lies the harbour. The sailor, in his affliction, is that much closer to disaster and the shore of the blessed; the waters of the abyss are indeed a great baptismal font.

The mosaic on the floor in Sant'Eufemia, the basilica at Grado, recalls the undulations of the sea floor, the curvilinear patterns that the waves print on the sandy beach and on the surface of the sea. Waves flow towards the shore and towards the altar, they curve, they curl, they break and they start flowing again. The harmony of that wave as it flows and ebbs, eternal in its fluctuating, is taken up in the ancient songs sung beneath the vault of the church; melody, too, is escape and return. Not the tempo of the church and the sea, but the brief, good tempo of life; waves and sand under the feet of those who pull the boat up onto dry land and ask for some mercy from the affliction of living,

lava quod est sordidum, riga quod est aridum, sana quod est saucium . . .
"Wash what is unclean, water what is arid, heal what is wounded."

A fish swims on the bed of the mosaic as out in the lagoon, the
symbol of the Lord incarnate in the daily food of those who struggle
between land and sea. Sometimes, when the tide goes out, a fish
remains stuck in a puddle and the children put it in a bucket; happily
they take it in their hands and play with it, but the fish writhes, its
gills rise and fall with the effort, nobody has asked him if he feels like
playing and even for the child something, for a while at least, changes
when the fish stops moving. *Hostem repellas longius, pacemque dones
protinus* . . . *vitemus omne noxium* . . . "Far from us drive the foe we
dread, and grant to us thy peace instead; so shall we not, with Thee
for guide, turn from the path of life aside."

The lagoon, the geologists say, is young. Some say one hundred and
twenty centuries, thinking of the far-off origins in the tectonic rise of
the Alps and the alluvial material brought by the rivers; others bring its
formation even nearer, placing it in history, measurable even by means
of man's short memory. The lagoon's time mixes history and nature;
for the most part its splendour lies in disasters and it matters little
whether they be man-made or natural: the Hun invasion that destroyed
Aquileia in 452, the fury of the sea in 582, the sack by the Longobards in
586, the flood of 589, the Saracen incursion in 869, the plague of 1237,
the fire raised by the English in 1810 – "Attila is God's scourge / and
the English are his brothers" – the *sión*, a cyclone, the one of 1925
and the one in 1939. Over the centuries and the years the *pescadora*,
the bell on the basilica tower has heralded the storms; processions,
rogations and even exorcisms have all been deployed in seeking
protection from the calamities, from each high water.

Grado is a literary landscape thanks to the lyrics of Biagio Marin,
who made a poetic myth of the city. Before Marin there was very little,

almost nothing – the conventional verses of Sebastiano Scaramuzza, more meaningful for the linguist than for the reader – but even this almost-nothing glints with the odd fleck of gold, it can move one just like the inlay on the shell born of almost-nothing. Domenico Marchesini, known as Menego Picolo and who lived between 1850 and 1924, with his Grado poetry and prose will have no place in the memory of his literary descendants, if indeed such exist. But in one of his lines the poor fishermen become *comandauri del palù* "lords of the marsh"; their hard work out there is touched with the glory of the Serenissima, whose own mother was Grado; but then the poem immediately states that even if their work makes them its lords, the marsh, on which they depend for their sustenance, is their *paròn*, their master.

A line of poetry is not insignificant, in a life. Neither is it insignificant to set up an inn, like Menego Picolo's "To the Friends", which he opened over a century ago after giving up his job as sea captain. This was not a step down socially; in the times of the Serenissima the innkeeper was an authority who dealt directly with the representatives of the Republic and was responsible for the quality of his wine – and his guests' behaviour. The inn and the church are the two most important places in every human settlement worthy of the name, and on every island too.

The two places are not dissimilar: both are open to travellers passing by and looking to rest for a moment in the shade before some ancient image or a glass of wine, both of which help to keep going. Two open-handed places in which no one asks the visitors where they are from and under which flag or insignia they travel; in church there's nothing even to pay – lighting a candle is recommended, but is not compulsory. Perhaps today the churches are one of the places in which it is possible to breathe more freely, almost like being out in a boat: one enters when one wants, nobody asks why one doesn't go to Mass or why the eight

o'clock service rather than the one at ten, unlike the organizing committees of cultural events, where one is required to account for each little
defence of one's own liberty, for each guilty desire to go for a walk
rather than attending the debate. Social rites are more intransigent and
insistent than religious ones; indeed, it is much more difficult to elude
them. Posters for parish events do not carry the intimidating R.S.V.P.,
at the most they ask, quite reasonably, all things considered, to go into
church somewhat more completely dressed than out in a boat.

San Pietro d'Orio welcomes us with a sticky, sterile heat: this realm
of dried up cuttlefish bones could, at least at this noontime, be one of
Melville's Encantadas. A crust of mud splits in the sun, a lizard on a
rock studies the unwelcome visitors for a long time; it's a direct gaze,
eyeball to eyeball, and one feels inadequate and oafish in front of those
age-old pupils; there's a feeling of relief when the animal disappears
under the rock. There are many mosquitoes, canes by the shore and
dandelions that cover a field right up to the point where an acacia wood
begins; bramble bushes which in just a few weeks will produce black-
berries, the bittersweet smell of wormwood, used to flavour *grappa*.

   On this island there used to be a shrine looked after by the
Benedictines and, before that, a temple to the god Belenus; later, in
accordance with changes in gods and their altars, it housed a German
bunker. Between the two wars a man lived on this island with just
the coarse grass and his goats for company, stubbornly refusing to
travel, neither to the city nor to any inhabited place. He'd probably
come to realize that in order to be a little less unbearable life has to
be emptied of all possible ballast, especially the ubiquitous human
presence. Every act of self-denial has its own grandeur, even if it be
naïve or arrogant. In any case on the sea one is never truly alone:
the silver lagoon, the continuous, varied background murmur that
requires interpreting, imposes a sort of dialogue.

*

There are many islands, without counting those surfaces that appear and disappear with the tide; the journey brushes distraitly past them, heedless and superficial like the journeys we make every day, which lead us to the end of our time without ever really having learned the road home. The *batela* wanders about like a fish, searching for the channels between one shoal and another, where in the duck-hunting season oystercatchers and coots fall plumb into the water; it skirts the nets set for the grey mullet, it passes long, blond seaweed, angled like waving hair, and then over the area near Marina di Macia where every now and then Roman *amphorae* surface. In ancient times there were probably warehouses here and the sandy bed yields up these beautiful vessels, figures of Eros emerging from the waters of sleep. To "emerge" and "surface" are really euphemisms for the often illicit work of recovering the *amphorae*, which generally lie at a depth of about a metre and a half beneath the sandy floor. There was a time when some leading families from Grado used to hold seances, ostensibly to discover the location of the much valued relics, but in truth their purpose was thus to avoid having to reveal from which fisherman, more vulnerable to the Law than the deceased, the precious information had come.

Up until a few years ago the now deserted island of Marina di Macia was the realm of the enterprising Papo Slavich, who subsequently sought refuge in Senegal. The island is rugged, a barrier of tamarisks doubled by its reflection in the water, it looks like a tropical rain forest: offshore the *tragio* spreads out, a wide section of shallow and tepid water, a nursery for fish and their eggs. In the last days of the Second World War the Germans, on their retreat towards Venice, were machine-gunned here by British planes and threw themselves into the water, hoping to escape on foot over the dunes and the marshes, but they became stuck in the silt that can take hold like quicksand, and they drowned in the mud, or were gunned down one by one. For days on end the corpses blocked that part of the lagoon, floating between the shoals and the gulleys. Rumours in the town spoke also of gold ingots abandoned by the Germans, their discovery attributed to some families from Grado who were suddenly well off, murmurings and quarrels that in some cases even ended up in court.

Papo Slavich's victims, however, were merely oysters. His idea was to replace the native Grado oysters with Portuguese ones – which in fact were Japanese – and he started breeding them in commercial quantities and designed facilities for their cultivation and harvest. On the island the abandoned tanks that have been invaded by the grass, the blocked rinsing pumps, can all be seen, the ruins of a small, fledgling empire. The Portuguese–Japanese oysters have prospered vigorously and cling even to the jetty, suffocating and ruining the Grado oysters. A successful venture then, except for the fact that those exotic fruits of the sea, so it is said, taste of water melon.

Morgo is the most beautiful of the islands, lost in a dream, a place of enchantment. Thick pines, elms, bamboo thickets, tangled bushes and a few agaves block access to the interior; in one section of the wood stand rugged, stripped trunks of trees devoured by the processionary caterpillar; they have a livid look, like survivors of some catastrophe. The water near the shore is all white from the feathers of the stilt-plovers, birds that resemble light-coloured herons and take to the air when the boat comes close, a white cloud in the sky, white foam rocking in the slight movement of the water. On the beach, crabs abandoned by the tide, they too dried out and white, crinkle and disintegrate underfoot like freshly-boiled crab between one's teeth.

This romantic island, once rich in animals and self-sustaining, has its own romantic story. Up until a few years ago in the depths of the wood in a dark, hidden clearing there was a plinth with an urn. Following the First World War Maria Auchentaller, a Viennese count's daughter, fell in love with the "little doctor", an irresistible Don Giovanni who lived in Grado and who even today is remembered by many for his macho boots, accessories that were apparently useful in seduction. Mothers are often more interesting than their daughters and the young countess caught her own *in flagrante delicto* with her loved one. She returned to Vienna and killed herself; her ashes were brought to Morgo and put on a little column in that dark glade. There's nothing there now. That emptiness suits death, its unimaginable void, more so than tombs and gravestones with their high-flown and uncertain messages of consolation. The boatman doesn't remember what happened to the mother; a brother who supported the Germans moved to Alto Adige after the Second World War where he slowly drowned himself in drink. There was also a good painter in the family, whose works were in the Viennese Secessionist style, dykes and sea storms; they embellished some hotels in Grado.

"Grado, 26 July, 1962. My Friend, listen to me. I've just finished copying your letter into my diary. This morning I've been out on the dune . . . we had luck enough to find a small *argonauta*, a paper nautilus . . . the wonderful form was sitting in the palm of my hand in front of me. It does the heart good, it's such an unusual shell. And here, on coming home, I found your letter which is no less beautiful than the paper nautilus . . . yesterday was the 19th anniversary of Falco's death and on the tomb we lit a flame of red roses and carnations. A great big flame. I would have liked you to be here, because you are part of my life . . . you certainly must return to Grado. I would like you to come one evening with the ferry, that way you'll be able to come with me out on the dunes in the early morning. You cannot be fond of me if you've not been with me on the dunes and in the San Marco pine wood. That way you could stay out on the boat until midday and go swimming with your girlfriend. Or we could go to the San Marco wood in the afternoon, about five o'clock. That way you can see plenty of things in a single day. I'm glad that your friend enjoyed herself at my house and with me . . . I embrace you and send you greeting; please say hello for me to your mother and father – Biagio Marin."

With Marin one never wasted time: he had an almost physical aversion to banality, that prevarication which exhausts itself in a vacuum and occasionally offers protection from harsh realities, keeping one from leaning out into the void. He had studied in Vienna and he was masterful in his evocation of the final years of the Hapsburgs, but he certainly had not learned the Austrian art of affable, sardonic reticence, the elusive grace of Hofmannsthal's "difficult man". Tactless in his pursuit of essentials, Marin was irascible or genial like a marine deity, but incapable of laughter. He immediately jettisoned the circumstantial and went for the absolute, or at least that which, life being what it is, came close to something absolute. He knew how to teach "how man makes himself eternal"; the gesture with which he resolved some anxiety or darkness that one confided to him – the carefree gesture of a hand dropping dirty linen into the laundry basket – dissolved the psychological misery and helped one confront the shadow and accept one's own limitations, submit to one's own rules, proceed along one's road with fewer fears and fewer idols.

In his vitality, his avid, insatiable vitality, Marin was childishly, sometimes deplorably greedy for recognition, like a child who wants a toy and tears it from another's grasp. But he recognized that this was simply an appetite that could be indulged but which in itself is of no value and which, if indulged, does not lead to happiness and, if unrequited, does not affect one's good humour.

Marin had the epic self-sufficiency of children and certain old men, those who simply are, like nature, and do not in any way depend on how others see them. In a rich life, rich even in mistakes and tumbles, he encountered difficulties, want, tragedy in the death of his son Falco, but never unease, that anxiety which makes the hands sweat and enervates more than pain does. Talking with a friend or speaking in a difficult and tense public situation was all the same to him, the concept and the reality of stress were perfectly unknown to him. This was one of the reasons why he lived to ninety-four in perfect lucidity and excellent health.

His vitality was prodigious, demonic; it gave him an unusual multiple personality, abnormal, tumorous, the sort to expand and crush those who were close to him. As Diderot said of Racine, Marin too was a great tree, destined to grow tall and provide life and shade but also destined to crush, in its growth, the plants that grew beside it. Sometimes it seemed as though he contained within himself many people of high and low degree, large-spirited and ravenous. Certainly he was not always able to learn for himself those values that he had an extraordinary gift for imparting to others. "I am ashamed of myself," he once wrote to Giorgio Voghera. Especially as a young man, but even later, Marin was also a devastating bully; the letters and the diaries of his son Falco, who was as straight as a die, testify heavily against him in their very affection. But his vitality and his overbearing behaviour were also capable of being refined into high spirituality.

Marin felt deeply the tragic conflict inherent in life and its passing, in its birth and its death; he felt it on the philosophical level, on the religious level, on the historical level, even in the drama of eastern and Adriatic Italy, in which he was both witness and participant, from the First World War to the turn towards Fascism, to the Resistance, to the fraught years immediately following the Second World War. "If the Spirit of the World has decided to obliterate the millennial Venetian imprint on the eastern Adriatic world," he said, "I will bow and I will say *fiat voluntas Tua*, but then, for my part I will add: *Pig . . .*" and the worst possible blasphemy was completed.

Above and beyond all of these conflicts, however painful, Marin said yes, amen to life whole and entire, beyond good and evil. He saw and heard and felt life's unity everywhere, even in pain and in death, and he possessed this unity with an inebriate and disturbing sensuality that found all things desirable, even death itself – not merely the gulls flying in the summer sky, but even the gulls dead and rotting on the sand: he would pick them up in his hands with something approaching desire. For him the eternity of creatures was their meaning in the life of all things, as it were the crest of a wave, not yet destroyed in its rapid breaking. All of his poetry sings this unity in which single existences flourish and wither, like the plant that dies and is reborn.

For him life, even in its tragedies, was thus part of a song . . . an affirmation: Marin didn't know the word for No, the word which, however much one may love people, animals, plants and living things, one sometimes has to be capable of saying to the universe, to the Big Bang and all the bloody carnival that has come after it; one has to if one wants to heed not simply the tears of Achilles, but the despair, too, of all the abject, nameless suffering that cannot even find a voice. But there was nothing edifying in Marin's love of life; it was a powerful love of the spells that life is rich in, despite everything, and which his poetry captured and recreated with a musical enchantment that seems to rise out of the inchoate murmur of becoming, still short of full articulation – a siren song that came before history, or reason.

That paper nautilus, that shell mentioned in the letter of July 1962, is a symbol of his poetry, a harmony in which, as in a face, the flux of life is given shape. As a youth Marin's brimming enthusiasm must have been hard to take, but in his poetry, as in his own character, he grew in refinement over the years, as though the years had rarefied his excessive vitality, had given it poise and nobility. The first collections already contain a few masterpieces, but they are scarce and isolated; if Marin had died at sixty or sixty-five, he would have remained on the margins of literature. He wrote his most beautiful poems at the age of seventy, seventy-five, eighty. He would get angry whenever anyone told him that of his potentially endless lyrical production, in its infinitely repeatable variations, only a small part would survive.

But this part, not so little after all, is the work of a true poet. He himself knew that praise was never given to an individual nor to his poetry, with their qualities borrowed like any other item of clothing worn in this life, rather what was praised was that which transcends the individual and his poetry and stretches out towards that transcendence. This lesson is a liberation from petty private fears. So despite his substantial failings one can say thank you to him in the way one thanks one's father, and at the same time one's brother, with whom one has travelled and clashed, and even a son who will outlive us; or just as one would like to thank one of those big, ancient trees that lived so long before our arrival and will continue to live so long after our departure.

Travelling, like storytelling, like living, is omitting. Mere chance leads to one shore and abandons another. On the island of Belli, "Beautiful", called thus because of the proverbial ugliness of some of its inhabitants, there once lived old Bela, a witch who stirred up the winds and ruined the fishing out of spite for those who were not kind to her, and for similar reasons she seems to have once made a reconnaissance plane fall with a wave of her hand. She was a demonic specimen – the water encourages evil spirits. On the dunes near Grado the people feared the Balarin, a malign goblin, or the errant Jew, and in the howling of the wind and the creaking of the doors on the night of Epiphany one could hear the Varvuole, the furies that came from the sea.

One can imagine old Bela's face, probably hideous from age and from the insults received out of cruel prejudice, and it is to be hoped that those who called her a jinx really did return home often with empty nets. Travellers are followers of the Enlightenment and when possible they discredit the blind and irrational ferocity of myths; Ulysses too – "he whose inner will is proof against sorcery", as Circe describes him, dissolves the brute power of witches, giants and sirens. Nastiness towards those branded as jinxes is a kind of racism worse than the rejection of the foreigner, because it is masked, as is every superstition, by a sophisticated vulgarity.

In his *casone* on the lagoon the poet Pier Paolo Pasolini used the cine camera to recount the tale of witch and foreign victim *par excellence*, the story of Medea. Medea was devoted to the grim (but to her familiar) gods of earth and night, and thus was close to the archaic and dark roots of myth – the indistinct totality of life – and she was therefore a stranger in the land of the man she loved, Jason, and a stranger too in Greece, which over the centuries has shone out as the universal homeland. So she was condemned to an even greater trial, to be the most alien of strangers, the most unacceptably different. She was even induced by the violence and the deceit she suffered to violate that most universal of all feelings, maternal love: killing her sons she becomes monstrously at odds with her own self, her own heart, after she had become a stranger in the land of her birth, Colchis, and in her chosen land, Greece.

Her tragedy re-echoes over the centuries, in countless reworkings, ancient and recent, but her terrible story will not answer to any modern psychological relativism. In the myth of Medea it is reason which ensnares and destroys the grim and ingenuous magic; the potions and the witchcraft of the sorceress are ineffectual against the calculating astuteness of Jason and the Greeks, and her own passion, as intense and wild as life itself, is easy prey for the web of mediations in which civilized society envelops and smothers it. The Argonauts who succeed in their quest for the Golden Fleece – thanks to her, for love's sake traitor to her own values – have the terrible and irresponsible force of Greek youth, at once innocent and sophisticated, and to them the whole world, even the unknown and threatening parts of it, seems to offer itself up to be seized and plundered. In the various Medeas created and recreated in world literature, the clear Hellenic light is a troubling illumination, a demonic transparency of horror. It is not classical harmony and neither is it Dionysian fury; the Greek spirit – the ship setting off to pillage Colchis – is indeed absolute and candid bad faith, the act of plunder that stops at nothing, a market for everything that is sacred.

The sea, insidious and boundless, is the space in which this unscrupulous adventure takes place; it corrodes laws, and altars and accepts no prohibitions; it is the space of sacrilegious history. The Greek spirit is precisely this mobility, untrustworthy as the sea; Medea – murderer of her brother and eventually of her own sons – is the custodian of the sacred, not of the archaic sacredness of her rites, which she is magnanimously ready to relinquish, but of the whole sacredness of life. The spellbound immobility of the lagoons of Grado might well be a symbolical backdrop of the myth, a communion of demons and gods, in which Medea grows and from which she is torn, through her love for Jason, by the strength of Greece's secular and rational civilization.

Greek civilization wins, but this victory involves a horror that is every bit as dark as the obscurity of Colchis with its dragons. Uprooted from her world, in whose eyes she has made herself guilty, betraying it and cooperating in its ruin, Medea is gripped by this sense of guilt and disorientation, she is rejected and despised by the Greek world to which she had sacrificed her own world and in which she can find no place; humiliated, betrayed and trampled on by Jason, for love of whom she has sacrificed everything, she falls prey to a searing pain, which leads her to the ghastly murder of her own sons, a vengeance directed at Jason, but also, and above all else, at herself.

In one of her novels Christa Wolf harks back to traditions more ancient than Euripides' tragedy and suggests that the victors' memory has falsified the truth, attributing to the barbarian foreign woman a crime actually committed by the people of Corinth, who killed Medea's sons in an explosion of violence. In mythology nothing really happens, everything is simply recounted and takes effect with each telling of the story. Medea as murderer of her own sons is more credible, more real because she is thus even more the victim: no one could be more of a victim than the person who is tortured to the point of being overwhelmed, to the utter loss of humanity, to being driven to do evil. In Pasolini's film Medea's savage vengeance is also the brutalization that western violence instigates in the Third World, alienating that world from itself, it is barbaric disorder reacting to a barbaric order.

But *Medea* is a tragedy, and it would not be a tragedy if it did not sanction the need for those horrible events of which it is nevertheless so morally critical. Greek civilization, despite everything, is a light which in the end serves to spread humanity, far more so than primitive Colchis with its dragons and darkness. The tragedy is that the man who bears this torch is Jason, the unworthy, and with him the rulers and the people of Corinth, of Greece. Jason is a liar skilful not only in deceiving others, but also himself, thus stifling his awareness of his own guilt and committing evil while convinced that he has no choice; he is prepared to do anything to the point of losing all substance, to becoming a man without qualities, with neither core nor depth, a mere surface cloaked in seduction, in diplomatic and erotic charm, in beautiful heroic gestures. He is the prototype of male vanity, unsure of itself and devoted only to its own image, cynically ready to absolve itself in the name of an overriding necessity.

Even in her homicidal fury it is Medea who is aware of the authentic sense of love, of feelings, of values. But Colchis, with its tribal ferocity, is not a possible alternative to the Greece of Homer, Socrates and Plato, of myth and *logos* which are rooted in being. It is tragically cynical, a whim of the gods, that the herald of Hellenic illumination in the midst of dark barbarism should be the wretched Jason and that his victim – the price paid for the epoch-making enterprise, the Argonauts' expedition – should be Medea, so much greater than he. But it is still more tragically cynical that this whim of the gods should be an essential element in Greek civilization. This relentless dialectic allows for no dreams of uncorrupted paradises and even less for any comparison with the West; in the film, too, the spellbound somnolent oblivion of the lagoon mitigates, but only for a moment, the unbearable horror of the story.

Every *Medea* is the story of a terrible difficulty in comprehension between differing civilizations; a tragically topical warning on how difficult it is for a foreigner to stop really being such for others. Medea reveals the triumph of extraneousness and objective conflict between different people and peoples. For this reason too, in Grillparzer's play *Medea*, she is able to say that it would be better not to be born and that when this happens all we can do – without falling into tearful self-pity, like Jason – is to bear the pain.

The Grado lagoon finishes at Anfora and at Porto Buso. Up until the Great War, just beyond it lay Italy, and the irredentists of Grado, the republicans from the Ausonia club, used to cross the channel at night to touch the homeland. In 1915 an Italian torpedo boat fired a few shells at the bunker on the island, the Austrians replied with a couple of shots and abandoned the bunker and thus began the worldwide bedlam which threatens to break out again today.

That channel was a fatal border, the front line in a world conflict. Grado itself is a border, a strip marking several frontiers. Between land and sea, between open sea and closed lagoon, but above all between mainland and maritime civilizations. Grado was born of Aquileia, but the eleven kilometres dividing the two towns mark a notable distance. From ancient times Aquileia extended its authority over the inland dioceses; its great history together with that of its patriarchs extends towards Germany, Hungary, towards central and imperial Europe. Grado became a metropolis for the dioceses of Istria and maritime Venice, opening up to an Adriatic and Mediterranean culture. Even the dialect changed over those eleven kilometres between Grado and Aquileia; Friuli set its mark on it.

Those eleven kilometres mark the passage from the airy marine ethos of Venice to a continental and problematic *Mitteleuropa*, grand, morose laboratory of civilization's discontents, expert in emptiness and in death. That cultural continent – and Michelstaedter's nearby Gorizia was already an extraordinary barometer for the apocalypse – was a world well wrapped up and buttoned down, in its heavy greatcoats, against the wind of life. Before the Great War when Marin, a schoolboy in Gorizia and founding member of the Ausonia club, used to swim across that channel to touch Italy, he certainly must have enjoyed getting undressed, stripping off all those defences learned at the big *Mitteleuropa* school and throwing himself into the water, letting himself drift with the flow of life. He would cross the channel and come back no longer knowing which was his place, his homeland, which side he was on. He did learn once for all a few years later when he declared at Vienna University, where he was studying, in a stormy interview with the rector, that he was an Italian patriot and meant to go to war against Austria. A few weeks later, however, in Italy, he was protesting to a boorish captain in the Italian army which he had joined as a volunteer, that he was an Austrian, and accustomed to a more civil style and tone.

Borders often require blood sacrifices, provoking death; in 1023 the great Patriarch of Aquileia, Popone, devastated Grado in a bloodbath and, between 1915 and 1918 Italy's eastern borders were a slaughterhouse. Perhaps the only way to neutralize the lethal power of borders is to consider oneself and to put oneself on the other side, for ever.

*

Myth has it that in these lagoons the Danube reached the sea through a river that rose out of its tributary, the Sava. This river was the Istro, which in other versions was the Danube itself. The Argonauts too reached the Adriatic up the Danube, carrying the ship on their shoulders and relaunching it in other waters until they reached the sea. It is right that the Danube – the river of continental *Mitteleuropa*, of its greatness, its melancholy, its obsessions – should flow into the Adriatic, because the Adriatic is the sea *par excellence*, the sea of all persuasion, all letting go, of true life and of harmony with life. The Argonauts, fleeing from the fogs and the monsters of Colchis, reach Cherso and Lussino, the perfect enchantment of the Apsyrtides, then the Isle of Circe. But those absolute islands were born of the blood spilled by the Argonauts themselves from the body of Apsyrtus, Medea's brother, who was treacherously killed through the sorceress's deceit – guilty again because of her love for Jason; he was hacked to pieces and thrown into those immortal waters. Even that beauty and harmony are children of crime and fraud; on these banks and in these ambiguous, yielding courses of water, the Danube carries Medea, her pain, her fury and her perdition and Jason's treachery.

Beyond the channel, which opens up in front of the On the Slate restaurant at Anfora, lies the Marano lagoon. The *Maranesi* pass for brave, aggressive fishermen, people talk about their casual incursions across to the other side of the Adriatic, challenging the Jugoslav, later to become Slovenian and Croatian, patrol boats; people also complain about their incursions into Grado's waters, and happily recall a certain Graziadio who in recent times kept them away from Porto Buso with his shotgun. From outside the Mistral arrives, a breath of the real sea. The line dividing the sea from the lagoon is visible, precarious and unavoidable like all borders, with their requirements and their vanities, it matters little whether they be borders between waters, colours, countries or dialects. A fisherman on his way back from the Banco d'Orio has caught a sea bass weighing almost three kilos, even the scales of that fish, sparkling and imperceptibly changing colour thanks to the sun outside and the death inside, are a heaving of borders.

Cristiano asks if we want to go with him on the dunes at Anfora, to look for clams. He is twelve and has a fresh, determined face; he is the skipper, he knows where and how to take the boat and, with instinctive respect for the hierarchies of experience, one follows his orders. His calm rowing inspires confidence. He doesn't miss the two dots on the sand freed by the tide, indicating the clams' hideaway. The knife disturbs the black mud, seething with minimal and obstinate life, extracts the animal closed in its valve. The beach is white with light, with shells, with breaking waves. Just over there among the coarse grass and the seagulls' nests, the carcass of an enormous sea turtle rots. A few days ago near that turtle Cristiano found and saved a dog. He found it by chance, almost dying of thirst and so exhausted that it couldn't manage to climb into the *batela*. It must have been on the dune for a long time. At home it drank one bucket of water after another and then slept for almost two days. Cristiano has grown fond of the dog, a beautiful setter, old and a bit deaf, with noble, puzzled eyes. He hopes that its owner had wanted to get rid of it, so that he can keep it, and he's called it Ivan.

He didn't invent the name: Ivan was a Maremmano sheep dog which some twenty or more years ago belonged to a policeman from the small station at Porto Buso, now abandoned; nearby, Giuseppe Zigaina recalls, was the house of the buoy-keeper who lived alone with his offshore buoy and had to keep its lamp filled. One day the policeman, tired of the animal, took it onto the dune and shot it. The dog was wounded but survived. It survived for a long time, never letting anyone come near, and learned to feed on gulls' eggs and the odd animal; only at night did it come to drink from the fountain at Anfora.

That white dog, appearing and disappearing among the sand and the tufts of grass on the shore, remained in the people's memory. Its name is remembered and giving it to another dog, as Cristiano has done, is a little rite that conveys an inheritance and grants authority to the new animal. The new Ivan was in fact a lost dog, and when his master came to collect him Cristiano perhaps felt that all stories have an end. But the name of the old white dog remains, while nobody remembers anything of the policeman, not even his name.

Knotty fisherman's hands, knots of wood in the boats or on the boards on which clams and lobsters have been emptied, knots in the nets that are thrown into the water or in the ropes that moor a boat: throughout the engravings of Dino Facchinetti these images of strength and patience recur, learned from the long slow rhythm of the waters, of the toil, of work down the generations. Poetry is *pietas*, humility – closeness to the *humus lagunare*, evoked in a work of 1991 – and the fraternal pleasure of living. The waters of that immemorial *humus* are dark, the *batela* glides calmly, the hand guiding it knows how to sculpt a face mined by the years, to etch the profile of a landscape. Grado and its lagoon have known artists who celebrate them in colours or in pencil sketches: the Siroccos of De Grassi, the twinmasted *bragozzi* of Coceani, the dykes and the waves of Auchentaller, who bears the same name as the unhappy Contessina of Morgo. Those patient and knotted hands are like the rough goodness of old trees; the ancient lagoon life suggests an art that is careful about things, that serves reality.

Starting back, to complete the circle. The island of San Giuliano, with its sixth-century church, glorious orchards and the *chiuse*, the locks for capturing the fish; on the mud of the shorelines the Istrian rock stands out white. The people of Grado used to go over to Istria carrying sand and come back with these bright stones. The islands of the Gran Chiusa, Casoni Tarlao, Isola Montaron, Isola dei Busiari; on the horizon the belltower of Aquileia, high up over the splendid basilica, hidden away from view, symbol of the city, of *civitas*. Like the *tapo* flower, the city rises out of these marshes, as does history. Out of these lagoons Venice was born. When Attila fell on Aquileia, heralded by a burning dry wind and reviled by the Aquileiesi in their dialect as *fiol de un can*, "son of a dog", the refugees who hid among the islands laid the foundations of one of the world's great states. A ballad, attributed to the Bishop Paolino, narrates the destruction of the forums and the palaces, the deserted churches became dens for foxes and nests for snakes. The lament for the ruin of the city – from ancient Sumerian Lagash to Bath in Anglo-Saxon elegy – recurs throughout world literature, a true literary genre dealing with the transience of all that is high and mighty.

As with Rome and the flight of Aeneas, empires are born out of exile; the foundations of the future are preceded by an exodus, by the painful loss of the past. On these waters the beginning and the end of the Serenissima are there for the touching; on the Centenara, now reclaimed, a Gradenigo, descendant of the family of the Doges, ended up as caretaker of the fish farm, slopping out when there was too much mud, burning the brushwood and the dry grass.

Towards the east, more or less in front of the Mula di Muggia bank, lies the small submerged island of San Grisogono, from the name of the Aquileiese martyr who, tradition has it, was decapitated and buried in those sands when they were still above sea level, in the time of Diocletian. Therefore the *batela*, in this brief diversion from the channels of the lagoon, if tradition is to be relied upon, slides over a family tomb, because from those Grisogono of remote Greek and later Dalmatian origin, minor magistrate-nobles who settled in Split and produced men of letters and science who gave lustre to various Dalmatian cities in the time of the Serenissima, there came, too, Francesco de Grisogono, maternal grandfather, who had come close to genius and visited every facet of melancholy, passing on to his grandson the nostalgia and the *hubris* associated with the business of enclosing the world in a cage of signs and words.

In one of his last pages, written to be read after his death, Francesco de Grisogono had written that, "He had ceased existing without ever having been able to start living." He had soon realized that his "burning vocation" was destined to burn in absolute solitude, and that his life would depend upon his capacity to prevent the bitterness of his misfortune and isolation from degrading his intelligence into sterile, brilliant eccentricity and the richness of his heart into compulsive resentment.

Born in 1861 in Šibenik in Dalmatia, Francesco de Grisogono grew up in difficult conditions and, after being prevented from completing his cherished studies in philosophy and mathematics in Vienna, he spent many years as an officer in the Royal Imperial Navy. He was an Italian irredentist, but was in love with German culture and knew and appreciated much of Croatian culture, to which another branch of the family belonged. Eventually he became a simple teacher in the vocational schools in Trieste. Frustrated as he was by all manner of adversities, he found himself excluded throughout his life from any contact with the world of research.

He was a philosopher and a scientist, inventing systems for space navigation and instruments for overcoming gravity in this field; he read Kant, Schopenhauer and Nietzsche as well as the great mathematicians, wrote philosophical aphorisms full of wit and revelatory in their disenchantment. But Francesco de Grisogono was – and he knew it – isolated from the great scientific and philosophical culture of his time, which was living a prodigious period of revolution, to which he probably would have been able to contribute and which certainly would have nourished his mind, freeing it from the asphyxia and the lucubrations of solitude. He himself observed that the projects and the ideas that proliferated in his head without ever being realized, seeds falling into sunless soil that rendered them consumptive, these things left him at once oppressed and excited, like a machine with too great a head of steam, blocked and forced into awareness of his situation.

Those "seeds of a new science" – to quote the title of his main and posthumous work, which caught the interest, many years after his death, of the Nobel prize-winning physicist Enrico Fermi – in truth these managed to bear fruit thanks to the most strenuous effort which he felt it was his duty – to himself and to others – to disguise in a genial levity. In his modest study and at the little fold-away table he used to carry with him even on Sundays when the family went for the day to picnic up on the Carso, while his three children played and his wife tried to get him to eat plenty of eggs to keep his strength up, Francesco de Grisogono wrote down stern aphorisms and pathetic fantasies, elaborated the acute principle of minimal distinctions, and contemplated the creation of a positive critical philosophy freed of metaphysics. He unmasked commandments and moral prohibitions and demolished the concept of truth with an ethical absoluteness and a dedication to the real that was worthy of his legendary martyr-ancestor. He developed his theory on power as the goal of knowledge, and lived the impotence of his condition serenely. Above all else he worked at the fundamental dream of his life, the "conceptual calculus", an *ars combinatoria* based on rigorous mathematical foundations and capable of producing all the operations, the discoveries and the intuition of genius.

Francesco de Grisogono sought to free human creativity from the whims of chance and from the injustice of fate which, as he well knew, conditioned it and clipped its wings. To this task he brought a titanic impetus compounded with a genuine scientific rigour, a prophetic intuition, outdated impedimenta and a naïvety that was unavoidable in an isolated provincial. And if genius is inevitably subject to hazard, then conceptual calculus, with its machinery providing every possible operation, and imposing on them its inflexible logic, floats free of the randomness in which men, even geniuses, are ensnared.

The most interesting aspect of this Promethean design is the arrangement of the tables that the writer composes in his *Seeds of a New Science*, to catalogue the infinite variety of the world, in such a way as to organize the material for those combinations that will extract from reality all possible inventions and discoveries. It classifies types and subtypes of elements (unentwineable: bacillary, arched, contorted, "circuent"), the thirty-six determinations of a "ponderal" or the twenty-one determinations of an event, the locutions and the translocational operations, the "electriferous" instruments and the "sonifers", the seventeen parts of the "alteragifers", the 143 modalities of an action, the twenty-eight physiological phenomena and the same number of psychic phenomena, the divers substances – the friable, foliaceous, mucilaginous, foamy, pungent. It suggests scientific research ranging from the brilliant to the hare-brained, enquiries into the influence of a vacuum on the variations in the electric resistance of selenium, through the effects of light or experiments to verify whether the given $X(2)^n$ contains properties that will arrest the decomposition of corpses.

Among those tables, those calculi and those mathematical signs, pigeon-holed and untouchable, sit the seduction and the prolixity of the world, the immensity of the celestial vaults and the chasms of the heart. That all-encompassing *hubris*, which toys with omnipotence, exposes the individual in his smallness and helplessness, lost as he is amid the infinite and even more so amid the enigmas of finite things, overwhelmed by love for life; all of this he tries to capture like a fisherman who seeks to capture the sea in his net. Only plain mathematics, with its signs as abstruse to the layman as hieroglyphics, can elicit the mysterious and terrible grace of living; here we have the glum, positivist, nineteenth-century honesty, with its rigour and its ingenuous faith in being able to eliminate metaphysics, which authenticates the sense of mystery – unstated and indeed doggedly banished like an error in a computation.

Those infinite spaces – which de Grisogono strove with his genuine acumen to render navigable for men – often contract into his solitary researcher's rented room, where he lacks even an interlocutor in whom he can confide, someone to whom he can present results and projects, and he has to be careful that the solitude does not lead him to start raving over nonsense.

Francesco de Grisogono knew the inner perils of isolation and melancholy, the excesses in which a heart, too rich and big for the cramped reality in which it may find itself, chokes and suffocates. As he said of himself, "Patiently and playfully he bore the sight of all his dreams dying one by one . . . and in this bitter disappointment he did not come to hate men nor things and neither did he tire of loving life which lavished only thorns on him. . . . Thus he grew old in a peaceful melancholy and carried the cross of his dark destiny in the guise of an ordinary man, in order not to render himself ridiculous as a misunderstood genius."

It is difficult to say which of the two, the martyr or the scientist, suffered the harsher fate.

"Well . . . I don't know," says Arcadio Scaramuzza, "at home he never spoke about it, and we never asked . . . you know in those days, between his arrest and the trial, he'd lost all his hair, that was when he went bald, and we felt it wasn't right to ask him questions, to remind him of that period. . . ." So at home his father, Antonio Scaramuzza, had recounted nothing of those days in Kotor, which under his leader-

ship seemed to have transformed the Dalmatian port into Kronstadt
and to have brought the Red October to the Adriatic. According to his
son he had brought his baldness back with him from the Revolution, an
upset which, in the eyes of his relatives, seemed to add more weight to
the courage and the glory of those deeds.

Antonio Scaramuzza was one of the ring-leaders of a revolt that
broke out in Kotor on 1 February, 1918, when the sailors of the Austro-
Hungarian fleet took over some ships, including the flagship, the
armed cruiser *Sankt Georg*, arresting the commander, Admiral Hansa,
with his officers and forming the Revolutionary Sailors' Committee,
elected by the crew mustered on the quarterdeck.

The *Sankt Georg* and the other ships – all but two of them ready to
join the mutiny – had raised the red flag, but among the sailors, of
all the differing nationalities in the empire, the echo of the Russian
Revolution and proletarian demands – the ending of the war, freedom
to establish trades unions, international brotherhood, the democratization of civilian and military life – were enmeshed not only with the
immediate reasons for protest arising out of the treatment they received
aboard, but also with the separatism of the various peoples of the
empire, each aiming at the dissolution of Austria and their own self-
affirmation, almost always at the expense of their neighbours.

Resolute in its execution, but hesitant in the management of
its brief success, the mutiny had been prepared in most efficient
secrecy; Scaramuzza, who had had a leading role in the organization, recalled the varied character of its objectives fifteen years
later in the *Piccolo*, Trieste's newspaper: "To the Italians we promised
freedom, to the Croatians a Serbo-Croat state, to the anti-Serbian
Slavs the sale of the ships to the allies (excluding Italy) and
the division of the proceeds, to the Bohemians a republic and to
the Germans and Hungarians better treatment from their officers,
good and plentiful rations and more money." But on board the ships

the *Marseillaise* was being played and the Revolutionary Committee's despatch, telegraphed to the government in Vienna, requested immediate peace negotiations, acceptance of the principle of self-determination, together with Wilson's Fourteen Points and above all the democratization of the state.

The revolution, which seemed to be spreading, in fact collapsed in three days: three days of discussions, messages sent to Vienna, negotiations, some shots which chased off three German submarines, a piece of shrapnel from the fort which decapitated the Viennese Zagner, one of the leaders of the insurrection who had climbed up on the gun tower of the *Kronprinz Rudolf* to give the command to return fire. He was buried solemnly in the bay, headless and wrapped in the red flag.

In those few hours the sailors of Kotor hesitated over the measures to be taken, but they behaved with calm, courage and even excessive liberality, such as when they sent to shore for a physician, Doctor Chersi of Lussino, because Admiral Hansa, their prisoner, had a stomach ache; and, as the doctor prescribed a meat-based diet, they sent another launch ashore to buy him beefsteaks for grilling. Just before being released, the admiral promised that not a hair on a sailor's head would be touched, but once he got over his stomach ache he forgot the promise and shot four of them; Antonio Grabar, from Parenzo, in particular died displaying remarkable and disdainful courage. Many sentences to hard labour were handed out at the trial, but on the whole Austrian justice was not too harsh on what had been an armed revolt during wartime involving eight to ten thousand men. Scaramuzza was saved because the commission set up to identify those responsible on the *Sankt Georg* declared, perhaps thanks to his friendship with Ficich, an Italian member of the commission, that he had not been seen among the mutineers.

That was just about the only stroke of luck Scaramuzza enjoyed.

The failed revolution, which he had skilfully helped organize, marked a certain vocation for failure that was to accompany him in his professional life, in the enterprises he embarked on that went wrong; even a cinema that he set up caught fire. But he evidently did not lose heart. In Grado they remember him as big, robust, and fearless under all circumstances. He could not have been too happy when, years later, Fascism sought to glorify the Kotor revolt – and his role in it – interpreting it as a movement driven solely by Italian patriotic fervour against Austria.

Indeed, in 1934 the *Piccolo* published a series of articles in praise of the Kotor revolt, with the Italian *tricolore* rather than the red flag flying over it, all Bolshevik references expunged. The writer, R.D., even went to meet one of the thirteen members of the Revolutionary Committee, the Triestine worker Angelo Pacor, and described him with great feeling, taking care to eliminate any possible communist connotation: "One of our typical intelligent workers ... modest ... forceful of character. . . . His face, deeply wrinkled by his resistance to the privations borne out of love for his children, is lit with a smile that inspires trust. Nothing here of the Asiatic revolutionary; nothing frightening in that honest face. . . ."

The spectre of Lenin is exorcised even from his facial features; the writer from the *Piccolo* portrays an anti-Bolshevik physiognomy, without ever asking himself why on earth this fine Triestine should have a Mongolian look. Four years earlier, in his play, *The Sailors of Kotor*, Friedrich Wolf – who in 1922 was a member of the Dresden workers' and soldiers' council and an active Communist – had celebrated with revolutionary and proletarian feeling the red flag flying in that Dalmatian bay. The protagonist is the group of sailors, the real chorus of that protest, of that hope, and of that disaster; with the play's social realism, Wolf brings to light the inadequacy and the contradictions of that revolt, the incapacity of its leaders to see it through to the end and above all the ever-present tragic conflict common to all revolutions, born to eliminate violence and yet constrained to use violence in order to succeed and if they hesitate in its use they are quashed, as happened in Kotor.

Today Wolf's revolutionary pathos might seem dated, but on this turn-of-the-century set which tends – with its intelligent special effects – to classify the tragedies and the hopes of redemption in a context of bloody farce, events such as those in Kotor find a searing, touching topicality, that reflects a strangulation point in contemporary history. Perhaps this was one reason why Antonio Scaramuzza did not like to speak about it; he also spoke of it very little because he could not contradict the Fascist version, ultimately so flattering to himself, and he felt embarrassed about acting the positive, admirable role which had been foisted on him. His contributions to those historical pieces of 1934 are in line with the newspaper's approach, but slight and laconic. He probably preferred to do other things, such as managing the Pine Wood guest house in Sistiana, although he ended up losing that as well.

Moments when history is made, and extraordinary adventures often render those who have lived them taciturn. Augusto Troian and the other seven from Grado, members of the "Legion of the Survivors of Siberia", also spoke very little about their incredible Odyssey, errant footnote to Universal History. That Odyssey too begins with the First World War, out of which all that still envelops and conditions us was born, all the possible and still incomplete parabolas of our destiny. Those eight men from Grado – narrates Luciano Sanson, distant cousin of one of them, Beniamino – were called up in 1914 in the Austro-Hungarian army and sent to the Carpathian front. When Italy too entered the war on 24 May, 1915, Troian, an irredentist, had deserted and given himself up to the Russians, and the others had done the same, or had been taken prisoner; at all events they had joined the volunteer forces organized by the Italian military mission with those from Venezia Giulia who had deserted from the Royal Imperial army for patriotic reasons.

Those groups were supposed to have been repatriated to Italy and then to have been sent to fight against the Austrians on the Isonzo front. The first of the staggered groups reached Archangel and before embarking were blocked by ice and by the Russian Revolution. Troian and others decided to head for Vladivostok, so as to reach Italy by sea, and in an epic *Anabasis* they crossed Siberia. But on arriving at Vladivostok they were asked to join up with an expedition sent by the allies – including Italy, via China – to try to block the Russian Revolution, which weakened the Entente because it was starving the Central Empires' eastern front of manpower. Troian remained in Vladivostok at the headquarters of the Italian expeditionary corps; the others went back to Siberia and found themselves in the chaos of that immense territory, the Revolution and the Civil War, in a space that was too big and empty of things, but too full of history and changes. Odysseys are long, all homecomings are difficult; the men from Grado did not return to Italy until 12 April, 1920, on board a Japanese steamship that took them to Trieste.

Of that journey through the snows of the steppes and history, of that wandering which traces in miniature the many escapes and peregrinations of individuals and peoples that mark the century, almost nothing remains, apart from Luciano Sanson's article in the *Piccolo*. There is no mention of battles, which the legion must have contrived to avoid, slipping between one military confrontation and another as though through showers and hailstorms. In any case, everyone who lived through those extraordinary happenings tends towards silence; perhaps because they do not know how to speak, perhaps because they think that if they speak they will get it wrong. Or perhaps it is because while living an adventure it seems like something exceptional, but then when one gets home, and is about to start telling the tale, the words don't come; those things that seemed remarkable have disappeared, flown away, or they no longer seem so marvellous, and little by little nothing comes to mind, after all perhaps nothing happened and one knows not what to say.

The "Anzolo" San Michele, who rotates around the top of Sant' Eufemia, is big and handsome too, with his wide wings, fluttering and fringed strips of cloud, his arm and index finger extended to indicate the direction of the wind, his body erect and ready for battle, an archangel aware that the fight, even in the heavens, is certainly not over with the provisional victory that resulted in Lucifer and his rebels being locked up down below. But every now and then the Angel Saint Michael is removed for some restoration work and is installed inside the basilica. Erudite chroniclers and journalists seeking local colour describe him, there on the floor, awkward and graceless, a clumsy and inoffensive giant, his pupils lifeless. It is known that captive albatrosses lose their nobility, their aura of distance. Up high, among the standards of the sky and the wind, the Angel seems to see and dominate many things; but once he's down even he is embarrassed, like a man who knows not what to say.

Barbana, the most famous of the islands thanks to its sanctuary, is beautiful from far off, with its maternal dome and the belltower protruding from the thick green and arching in a harmony of curves over the water. On landing it's the wind blowing through the great pines, elms and cypresses that strikes one more than the church, and the ex votos which, like sacred ancestors of the strip cartoon, recount disasters and catastrophes of all kinds miraculously averted. The Perdon de Barbana takes place on the first Sunday in July; it is a great procession of boats all decked out in honour of the Madonna who, tradition goes, was brought to the island by a storm at the end of the sixth century: the wooden statue was found among the branches or leaning against the trunk of a tree. Today's statue of Mary, looking anxiously into the distance, with her son in her arms, is more recent, albeit still many centuries old; it is not the first and perhaps not even the second image of the Virgin to be venerated on Barbana. Perhaps the first was a black Madonna on the prow of a dromond or a Byzantine bilander and came from distant seas, or perhaps it was simply a female carving, a figurehead gazing at the sea with her awestruck eyes and looking out for imminent storms; perhaps she became a Madonna only when she touched land.

Surrounding the chapel, built where a tree used to provide refuge and shelter to the image brought on the waves, there is a small cemetery. Among the others there lies a Rev. Fr. Mauro Mattessi, "industrious and joyful servant of Maria", who lived and died in the sanctuary. Literature has long been capable of telling the tales of people who retreat from the world like the reclusive Saint Peter of Orio, of melancholy hermits and refugees who hide themselves away on an island or among the anonymous crowd, stripping themselves of everything and perhaps attaining freedom, but not joy. This last is reserved for the Benedictines or the Franciscans and seems to be denied to modern, lay hermits, who, in a search for life's essence, make sacrifices more radical than religious vows, so radical indeed as to strip life down to the point of total sterility. Modern civilization is marked by these flights which achieve an absolute that is close on vacuity.

Another tack and the return is complete. Pampagnola again, with the beached *burchi*, under a sky that is retreating into the evening. The same images as on the outbound trip, photographs from an album leafed through backwards, towards the point of departure. A journey is always a return, the decisive step is the one that brings the foot back onto land or back home. Augusto Zuberti's restaurant, where one stops before leaving for Trieste, is almost home and has been so for many years. Here Marin's birthdays and name days were celebrated with memorable suppers – he didn't mind these continual celebrations. Each year the appointed orator would extend everyone's homage to Marin, exorcising with due discretion the shadow of his possible and impending end, while he himself listened without batting an eyelid. The years passed and the orators, they too no longer all that young, passed on to better lives while Marin carried on, prolific with new books, naturally called upon to outlive his commemorators.

Here one evening he said that he was a gulf, the confluence of other people's lives. In that gulf all the loved ones were together, companions inseparable from the fabric of one's own existence, parents, the girlfriend from that day on the dunes and from forever after and, years later, the boys, in the meantime of an age to go out on the dunes with girlfriends of their own. Places and things, too, difficult to separate from loved ones and from the image of the world that envelops them: the sea, the wind in the pines, the chattering of the cicadas, the seagulls, the summer's amber. A true inn is a gulf too, a seaport welcomed by those who journey and are anxious above all else to come to rest. Marin's grandfather used to keep an inn, the Three Crowns near the early Christian Basilica of Santa Maria delle Grazie, and perhaps that was the future poet's true academy.

Nevoso

In the beginning was Mr Samec's voice, low and a bit croaky, with the imperceptible hiss of his Slovene *s*: "And then I said to him," he began again, just touching the person next to him with his little finger which mild arthritis, perhaps the result of so many years spent in the damp woods, had curved like a hook, "'Excuse me, Your Excellency, but with your permission . . . .'" In the beginning or almost, because in the forest everything had always already begun and indeed everything was always beginning to end, disintegrating into the soil and sinking into the rust-red layers of so many fallen leaves and years, no longer distinguishable. On entering the forest for the first time, as a boy, one had felt in some way that it was not the first time and that one's own story must also have begun so long ago, time stored and measured in the circles within the tree-trunks and even farther back than that, and in this awareness there was neither excitement nor melancholy, but simply the silent feeling that this is the way it was and that was enough.

Mr Samec almost never managed to finish his story, which the others thought they had heard to the very end many times already, because Rudi would start playing "Za kim" or recalling his ancestry, conceivably noble or even imperial, since his grandfather – or was it his

father or his great-grandfather? – had been found newborn, crying in
a bush in the park at Schönbrunn in Vienna, and so may have been the
illicit fruit of sins in very high places. Or, once again at that table in
the clearing at Sviščaki opposite the Planinski Dom, the mountain
refuge, someone, taking no notice of Mr Samec, preferred to observe
the continual improvements and enlargements made to the chalet
belonging to Mr Voliotis, who some time previously had celebrated
there his silver wedding with his wife, children and grandchildren. This
same person remarked that the management of the porno cinemas,
which Mr Voliotis had taken on a few years before in Trieste, where he
lived, must be more lucrative than the timber trade. Timber had been
Mr Voliotis's earlier line, and he explained that he had switched jobs
so as to avoid having to travel and to be able to spend more time with
his family. But if Mr Samec's story was destined to remain unfinished,
this was above all thanks to his wife, Mrs Anna, beautiful and unfathomable with her snub-nose and slanting eyes, with a look of tender
rapacity in her face marked by the years, as she signalled for him to
stand up and take her back to their chalet.

The Excellency about whom Mr Samec was trying to tell his story
was a Fascist Party official from Fiume; he had got into the man's good
books when he accompanied him on a bear hunt and discreetly talked
him out of some act of folly that could have been fatal, and as a result –
but the narrative became confused at this point because it was here that
his listeners' impatience would get the better of them and the story – it
was a gamekeeper or a woodsman, rather, who paid the penalty when
his jaw was crushed by a bite from the bear (occasionally a she-bear), so
that for the rest of his days the victim had to nourish himself by sucking
food and drink through a straw. Not that this tragic element in any
way jeopardized the few benefits (the odd permit, a commission here
and there) that the Party official's gratitude ensured for Mr Samec's big
hardware store in Ilirska Bistrica, back then known as Villa del Nevoso.

Then and now, so that back then it was also Ilirska Bistrica, because names do not disappear as those who move frontiers like to think, rather they live on whenever there is a retelling of the story that happened when that person, that place or that bear was so called – and thus continues to be called so. The forest is pure memory of names: *Volk samotar*, the lone and uncatchable wolf that terrorized the woods of Mount Snežnik, the Nevoso, the "Snowy Mountain", between 1921 and 1923; Josef Ronko, the bricklayer, who lived in a small wooden cabin at Prevale after 1903 and who is remembered as if he were the lord of some castle; or Fajstric, the marksman who in 1893 was supposed to protect Prince Hermann von Schönburg-Waldenburg, Lord of the Nevoso, on his first bear hunt and instead ran off up a tree when faced with a wounded bear; it was the prince who had to rescue the marksman.

Above all the memory of the forest tells of the vanity of possessing it. The deep breath of the forest is a lesson in how to feel life as something impartial, indifferent and yet welcoming and inexhaustible; one knew this feeling from the very first time and meets it again each time one enters these woods. Then one saw the children feel it and they too learned it for ever in their turn, so that in time it was a feeling that everyone considered to have existed always and whose beginning no one could recall, like breathing. The forest, first Austrian, later Italian, Yugoslav and then Slovene, mocked those changes of names and borders, it belonged to no one; if anything it was the people who belonged to the forest, at least to that limited extent to which one can belong to someone or something. Even the forest that has existed for a long time is mortal, like the roebuck that suddenly appears on the grass at daybreak, either in front of the shotgun barrels or in front of no one, and whose life – even the life of his species, so much longer than that of an empire, however revered, or of a fleeting Federal Republic – lasts only a moment. If one turns one's gaze to the Great Bear or to the

morning star that fades in August above a red fir in the Pomočnjaki
clearing, it lasts just the moment of the roebuck's apparition and his
leap into the clearing.

Ilirska Bistrica, the busy and anonymous industrial town at the
foot of the Nevoso, is the capital of the wooded mountain that rises
immediately towards the north-east and descends on the other side,
beyond the summit, in one direction towards Mašun and in the
other towards Leskova Dolina, the hazelnut valley, and Kozarišče, in
the direction of Postumia. Then it extends and thins to the east where
it stretches as far as the Slovenia–Croatia border. A wooded lung –
predominantly beech, fir and larch – preserved and intact in its green
life, cared for civilly and wisely by a forestry administration that has
no drive to innovate and to rush things, but respects the trees' rhythms.
Every now and then they open a road in the wood, but in the meantime they wait for others to become harmoniously integrated with the
forest, to the point where the roads are almost camouflaged. Some
areas are left in peace for years while work goes on in others – protecting
the woods and defending them from construction, exploitation, abuse,
except perhaps for some indulgence towards hunters, especially if
Milanese.

There are no hotels in the Nevoso's 227,600 hectares, only a few
houses, some chalets and cabins, the ruins of a couple of Italian
barracks, a refuge on the summit and one in the clearing at Sviščaki;
the Planinski Dom, its three rooms equipped with bunk beds, is the
palace and centre of the Snežnik. If the maps – the noblest of which
is reproduced on a postcard, and was hand drawn by Professor
Drago Karolin, well into his nineties and the tutelary deity of the
Nevoso – indicate Mater Dei or Saints Cosmas and Damian, this simply
means a stone with the names of the saints or at the most (a recent
innovation), a small niche with a Madonna which replaces an earlier
dressed stone. The road-building on the Snežnik brings to mind Josef

von Obereigner, Prince von Schönburg-Waldenburg's forestry director. It was he who in the nineteenth century planned and maintained these lanes and paths, giving them name and form. Following 1929 the Italian army contributed to the network with a number of good, still-solid and useable roads, like the one that leads to Orlovica, Monte Aquila. Today the postcard–maps of Drago Karolin are the chart of that universe, in which every least detail is worthy of attention and identity, almost as if the cartographer sought to rescue it from the indistinct mass of the woods.

The Nevoso's architecture consists of platforms built in the trees, shaky chairs and solid wooden cabins, their boards fresh and solid or rotten with the years and the damp, hides built for waiting for the animals and, thence, either to kill them, as the legitimate owners of the platforms do, or simply observe them, as the unauthorized users do. The hunters, who pay up to $15,000 to kill a bear, maintain that the smell of the intruding animal-watchers pollutes the forest and scares off the animals, chasing them away from the hides and thus from death.

But Ilirska Bistrica is only one hurried break along the journey – the Nevoso is halfway between Trieste and Fiume – and it is where one stops merely for fuel or to repair a tyre, inevitably punctured on the rocky roads, rough with all sorts of pointed things. The true capital of the province is Sviščaki, a clearing a little wider than the others, at 1,242 metres above sea level, traditional point of departure for the brief excursion to the summit. Some chalets surround the clearing which orbits around the Planinski Dom, the Slovene Alpine Association's refuge; not far off stand the recently built small houses of a new Sviščaki: a tasteless huddle, camouflaged by the trees.

History: even many years after the first encounter with the Nevoso, now that the children travel the world and yet continue to know all there is to know of every valley, every old path swallowed up by that wood, each apparition of that bear, the bigger one with darker fur, the one that everyone had seen, perhaps by chance on arriving at the refuge by car. But we four never did see it, despite the nights and the dawns spent waiting for it motionless in the clearing. History has been cadenced by the summers spent at the Planinski Dom and by the succession of caretakers/hoteliers at the refuge, names learned . by heart like those of ruling dynasties.

Indeed, each change of dynasty was painful, an embarrassment because for the new managers the family were strangers to begin with and it was humiliating to be taken for tourists or ignorant new-comers, to feel oneself being treated like a foreigner in that place which was in fact one's home and homeland. "Up there I know who I am," the great Julius Kugy used to say of his Julian Alps, and this was true for us and the Monte Nevoso; but the others, or at least the officials in charge of that refuge, also had to be aware that it was one of our abodes. Thus, when an Ivanka succeeded a Meri or the Pugels followed the Valenčičs, one had Professor Karolin write a letter of recommenda-tion, in Slovene, praising the qualities of the entire family, referring especially to their love for the Snežnik and their adaptability to hard-ships. That letter was an introduction to the new managers, taken aback at being asked to welcome into the room under the eaves the only family who ever stopped up there for any length of time and who thus enabled the custodians to earn a few dinars that had not yet become thalers.

The Snežnik, looking like Fujiyama, rises over Sviščaki, above a sea of woods. The house facing the Planinski Dom, on the other side of the clearing, was used almost every year for the holidays of the workers from the timber mills in Ilirska Bistrica. It was managed by Milivoj, a Serb with a long moustache and Mongolian eyes who had been given that safe job, it was said, thanks to his record with the partisans during the war. Even when people did not yet seem to think – or had not yet gone back to thinking – that to be a Slovene or a Croatian or a Serb and Yugoslav was a contradiction to be resolved through bloodshed; even when they seemed if anything to be proud of the red star that had not merely restored the Snežnik to Slavia, as was right, but had even brought excessive wealth to this last of Italy's lands – even the air was full of suspicion about Milivoj and vague allusions to cruel deeds of his. It is true that some evenings, when he was drunk, he used to shoot into the air and Milka, the custodian at the Planinski Dom, would proudly assert that her husband – "our" husband, she would say – went happily to bed when he got drunk. Anyway Milivoj died before the collapse of the Federal Republic saw these latent contrasts regarding differences between civilizations resolved with shooting that was not into the air and was not limited to merely drunken outbursts. Even the Bosnian woodsmen, who used to work meekly and industriously in the forest, never shooting in the air or anywhere else for that matter, have gone now, while the lynxes flourish.

A postcard on sale at the Planinski Dom summarizes the history of the refuge from 1907 to 1972, but it says nothing of D'Annunzio's refuge which was alongside the present-day one and was blown up by the partisans. Until just a few years ago there still was some minimal trace of its existence. It seems the poet never actually set foot there. For D'Annunzio the Nevoso was a word, it was the music and the light of that word, its clarity. Indeed, in 1924, from his Villa "Vittoriale", on the eve of the unification of Fiume with Italy, he asked for "a token" of recognition for his own merits and suggested being given the title *Prince of Mount Nevoso*, or *Prince of the Adriatic*, he did not mind which. But before putting in this request for a D'Annunziesque word, the poet who perhaps more than any other had understood the Odyssean charm of technology, the Medusa and Muse of modern life, had also expressed the wish for a small private airport at Gardone. He had to make do with that melodious trisyllable.

In the beginning there was no bear, only the story of the bear. The

Sviščaki group paid no attention to Mr Samec because long before
they came to know Mr Samec himself, they knew that story about the
hunter with the smashed face who had to eat through a straw. In
the various tellings it is linked to all manner of bears, hunters and
places. According to the version set down by the authoritative
Drago Karolin, reproduced in the small green volume, *Snežnik*,
published in 1977, the incident occurred on 19 July, 1900 and involved
Andrej Znidaršič who was accompanying Duke Heinrich von
Mecklenburg, guest of Prince Hermann von Schönburg-Waldenburg.
Director Bercè, who from Kozarišče manages and protects the
Snežnik forestry reserve with a genial meticulousness, denies this
episode, which he claims took place in fact elsewhere; he gives a
different version of the duke's hunt, one no less perilous but which
concludes happily for the aristocratic cub killer only because maternal
love prevailed over the fury of the bear that attacked him, forcing her
to concentrate on saving the other cub; anyway, in this version,
certainly reliable, there are no smashed jawbones and no straws either.

These last features recur in other tales and in other places; the most
illustrious archetype is certainly Julius Kugy's story – dating back to
1871 and set in the Val Trenta – where the wounded man is his trusty
climbing and hunting companion Antonio Tozbar, a.k.a. Spik, who
loses even his tongue and the power of speech. The episode is
renowned not only because of Kugy's fame but also thanks to the
authority of Giovanni Gabrielli, prestigious legal expert, who repeated
it for years during his trips in the Carso area and in the Vipavo Valley,
until even his most tolerant friends obliged him to give over. A variant
on this topos is the story of a man who, attacked by the bear or running
to help someone who had been attacked, brandishes an axe and in his
excitement wounds himself to a greater or lesser degree, hitting his
own thigh and cutting his leg off, or inflicting slightly less gory injuries.

Every two or three summers this story cropped up and was

recounted and expanded; on one occasion it took place at Stare ogence, on another at Sladke vode. The bear was always a female defending her cubs, even if there were kinder episodes, such as that of the female bear that fell with one of her cubs into a cistern at Koritnice and was helped out by the lumberjacks, who let down a trunk which she was able to climb up.

The recurrent motif of the man who injures himself in a fight with a she-bear can also be traced back to an origin, to an event that took place near the Mater Dei and was set in motion by a Magyar count on holiday at Abbazia, who wanted a bear cub and sent someone out to capture one. But the suspicion is that each event, real or invented, is preceded by its story, the fantasy that conjures up the bear by thinking of it, the word that founds and forges reality. In the beginning was the word; the heavens and the earth come after, and even the forests and the bears. The forest has no word, it is the primordial inchoate, that pulls back into its womb all things and all forms, it is Artemis who must not be looked at and whose name must not be spoken; it is Life that dissolves lives and knows not the language wherein the never-ending metamorphosis is articulated. Story lays hold of a form, renders it distinct, retrieves it from the ebb and flow, from oblivion, fixes it: those legends and those fantasies about the bear impose a meaning and an order on the dark beast that moves through the thick of the forest, for civilization they are a squaring of accounts with the darkness of the wood.

Where does the forest begin? The entrances are invisible, and yet one clearly feels them as they open and they close, and when one is inside or outside, quite apart from the fact of being or not being surrounded by trees. One entrance, a personal one maybe, is the Pomočnjaki ("very damp") clearing alongside the road – a *gozdna cesta* ("path in the woods"), which offers no guarantee of being passable – connecting the Padežnica plain, where the snow falls in abundance, Mirine's two houses and the clearings of Grčovec clearing, with their knotty trees as suggested by the name and the richly turfed Travni dolci. Then it rejoins the main road, so to speak, that leads to the summit. For a few seconds one morning in the Pomočnjaki clearing the newly risen sun created a perfect cathedral of light out of the vapour that was rising from the grass, a form that became thinner and thinner as it rose, culminating in a cusp; the door, a great Gothic portal, was a luminous cloud, a gleaming, dense curtain that hid the wood behind. The figure sitting nearby in the grass, close both at that moment and over the years too, had stood up in the meadow at the forest's edge where we had both been waiting for the things to emerge from the dark, to emerge foretold from the unmistakable smell of dawn, or for the morning star to fade out at the apex of the red fir opposite, suddenly invisible in the brightness. Then the figure had set off slowly towards and in through that door of light, entering and fading in the impenetrable clarity, out of sight.

At that moment one could have believed that every disappearance, even over the ultimate threshold – the one that the roebuck in the clearing would no doubt soon have crossed, what with the gun-shots beginning to echo round the mountain – meant no more than passing through such a curtain, so there was no need for that dark, anxious fear that increasingly strips things of their meaning as the years pass. But unlike that clearing where the figure had reappeared in the gold of the grass with the daisies and bluebells, white mugwort and purple-red thrifts beginning to materialize, the wood restored nothing; that which had disappeared was gone for ever, devoured or decomposed in the moist soil, without compassionate lies or any illusion of burial, like that stag with its throat cut in the Dolčice clearing or that badger by the roadside on the way to Trije kaliči, the highest and most disturbing of the hollows, just below the summit of the mountain. The gold of the

grass was turning brown, gold tarnished by time which simply flows
and decomposes and disappears, as finally you spit out the fir bark that
you've been chewing for a long time as you wait for the arrival of an
animal – good, fresh and bitter bark that forms a grip on your teeth
and stimulates the saliva until you spit it out and it mingles with the
moist soil.

Anyway, there, beyond the door of that cathedral which evaporated
immediately, the forest opened, while on other occasions it was ready
to exclude whoever crossed it, to lead him to feel himself estranged
from the thick wood, even though it surrounds him. Padežnica,
Pomočnjaki, Grčovec, Travni dolci, Dolčice, Trije kaliči, Črni dol, Črna
draga ... these clearings were a shared history, with the years they
turned more or less into the lineaments of a face, assumed the colour
of thoughts and feelings; certainly landscape of loving, perhaps because
it was easier, in the dawnings, to love the face close by that emerged
pure from the dark. In that shadow you were no one and thus, stripped
of all personal shabbiness, it was easy to love, because nothing came
between love and life, which so often presents obstacles, perils and
traps for love just as the hunters set traps for the wildlife. In the
strong animal smell of dawn there was no need to clean any mud off,
like that doe which for a moment threw herself into the pond at
Pomočnjaki and came out running off happily with all that mud on
her back, fresh and clean as clear water. She did not shake it from her
and it had all the goodness of her own skin.

The roe at Pomočnjaki, the buck at Travni dolci which ran to the
mating call (imitated with a skill worthy of more serious ventures), and
then disappeared, barking disappointedly; the wolf at Trije kaliči, great
tawny beast, really close, as he turned slowly; the two deer bent over
the small spring of Saint Andrew; that frightened, sleepy hazel mouse
on the path to Planinec; those careful, vigilant boars at Pales; the
falcons, the wildcat, the dormouse working away all night above the

tree-platform, while yet again one hoped to catch sight of the bear. . . . But for years and years everyone else saw the bears, even those who went around in the woods making a racket and spreading litter. We alone, who even knew where to find the dens where the animals went to hibernate or to cub – we were the only ones who never saw them, and summer followed summer cadenced by this expectation and this quest and above all else by their failure.

Not even Boris managed to take us to the right place at the right moment – Boris, the gamekeeper of the aristocratic face, had seen countless bears, once even four together. Whenever he scattered some corn or left a carcass out as bait at Pales, it was like fixing an appointment with the bear; once it even came to uproot the post to which a cow was tied, two days dead, and dragged both off into the wood. But when he took us with him, the bear never came, not even when encouraged with a dead horse. Bearless year after year; at the most there was some fresh track or recent dung, which on our return were announced triumphantly, while the others – and the children too, although even they, without admitting it, made that elusive bear the focal point of their summers and perhaps even something more – the others congratulated us, laughing, on this excremental coronation of the season we'd waited all year for.

At Gomance, under a thick and twisted fir that covers the soil beneath, that German helmet must still be there, complete with bullet hole. It was right to put it back after having stumbled upon it; perhaps it is the only tomb, albeit vicarious, of whoever wore it and has probably disappeared completely now, because the forest, unlike the fields, provides no recognizable burial plots to bring a little order into the world. The woods of the Nevoso were a nerve centre in the partisan war; there were small groups here that moved like lightning and important headquarters were set up on the mountain, especially the bases for the couriers who maintained the clandestine links with the distant units of Tito's Ninth Corps. For the Yugoslav resistance the Snežnik was a theatre and in it they displayed an extraordinary capacity for political organization, military efficiency and courage. These qualities soon evaporated, however, when the valiant and merciless rebels of the woods mutated into a managerial class that was, all things considered, shoddy and parasitic; it survived artificially long after its actual demise thanks to the cover afforded it by the genius and the ingenious deception of Marshal Tito.

Partisan hospitals were hidden away at Beli Vrh and Požar, the Germans' headquarters were at Ilirska Bistrica and a few kilometres off, at Zabice, there was a group of the Germans' Chetnik allies under the leadership of Dobroslav Jevdievič. The Italian barracks at Morele and on Monte Aquila had been abandoned in 1943 and destroyed. A number of Italian soldiers had joined Tito's partisans, but soon realized to their cost that the proud and rightful rebirth of a nation oppressed by the Fascists was in its turn becoming savage and oppressive nationalism. Wandering through those woods in search of the bear it was strange to think of Father – or of Grandfather – who, in the hour of defeat had come this way, leaving behind the devastated barracks, to return to Trieste, and this at a time when a man's life on these very paths was worth no more than that of a beast. Thus a track led to Morele as well, under the rubble beneath which there had been a home – or den or prison – for a person whose face and gestures, with the passing of the years, are ever less distinguishable from those of his son, who would like to be even more like him than he is.

The partisans fought well, their rifles oiled with dormouse grease; even the woodsmen executed by the Germans at Klanska Polica knew how to face death. The worst clash came at Mašun, where the Tomsič brigade put up a fierce fight for the pass, before retreating to Leskova Dolina and burning the little town's fortress. In that war in the woods the fabric was being woven of a policy that had a global view and aimed not only at liberating a country, but at creating a new society. When the partisan groups met at Mašun in September 1943, along with the military commanders there was the Slovene leader Edvard Kardelj, possibly the only one of Tito's heirs who might have saved the Federal Republic from its shameful collapse. He was the inventor of that self-management that for some years seemed to be – and for some years therefore was – a true third way for socialism, available as a model for a large part of the non-aligned world in the Cold War and an instrument for genuine internal liberalization, unknown in the Communist countries. He was also responsible for the policy pursued by Tito on the international stage, combining as he did gifts of leadership with those more befitting Baron Munchhausen.

Kardelj was involved, furthermore, in the creation of Golj Otok, the gulag on the bare island in the western Adriatic established by the Tito regime for the imprisonment and torture of its political opponents, not least – following the rift with Stalin – the Stalinists, including those Italian Communists who had chosen to move to Yugoslavia in order to contribute towards the construction of socialism.

Thus in those days of war these woods, peaceful and secluded from History, which at the most had known the raids of the Turks in 1528 or the Islamicized Wallachians in 1758, became the place where an intricate web of hopes and lies was being spun, projects for freedom and plans for totalitarian violence, a spirit of sacrifice and of rapacious domination. In the forest a small anonymous pyramid recalls the unknown partisans buried there; the woods know not illustrious tombs or gravestones.

Kardelj, Tito, the Nevoso and naturally the bear are all found in an anonymous painting which lies in an attic in Ilirska Bistrica – the client, the Party, never collected it. The painting depicts the wood, a fire and a bear killed by some hunters – Tito with his hands on his knees and

Kardelj with his florid sausage-eater cheeks, gesticulating in evident imitation of the threatening lunges of the bear that has just been killed. Unfortunately Kavčič is also there, a leader who fell into disgrace immediately after the painting was completed, and thus it never found its rightful place and had to be removed from circulation. The bear lies on the ground, looking well nourished and blissfully asleep rather than dead, and one can almost hear him snoring. He's the only one enjoying himself amidst all these *coups de théâtre*: one eye looks half open and peeks mockingly at the leading politicians-cum-hunters; the right way to look at History, a sly, sideways glance.

And so even the woods are penetrated by History, with its continuous scene-changes and relocations. When the people fought in these valleys they felt Yugoslav, they were proud to have recovered from Fascist oppression by their own merits; this had been rendered possible thanks to Yugoslav unity; they did indeed consent to those injustices inflicted in the name of their country against the Italians – not on the Nevoso, which had always been Slovene and was usurped by its annexation to Italy following 1918, but in the Italian territories of Istria that can be seen from the summit of Snežnik or the Orlovica and which Yugoslavia would contrive to annex after 1945, cruelly persecuting the people who lived there. Until recently Josip Križaj was a Yugoslav hero, a Slovene Air Force ace who had fought in the Spanish Civil War, too, and came down in these woods near Mount Cifre by the Jarmovec in a mysterious accident in 1948; a monument there still commemorates him. For some time now the rumours have been that it was the Serbs who shot him down in 1948. In the museum of Kozarišče castle they are waiting for the return of the portrait of Princess Ann, Prince Hermann von Schönburg's sister. The portrait, together with paintings and precious objects from various castles, had been taken to Brdo to adorn one of Tito's luxurious and kitsch villas. Now, as with the other articles, it will return to the ancestral home. History is about moving

house, arranging and removing furniture from the attic to the best
sitting room and vice versa.

The Nevoso Castle, at Kozarišče, mentioned by old Janez Valvasor in
his monumental eighteenth-century work in praise of the Krain, was
neither destroyed nor burned during the Second World War, unlike
the other castles in Slovenia. Credit for this goes to the bursar, Leon
Sauta, a Czech who administered the castle for its owner, Prince
Schönburg-Waldenburg. Whenever the victors of the moment arrived –
those who had taken possession and wanted to raze the castle to the
ground – Sauta explained that they were now the new owners, that
the castle therefore was and would remain their property, hence it
was absurd and against their own interests to destroy it. He said this
to the Italians, the Germans and the Partisans and time and time again
that simple, impeccable reasoning convinced occupiers and liberators –
evidence of the fact that logic and grammatical analysis, if we had
more confidence in them, might spare us many ruins. Leon Sauta
would have many things to teach many people today even, especially
those former Yugoslavs who take it in turns to destroy one another,
intent on razing their cities to the ground and cutting one another's
throats in a crazy bloodlust, regardless – in the stupidest of fratricidal
wars, the tragic failure of Tito's great attempt at founding a state – that
the life they are destroying is their own. But the civilization of these
woods, like that of Slovenia in general, is far removed from this
barbarism that came before civilization.

The chronicles speak of borders and frontiers with obsessive insistence.
A compendium of them, in manuscript, is kept in the castle at
Kozarišče. It is in German, and its author, Franz Schollmayer, compiled
it in 1923 as a summary of the vicissitudes of those lands and especially
of the princes Schönburg-Waldenburg, for whom he worked. Over

time there were repetitions of the conflict between the lords of the Nevoso – or Schneeberg as it was known to the author and previous chroniclers – and the city of Laars, with all the ensuing jurisdictional complications. Even more recurrent were the conflicts between the woodsmen of the Nevoso and those from Cabar, beyond Klanska Polica. That line represents a persistent and fatal clash: the Romans' frontier against the Scordiscians which was perhaps already contested between Gepidae and Celts; much later it became a disputed tract of the frontier between the Austrian empire and the Hungarian kingdom, settled for once and all by a mixed Austro-Hungarian commission in 1913; then the frontier between Italy and Yugoslavia, and now between Slovenia and Croatia, in other words until recently the border between two Republics in the same Federation and today the border between two states, not at war but inclined to look upon each other with mutual wariness. "It was inevitable, he's a Croat," said Milka, the custodian of the Planinski Dom at Sviščaki when she told the story of how her daughter had come to divorce.

Wars between empires and between poachers, family rows, street fights, turning points in history and the daily simplicity of chalets in the wood; those woodsmen whose incursions are often complained about in the news – in Slovenia or in Croatia – are the symbol of the centuries-old toll paid in violence that a border often demands, an idol that requires blood sacrifices. Borders: a need, a fever, a curse. Without them there is neither identity nor form, there is no existence; they create existence and arm it with its all-pervading talons, like the hawk that in order to exist and to love its nest must make its dive for the blackbird.

The woods are at once the glorification and the nullification of borders: a plurality of differing, opposing worlds, though still within the great unity that embraces and dissolves them. Even the light, in the forest, makes clean cuts that create different landscapes, and, in the

same instant, different times. There is the black light in the deepest
darkness and that deep underwater green beneath a vault of branches
that twines above the path; and while in the golden clearings there
is still the light clarity of bright daytime, just a few metres away, in
the wood, it is already evening, a grave shadow.

But the forest, ever since Actaeon was savaged by his dogs, has
been indistinctness and Dionysiac destruction, a return to the primeval
magma; legend speaks of fear of the wood, which is fear of losing
oneself and being annulled. The long summers and the familiarity
with the hollows, the thickets and the paths are not enough to penetrate
that unknown in any true sense, it remains untouchable even when
one crosses it in autumn, in a crystalline and gusty air that freezes the
tiniest noise, the creaking of a branch. Old Drago Karolin, he was
certainly in the wood and he never came out of it not even when he
went to town; his entire life was wrapped up within the clearings of
the Nevoso. To be in the wood as he was it was not enough to walk
beside him for hours on end across the Snežnik, as he placed signs at
the forks, repainted old faded words, drew maps that recorded even
the smallest of paths, collected and polished bizarrely shaped roots,
angrily stamped on his hat when he took the wrong way and then
immediately resumed the conversation in an old-fashioned and high-
flown German, peremptorily hushing his wife, the ebullient Mrs
Ida. He also dedicated fine paintings and poems to the Nevoso, thus
finding a place for himself in the small tradition of homage to the
Muses that flowered in the shadow of the Snežnik: the nineteenth-
century local stories of Janez Bilc, the poems of Župančič or Marička
Žnidaršič, Avčin's descriptions, Poročnik's photographs.

For Karolin the forest was open, a garden or a house to look after
and keep tidy; the lynx was like a pet cat and the centuries-old, mouldy
fir trees of the wood around the Andreas Quelle were like a piece of
furniture to be polished. The forest did not give much away to anyone

else: it rebuffed them ironically in alien clumsiness, their enthusiasm
was in vain; perhaps this was why not even the bear would make
an appearance. To be at home in the wood one probably had to
know how to write Karolin's clichéd, rhyming verses, "Yonder rustles
the forest remote . . . "

Being a Slovene raised in old Hapsburg Austria, "Professor" Karolin
always spoke a ceremonious and old-fashioned German, favouring
the use of indirect forms: "I told my wife," he said for example, as we
cautiously entered a clearing frequented by wild boars, "Ask our most
esteemed friend, that is your good self, if his respected consort prefers
her *gubanica* with grappa or without. . . ."

Once, on hearing he was ill, we paid him a visit. Ninety-two years of
age, he had been in bed for a few weeks because of circulation problems
that also affected his speech; he was sweating, feverish, exhausted, but
in his eyes there was the same vivacity and kindness as ever, the same
tenderness that the decades had sculpted into an expression of stern
authority. Next to his bed there were some parcels and crates into
which his wife, adhering to his wishes that he expressed with difficulty
but still in the usual tone that brooked no contradiction, had the task
of collecting and sorting his things – the books, the weirdly shaped
roots, a stag's head, a stuffed marten, paintings, drawings and
photographs of the mountain, letters, documents and relics – thus to
proceed then with their elimination.

He was packing up his existence, emptying it of the things he loved
and had collected with pedantic passion; he meant to tidy up his life
and relinquish all that had adorned it, just as the Hapsburg emperors
in the Baroque ritual had to strip themselves of their titles and all
insignias of their glory before being accepted into the Capuchin crypt.

On saying goodbye Karolin had made a present to the visitors of a
postcard of the Nevoso, on the back of which were printed – in Slovene

naturally – a few lines of his poetry. Raising himself on the pillow with his wife's help and making use of two enormous lenses, he had translated these into German in a large, trembling hand.

That card with its four lines in German seemed to constitute a testament, a definitive seal. But some time later a letter arrived, in German of course. The large uncertain characters on the envelope immediately revealed who the sender was, but they gave no clue as to the firm yet dissatisfied precision expressed in that venerable hand, shaky yet rigorous in its sequence of logic and syntax, in its punctuation and spelling, in its spacing, its line-breaks. "Most esteemed friend, last time, when you came to visit us with your dear Wife, I gave you some of my verses, which I translated into German. My Wife, watching beside me as I wrote, maintains that I wrote *das Berg*, instead of *der Berg* ("the mountain"). If it is so, I beg you to correct this disgraceful error and to forgive me. I have had various circulatory disturbances, with some momentary amnesia, and if I committed such an error it was certainly done under such circumstances. I am better now, I have been on my feet, I have taken a brief stroll on the edge of the wood."

It was unthinkable that Professor Karolin might go leaving the mistake uncorrected or before he had clarified, for himself and for everyone else, all doubt regarding it. He must have spent some weeks mulling it over, trying to remember if he'd really used *das*, the neutral article, instead of the masculine, or whether this was just his wife's false impression, and he must have nagged her considerably on the topic. Passion is born out of vitality, but it also stimulates vitality and thus, thanks to his torment over a grammatical error, the professor had found once more a little piece of his forest, the world, life.

Correct usage is a premise for moral clarity and honesty. Many a dirty trick and violent abuse of power arise when grammar and syntax are messed up and the subject is expressed in the accusative or the object in the nominative, mixing up the cards and exchanging roles between victim and perpetrator, altering the order of things and attributing events to causes or players not effectively responsible, abolishing distinctions and hierarchies in a beguiling heap of concepts and feelings, deforming the truth.

This, indeed, is why a single misplaced comma can result in disasters, can cause fires that destroy the woods on this Earth. But Professor Karolin's story seems to say that by respecting language, or the truth, one reinforces life itself, one's legs become that bit stronger and one is all the more capable of taking a stroll and enjoying the world, with that sensual vitality that is loose-limbed in proportion to how free it is of the tangles of deceit and self-deception. Who knows how many things, how many cherished pleasures and joys are owed, all unwittingly, to the schoolteachers' red pencils.

The chronicle of the faithful Schollmayer, which begins with an invocation to Clio, summarizes the entire history of the Schneeberg, but it is dedicated to the "Nevoso, owned by the princely Schönburg family." Over the course of the centuries and events, the castle and the mountain passed from one family to another, but the one most clearly identified with them is certainly the house of Schönburg-Waldenburg, who had acquired them in 1853 and held them right up until nationalization in 1945. They were the last of the feudal lords, Germans who were used to centuries of contact with the Slav world – with the Czechs in Bohemia and the Sorbs in Saxony – and have left a good memory behind them. While the first lord, His Highness Anton Viktor, who owned some thirty castles, never set foot there, Prince Georg, apart from organizing schools for the woodsmen's children, instituted rudimentary social security and founded the first Slovene forestry school, while Hermann restocked the forest with animals, which the peasants had massacred in the 1848 uprisings.

Prince Hermann was the lord of the Nevoso *par excellence*. He was

German and lived near Dresden, but he spent many months of the year in the castle at Kozarišče, where the oriental room, the Venetian and the Egyptian rooms are still to be seen intact, together with the library, rich in literary and legal works not to mention bound volumes of *Jagdzeitung*, the huntsman's magazine, and an eighteenth-century *Universal History* in twenty volumes. In those feudal rooms the lineage takes precedence over the individual and his own sentiments. "Günther arrived at twelve and at a quarter past twelve we were betrothed," thus the Princess Anna Luise von Schönburg-Waldenburg summarized in her diary the meeting and the courtship that determined her love-life once and for all. The portraits of Prince Hermann show a drawn, melancholic face, a bourgeois introspection more reminiscent of Chekhov or Schnitzler than of aristocratic vitality. Vinko Sterle, hunter and descendant of a mythical family of hunters in the prince's service, as well as bard of the deeds of times gone by, has handed down testimony of the kindness of the lord of the Nevoso towards his subordinates and his strictness with his grandson who once wanted to shoot a stag in the back and was prevented from doing so by a sharp movement by one of his men, Matja Martinčič, who forced down the barrel of the shotgun.

The Nevoso's legendary head huntsman was Franc Sterle, Vinko's grandfather, whose role entitled him, when in the woods, to sleep in the cabin with his master. On one occasion, undressing on the eve of a grouse hunt, Franc, who was wearing excellent, and recently purchased thick flannel underwear, observed that the prince's drawers were a miscellany of darning and patches in ten places and said to His Highness that he could surely afford better underwear. "Oh Franc," grumbled His Highness, "you're just like my housekeepers – they won't wash or sew and would throw away a shirt rather than darn it."

The prince bagged his first bear on 16 May, 1893, a 220-kilogram beast that today stands erect, stuffed, in the atrium of the castle. Rather than climb up into the safe hide among the branches, he waited for the bear face to face, because – according to Vinko – this test of his courage was a moral confirmation of his right to be lord of the woods. Despite his introverted gaze, the feudal legacy had probably left him with the atavistic superstition which says that blood is a necessary baptism, killing is a way of loving and death is communion between victim and killer. But on one occasion he must have opened his eyes to the paltry deceit of this glorification that seeks to confer nobility on the suffering of life and death. He was old and was hunting a stag with Lojze Sterle, Vinko's uncle, another master of the Nevoso, who had even been given an education in languages. The prince's shot had found its mark and he had gone into the thick where the animal lay. Lojze wanted to go with him, but the prince shouted that he was to remain where he was; he waited for some time until, out of curiosity and anxiety, he went in through the bushes. The old prince was crouched down, holding the dead stag by the antlers and crying.

Perhaps it was not just pity; in that moment he must have seen the vanity of what he was doing and of everything else – as if on shooting and entering the thick of the wood he had stepped into reality through the back door and seen the stereotype from backstage. Those antlers would become yet another trophy, idiotically fixed to the wall; those hunting trophies all piled and lined up on the walls and on the stairs – birds with glass eyes, awkward bears grimacing like clowns, rugs that terminated in wolves' heads like threadbare rag balls – a vulgar and inevitable parade, the destiny of every life which charms for a moment but all it takes is a little powder and a well oiled barrel to take it apart and undo it into straw, springs and buttons, like a stuffed animal.

The prince carried on shooting. But a small wedge of the void the prince met in the thick beside the dead stag penetrates the endless hunting stories recounted passionately by Vinko Sterle. As when Franc, near the Gašperjev hrib, follows and wounds a wolf, killing it with the

stock of his shotgun in mortal combat only to realize that it was a
female with four cubs that sit there looking around; or Matja's hunt for
the much-feared lone wolf in 1923 – hours and hours over the snow in
the moonlight, obsessively tracking it down, even though he is no less
exhausted than his quarry, moving forward almost without realizing
where he was putting his feet, until he shoots at something behind
a bush and hits the wolf. The exhausted beast is sleeping and fails to
wake up, not even to die.

These stories tell of the elusiveness of the forest, which draws back
inaccessible, and does not allow itself to be caught, but lays false trails
and pitfalls along its paths, clumsy misunderstandings akin to the
accidents that befall the weekend hunters, who regularly fill each other
with lead. And even if every day tractors and concrete annex a little
more of the forest, rendering it no longer threatening but threatened,
in some way it does evade everyone's grip and one understands that
despite the love-drunk butterflies on the Peklo road that let themselves
be picked up delicately between one's fingers, or Rina, the red bitch
who once chased a marten for a whole afternoon yapping and howling
as she vanished deep in the trees, there is something missing every
summer: like the bear that one never managed to see, or Mr Samec's
voice that died away before he finished his story, left caught up in
the trees of the forest somewhere, suspended and unfinished, "'Excuse
me, Your Excellency,' I said to him, 'but with your permission . . .'"

Collina

"That's right . . . that's where it is, near the well at Madonna della Scala, one of the most beautiful places on the Collina," Piero had said once when he was on the night shift and was trying to keep everyone up for as long possible, playing with the room keys before handing them over to the guests as they came in, or at any rate to the regulars, the ones he knew. "I'd really like to take you there one day." They used to arrive around the mid-August holiday, he continued, all three of them together from Cambiano, just a couple of kilometres away and they would stop for four or five days, a week at the most. They pitched the tent, put down the barrel of marinated anchovies and tench next to the well and a bit farther away the bottles, covered with a cloth. They'd spend the whole day there, pulling out the tench and the anchovies, playing cards, emptying the bottles of Freisa, every now and then taking a sip of water or, when their hair and shirts were sticky with the humidity, pulling up a bucketful from the well and tipping it over their heads. Everything was still, only the stars trembled in the bucket as it came up out of the black hole of the well – a porthole to another universe, but it was not a good idea to look out on the other side to find oneself heaven knows where, at least not during the week's holiday.

It was so good sitting there on the grass, especially in the evening when it was a bit cooler and they would let me sit a while with them, if I happened by, even though I'm not from Cambiano, only San Pietro, he would add. The water in the well was dark as wine, a beautiful deep demijohn, and no one wanted to sit there thinking about what was down there or up on the face of the moon, things we'll never see anyway, and if it was decided that these things can't be seen, then that's the way it has to be.

Drinking, munching, dealing the cards, but most of all discussing politics and their respective wives and families left behind in Cambiano. Backbiting, rather – certainly there was never any shortage of material. Or they would drag up old gory tales from the area: that tart with her throat cut in the acacia and poplar thicket, or Hanged Man Wood, so called because of the stranger found there dangling from a large plane tree, swaying in the evening wind as if busy in a slow dance. Minot was obsessed with the murder in Valle San Pietro: at the front of the house the only footprints were those of someone entering, the man had been killed with an axe that couldn't be found and which they thought might have been hidden in one of the barrels, so the carabinieri broached them all looking for it and ended up drinking a bit more than they should have done.

And so, said Piero sitting down on the sofa in front of the mirror that doubled the small hotel lobby, they purged themselves of all the year's poison and a week later home they went, at peace with their spouses and ready to get down to work. One of them died a few years ago. He had been losing more and more blood for months, but he kept saying he wasn't bothered about haemorrhoids, and when he did finally go to see someone about them, it was already more of a job for Father Brin than for Doctor Beraudo.

Father Brin heard his confession, knowing full well that his only sin was the curse he came out with every time he banged his finger in the timber yard; certainly he was always banging it. He gave him his blessing too and noticed his stunned face, damp with sweat and holy water, looking up at him with an air of doubt, as if urging him not to spin too many tales and to stop pretending to know everything about the dark side of the moon. So the priest gave him a pat on the shoulder and said, "You're thick as two planks," and the other man was left with his mouth open and stopped breathing. But he'd drunk his wine, the Freisa and the Barbera, right up until a few days before, despite the nausea in his mouth – like chewing iron, he said – and everything (or nothing, since he'd almost stopped eating) kept coming up in retches and belches. And so he went down through the well. At least he had enjoyed those holidays over so many years. "Well," Piero concluded, "I'm sure that once you've had days like that, like those at the well at Madonna della Scala, with the cards the bottles the tench etcetera, then you've had your life and you can't complain."

Piero tried to drag things out with this and other stories, because the hours never finish in a hotel like that where there aren't many distractions and the only things that might happen in the thick of the night are a few unpleasant events – unforeseen, but never too much of a surprise – in that area near the Porta Nuova station. Like the guy that time who came rushing in holding his belly in his hands and when he put them on the counter they were covered with the blood that was even coming out of his trousers – he must have been stabbed from the bottom up by someone who knew what he was doing. But gradually even the guests who stopped for a chat said goodnight and disappeared. The last to go up to her room was the Countess, always half asleep under the big hat pulled down over her face, but awake just as much as was necessary. Whenever possible she found some way of mentioning Stefan Zweig's *The World of Yesterday*, so as to make a good impression on some well-read guest, he too at home in that hotel; but it was said that when she went ten-pin bowling with two commercial travellers, occasional guests, her language was far from irreproachable.

The Countess had lived in the hotel for many years; she was on her own and above and beyond bed and breakfast, the modest monthly rate guaranteed some company which kept her mind off the idea of a family. "You see, Professor, I was married at twenty-two and widowed at thirty-one, now I'm eighty-three and – how shall I put it? I don't want you to misunderstand me, I have no criticism to make of my poor husband but ... let's say that the experience left me with no desire to repeat it."

Old single ladies were a mainstay of the hotel's clientele; apart from the Countess, there were retired teachers, widows of high-ranking officers, especially Air Force, a time-weathered woman with a mad glint in her eye, always dressed in green, the heels of her shoes always worn, who used to write feverishly, filling sheet after sheet and every now and then asking whoever was nearest to hand if in their opinion the President of the United States and the Commander of the Nato troops in Verona – the two of them spoke on the phone every evening, she explained, at seven o' clock, Italian time – had received her manuscript, the one that provided once-and-for-all solutions to the world's and everybody's problems. It was essential that they read it, she added, for the sake of universal good and salvation, but when once she was asked in which language she wrote to the President of the United States, she replied that she wrote to him in Italian of course, because he had plenty of translators at the White House and anyway, "I tell you, when it comes down to it ... let him sort it out."

Let him sort it out – perhaps that was the right answer to all the brazen demands with which the world ensnares and makes mincemeat of any poor devil, if he's so inexpert as to make himself the least bit available. Go up to the room and leave the world to sort itself out, while the evenings and the years mingle and fall into the black opening of the elevator, sleep's antechamber. And the porticoes too, the ones crossed before entering the hotel are archways of sleep, geometry of things that become ever more equal and regular under the eyelids until all differences are extinguished. Falling asleep – there's nothing to it: but when it doesn't happen any more, only then do you realize what it means. Those three around the well at Madonna della Scala used to fall asleep quickly, sometimes when in the dark one could still just make out the red of the evening, a sombre red, dark as blood. Perhaps it is true that they were happy back then. Anyway, Piero's right, it is a place that should be seen – like all the Collina, of course, which Rousseau considered the finest painting that a human eye could ever meet, while Cesare Balbo went so far as to call it an earthly paradise, quite forgetting that (very Piedmontese) advice about not exaggerating.

In one of his little books of delightful walks, published in 1870, Maurizio Marocco, the clergyman who enjoyed exploring and describing the Collina, suggested crossing it by starting from Turin and climbing up to Pecetto. Others instead suggested following the route of the mediaeval merchants, for whom the Collina, the Hill, was the "mountain" to be crossed from Chieri to Pecetto and the River Po, and then on towards the Alps – a thick wood full of traps and dangers, both barrier and road to France and the world beyond. Now it is fresh green countryside, but in order to enjoy its beauty, even in this the age of disenchantment, it is a good idea to "have suffered some misadventure" – an opinion propounded in 1853 by Giuseppe Filippo Baruffi, professor of positivist philosophy in the Royal University of Turin, priest and great traveller, on foot, throughout Turkey, Persia, Hungary, Egypt, Russia and Turin's Collina.

There is no danger that the Collina might find itself lacking in admirers, given the constant ubiquity of trouble. But why should it be necessary to suffer in order to love the light-blue rows of the vines, the undulating lines of the supports that intertwine and fade into the shadows, the brown and gold splashes in the fields, the blue of the sky – sometimes so intense and dark over the hills that it looks almost scarlet? Baruffi had seen the world, the pyramids in the desert and the hostelries of Baldissero, and he must have known that only a very hard heart would ever have need of any such painful initiation before letting its eyes roam agreeably over the glory of these uplands, massed in serried ranks like battalions. Rather perhaps the opposite is true and it takes a strong heart and a clear mind to prevent the impropriety of a mishap or even just a toothache, from ruining the view of a meander of the Po, as sweet as the hips of the one who sleeps beside us. But perhaps, as a priest, Baruffi thought it necessary to lend sense to the cruel chaos that assails us and to pretend that it constitutes a year's foundation course for the holidays and walks through the Collina.

Anyway, the person who for years has taken every opportunity to go walking along the highways and byways beyond the Po has certainly never gone looking for troubles, but seeks to forget those already lived through, and to dodge those that lie in wait; he wanders back and forth and takes a detour down the first path that comes along, just to throw the world off the scent for an hour or two and make it that much more difficult for it to catch up with those who are enjoying themselves and empty more horrors from Pandora's box on their heads.

The asparagus soup one is entitled to expect on spending an evening at Sciolze – at least that's how it was last time, the culinary powers of our student, hospitable and indulgent as she is, do not disappoint – that soup is more than tasty and may be fully appreciated without any condiment of mishaps. And if it isn't asparagus soup, it will be something equally good, especially if her daughter does the cooking, and now it's almost time for *her* to graduate. That memorable cotechino sausage, for example, it must have been three years ago. On reaching Sciolze there's no point worrying about what to do with the others, maybe one or two will be able to come for supper even though they haven't been invited, the house among the trees has a big terrace, the rest will sort themselves out. At all events, once you're at Sciolze there's nothing left but to carry on down a bit and then you're back on the plain, the trip across the hill is over.

For the moment it has just begun, near Madonna della Scala. Amidst dilapidated farmhouses, tall poplars that rustle like birds in the evening, maples, acacias and thorny weeds, an old villa confirms Baruffi's sad observation with its name: Villa Passatempo. That harmonious quadri-syllable – *passatempo*, pastime – carries echoes of a deep, mortal anxiety. The thick shadow and the tall upright trees must be there to stop time passing or at least to make it slow its pace, golden resin sliding down the trunk and not a gushing cascade. And yet what the name recounts is that in that neoclassical villa, with its double stairway on the façade and the triangular pediment in the imperial style, the two ladies of Verrua wished that time would pass quickly, that it were already past, that it were already near its end.

Perhaps this is the original sin, the inability to love and be happy, to live time, each instant to the full, without craving to burn it up, to use it all quickly. Incapacity for persuasion, said Michelstaedter. Original sin introduces death, which takes possession of life, making life seem unbearable in every hour it proffers in its passing, forcing the destruction of life's time, trying to make it pass quickly, like an illness; killing time, a polite form of suicide.

It is quite right to take one's hat off to the Baroque and neoclassical villas, to pay due homage to art, but then it's a good idea to move on and to seek shelter under some inn sign, where it is as though everything's immobile because there is no need of anything else. The trip through the Collina does not follow time's rectilinear track and its irreversible arrow, rather it zigzags, sabotaging time, flinging it away and then finding it back in the hand like a yo-yo. One might end up never reaching Cambiano; it's only a few kilometres from Chieri, but one can never tell because all roads are long and there's never any shortage of complications. That priest from Cambiano, for example: often during Mass he would have trouble opening the tabernacle to get the wafers, and it was a real torment for him, he used to turn and turn the key, muttering, with the altar boy kneeling behind him, "What the devil's in here!" and so the Mass, too, became a drawn-out affair.

One walks here and there, death waits at Samarkand and other such destinations, but for whoever dreams of running off to Samarkand it's already an achievement if they reach Pecetto; Baruffi, too, after travelling to Samarkand and Trebizond, chose to set course for the Collina.

One turns for Cambiano. Chieri is left behind with the red of its towers, its palaces and its churches, a red that in nearby Monferrato is even redder still and is the martial, wine colour of Piedmont. From Chieri one leaves with Father Bosco's blessing – object of a rather excessive personality cult, which in the church of Santa Margherita places him in a privileged position near Jesus and the Madonna while in the cathedral he is flanked, in a *Hellzapoppin'* effect, by Pope Woytila. A little farther on a large stone Father Bosco watches and commiserates with San Giuseppe Cottolengo, whose surname entered the Italian language thanks to his work with the severely disabled. Perhaps the idea that God made man in His own image and likeness is not blasphemy and neither is it boasting, because to realize, as Cottolengo did, that monstrousness does not exist but there is only unspeakable suffering that warrants love, is greatness worthy of a God.

They say he often slept on a chair, moaning in his sleep, and that he loved to take snuff; it seems that this was something of an obstacle to his canonization. It's not easy to be a saint; not only do you have the whole world and your own self against you, but the Church too. They didn't want to canonize San Domenico Savio either, revered though he is at the church of Santa Margherita, because it came out that he was afraid of dying. On the cathedral tower there is a sundial that shows not only the solar time of any given moment, but also average solar time. It is not clear what this last means, especially for someone who already has difficulty in understanding whether daylight-saving time means going to bed a bit sooner or a bit later. Those hours, up there, think they're God's gift; the sundials, with the obsession of all those high-flown inscriptions that proclaim them ineluctable, inevitable, irrevocable, have made them more than conceited. But all it takes is a cloud to make them disappear and it warms the heart to see that face in shadow, empty, the vacant throne of time deposed.

Chieri and Asti were the chief contenders for domination of the Collina, in wars, alliances, and *volte-faces* that involved several large powers and shifted frontiers; all of Piedmont is a frontier along the Alps that gradually becomes a state, a no man's land that becomes a centripetal and magnetic force. The Arimanni of Cambiano, it is said with pride, have never submitted to Chieri. The entanglements of the frontier, resulting from the intricacies of mediaeval geopolitics, created these communities of free men – Arimanni in Cambiano or Kosezi on the Monte Nevoso – in conflict with the regulating power of the state and prepared at most to obey a distant and abstract sovereign such as the Empire, a star still shining, but perhaps dead.

The sovereigns who forged or invented Piedmont – from Amadeus VIII to Emmanuel Philibert and Victor Amadeus II – were great levellers, and gave order and uniformity to the diversity of the frontier. Amadeus VIII's statutes even governed clothing, Emmanuel Philibert emphasized his control over the lives of his subjects, Victor Amadeus II created a bureaucratic and enlightened despotism which rather than ratifying the old habits stratified in the variety of the centuries and places, proclaimed laws inspired by the universal principles of Reason.

The Collina is rolling, varied countryside; the big city at its feet is geometrical, square. Which is more mysterious, order or (at least apparently) disorder? The Collina, too, is organized, and subdivided according to precise rules, but this does not diminish its seductive powers. One can lose oneself there quite happily, aimlessly, but even this sort of wandering is order, conjugation and declension, perhaps irregular and stilted, of the syntax that governs a life and unites it to the other lives that walk alongside it; existences intertwined and distinct like the elements of a theorem or the notes of a song, and so we move on together, obeying a common law, a battalion that finds itself in disarray as a result of the stronger blows, but then its ranks recompose, even if they are thinned. Mysterious passions of order – the rows of vines, the line of march that sets off fraternally towards the inevitable final fiasco – but in the meantime, before reaching the other side, one crosses red hills and pauses awhile under the shelter of trees and inkeepers alike.

Even if the lives of this and that person criss and cross regularly like the spears in a bronze balustrade, the climbing plants bind themselves around everything and blur the design. And this confusion is beautiful too, with the crinkled leaves, the branches that wind and twist as they will, and the flowers that bloom on the balcony before dropping into the road.

Piedmont mysterious and geometric, mysterious because geometric, dry and essential like the great style of the epic that reduces life to unity and lends it sense, reduces to the bone the scattered multiplicity of things and unites them in a single breath that pervades them and comes from far away, not from the past but from life itself in its time-less anonymity.

Perhaps order leads to sulkiness. It is said that it was Emmanuel Philibert who created the Piedmontese devotion to sober duty, while Victor Amadeus II was concerned with purging the rigour of scholarship of all hair-splitting quibbles and other such like frivolities. Even Turin's architecture, for De Amicis, was "democratic and levelling". There is in all of this a soldier-like glumness, as of feet keeping in step. Seen from Superga the Piedmontese Alps struck Balbo as a "military panorama" and Piedmont does indeed carry the mark of those engineers – the Papacinos, the Bertola d'Exilles – who planted fortifications throughout those mountains, squat look-out posts destined to redundancy.

The poetry of discipline and order is the poetry of an order that disintegrates, of a defence that is overrun, just as the old Piedmontese fortresses were overrun by Napoleon in his lightning campaign of 1796, and it is the poetry of resistance to the raids that continually overrun life. The *Animula vagula blandula* sets off into the dark and entrusts itself to the cardinal virtue of fortitude so as not to be overcome by fear and death, to stand up to the necessity of History – whether understood as the troubled history of salvation or as thoughtless ruin – and to never lose the thread of things, even if, in the disarray of battle, that thread gets tangled and breaks.

Side by side with modern Piedmont, which attains expression but is also superseded in the realization of Italian unity, there survives a nostalgia for the old Piedmont, more French or Savoyard than Italian, in all its many shadings: the old Piedmont of Costa de Beauregard, Calandra, Carlo Felice, or Solaro della Margherita, wholly resistant to Savoy's voluntary dissolution within the state of Italy and disdaining the modern trends for rationalizing agriculture, as with the technical innovations of Cavour – modernizing his lands and the whole peninsula – in his estates at Grinzane or Leri.

Nostalgia for old Piedmont, rekindled during moments of the

most violent social transformation, lends support to the possibilities of a different development, latent in History, possibilities crushed by the course of History. But the robust modernization reproached in the name of old Piedmont, is a child of the values and the traditions of that same ancestral Piedmont. The creators of this last – those Piedmontese ministers who were so much more Savoyard than Italian, those military engineers who built fortresses in the Alps, those country squires who as early as 1561 were being taken to task by the mayor of Villarbasse for having worked with hoes and scythes alongside their labourers – these were the very ones to forge those famous, prosaic virtues that enabled Piedmont to transcend itself and create the Italian state. Those qualities were: duty, moderation, patience in the face of history and life.

Old and new Piedmont are fused together in the grand perspectives of the modern drawn by Gobetti and by Gramsci. The first sees the eighteenth-century Piedmontese monarchy continue and come to fruition in Cavour, in liberal entrepreneurial capitalism, in the workers at FIAT, who were to be its heirs and its fulfilment. The second celebrates in "modern and cyclopic" Turin the "organizability" of a civilized and emancipated Italy, thanks above all to the industrial proletariat and a liberal class open to progress.

Such perspectives today appear, at least for the moment, to have been defeated by the gelatinous "postmodern", in which everything is interchangeable with its opposite and the Black Mass and its junk is placed on the same level as Saint Augustine's thought. It is no mere chance that this triumph of the postmodern coincides with the crisis of Turin's leadership in Italian culture, a line that starts from Einaudi and Gobetti and Gramsci and reaches Norberto Bobbio. Faced with such an indistinct miasma there seems to be all the greater need for that military virtue of "keeping things meticulously dressed in one's mind", praised in Carlo Allioni, eminent botanist of Victor Amadeus II.

*

In Cambiano there is a man who is well known because of his longevity. He'll soon be a hundred and one, but for the past few months he's been feeling unwell and he is angry because ever since they threw that party and that supper for his century, he hasn't felt right: he was touched and being touched did him no good at all. One has to be careful with anyone of his age he says, and please don't let anyone dream of celebrating his one hundred and first birthday. He has no desire to end up like Norberto Rosa, vernacular poet and patriot ("Metternich and his great wig, we'll send him off to Old Nick") who had died while writing his little poem, *The Elixir of Long Life*.

Some decades ago, on his retirement, the old man went to live with an unmarried daughter in a house belonging to a nephew of his from Chieri, on the tacit understanding that no one would chase him out of there for as long as he lived. This was something that never even crossed his nephew's mind except that with the passing of the years the old man's daughter, no longer a spring chicken herself, started feeling guilty about their prolonged occupancy of the house and would say sorry every time the nephew came to visit, as soon as she opened the door to him. "You understand, it's embarrassing," the nephew tells everybody, "I won't go back any more, I don't know what to say to her; I can't really tell them to take their time, please, there's no rush, but then neither can I ask them to hurry up ... "

Cambiano has cultural ambitions: weeks dedicated to roadside art, theatre in the squares, street corners brightened up with the colours of the paintings and special tomatoes on show just a few metres away. In front of the church stands the house where Stefano Jacomuzzi wrote the first draft of his *Subtle Wind*, a novel of unforgettable intensity: its theme is the evanescence, the vanity and with it the grandeur of life, the seasons' light, the coming of the shadows; it melds charity and disenchantment, a footloose *pietas* and picaresque irony, into a sense of mankind's common, epic approach towards the darkness in which "metaphors die".

A character in another novel of his, a dying Pope, thinks that "to listen to virtually unknown stories of the life that has passed by alongside us is the happiest way of taking leave of life," and it is in this sense that the great and fragile mystery of life on earth can flash forth, as for Roth's holy drinker, a hope of salvation. The narrator knows that everything gets misplaced and is lost, as though it had never been, and that nevertheless it does not have to be only that way; just as Panama Al Brown, the protagonist of *Subtle Wind*, does not know where to find the sense in the things he cannot grasp: "In the heart, they say, but everything's all mixed up in there and you can't trust anything."

Disenchantment defends an irreducible capacity for being enchanted; the sad awareness of the ambiguity of the heart allows us to preserve the fear and the trembling with which life has to be faced, to love its harrowing errors and to know its prosaic weights, loading them onto one's shoulders so that they are not too much of a burden for one's brother.

Stefano, salt of the earth. With him one felt less alone in the shock and the turbulence of things. Since his passing it has been more difficult for many people to live and to laugh in spite of everything, to savour fully every instant for itself. "What would you do," [Stefano again] "asked a pious and supercilious relative of San Luigi Gonzaga, in childhood, while at play, if you knew that you were going to die in a few minutes? 'I would carry on playing,' replied the child."

San Pietro is to Pecetto as Alba Longa is to Rome; when its name was Covaccio, forty-four of its armed men built a new quarter, Pecetto, which in a short space of time became more important than the cradle out of which it sprang. The stream, which was called Canape, took the name of Vajors – the river of bones – because of the many bones buried there following the battle of 23 April, 1345, when the marquis of Monferrato turned its waters red with the blood of the soldiers of Robert d'Anjou. A poet who accompanied the defeated Anjou prince sang of the bloody battle. The ballad's opening gives no clue of the massacres to follow: "Sur les doux temps, que renverdissent/ toutes choses et bois fleurissent . . . " But every song begins this way and many of them end badly; playing cops and robbers in childhood gives no hint of the cancer or the car that will cut down the child, neither do a night's tender manoeuvres presage the rough hands of the doctor who will carry out the abortion or the quarrels that will find their way into court over an apartment bought together as a shared asset. And even when things go better, the finale is anyway a disaster.

Of a summer evening it is pleasant to lie down in the grass, next to the canes. The night is high, overarching like the apse of a church, a black sky that looks blue; some people's black hair also seems blue, and sometimes, staring up on high, it is difficult to find a particular star, perhaps it has fallen into the dark, swallowed up by the darkness like a firework. The Milky Way shines, black, luminous waters; there's no need to worry about falling in there together, as at the seaside, falling up there, down there – even disappearing might be a celebration, like getting lost among the hills that in the evening look like a sea, large and calm waves coming in a long, powerful breath.

San Felice, not far from Madonna della Scala. The small village is lost amid the greenery; vines and climbing plants, silence, yellow autumn Jerusalem artichokes, further off the tawny towers of Castelvecchio. To stop, to sleep, to disappear. But it is always time to move on. "Gentil galant, faites votre voyage," says the shepherdess in the ballad.

Revigliasco, where as a young man D'Azeglio came to blows with his preceptor Don Andreis and later the quadrumvir De Vecchi set himself up in a fine villa. In the village square, named after Don Girotto stands a headless angel near the parish church; he turns his back on the Madonna, evidently reluctant to give her the news that will change the history of the world. But the little bridge, adequate for the modest stream and also named after Don Girotto, has disappeared, having been demolished in the course of progress. Revigliasco is still "a place of the most perfect air", as defined in a 1760 essay on some Spiritual Exercises, and for this reason too the place flourished; no wonder then that the construction of a wider road eliminated the hapless bridge. History, unfortunately, in order to facilitate access to the new villas on the Collina, also passed carelessly over the plaque that indicated the name of the bridge.

That plaque – whose existence is confirmed by Mr Felice, carpenter from Revigliasco and enamoured of every stone of his home village – summarized the life of the personage to whom the bridge was dedicated in an epic synthesis, like a gravestone. As *Spoon River* teaches, the graveyard inscription is the laconic novel of a man's life, the epitaph that encapsulates its meaning. Probably everyone composes a single poem with the deeds of his or her existence and the gravestone condenses it, transcribes it and entrusts it to that voluminous and interminable *Complete Works* – the world's graveyards.

He must have been an enviable man, the subject of that missing plaque in Revigliasco: *Bridge Don Girotto, 1857–1943, Philosopher – Latinist – Oenologist, Archpriest of Revigliasco for 52 years.* That trinomial designation (Philosopher – Latinist – Oenologist) is in its concision a yet more expressive monument to Don Girotto than his autobiography and his memorable sayings, collected and published by his successor and very much present, as is his personality, in the memory of the people of the Collina.

Philosophy, for the archpriest of Revigliasco, seems above all else to have been humour, irony, a sense of the smallness of all finite things – and even of oneself – compared to the big background of the infinite, against which all human experience is set. This feeling prevents one from taking oneself too seriously, and thus is a liberation from the poisons of insecurity and arrogance; but it also prevents one from taking any vaunted greatness all that seriously and thus frees one from fear. Compared with the eternal, each single thing looks tiny, but, in its smallness, shares an equal dignity with the next, even with those that flaunt a menacing power. Irony becomes the bulwark, inflexible yet loving, of every creature, even the weakest and most reclusive, against the vacuous pomp of the world that seeks to trample them underfoot.

Don Girotto's anecdotes – his "pleasantries" collected by Don Nicola Cuniberti – describe his good-humoured and biting inventiveness, the blunt and irreverent language of his celebrated bulletin that upset his superiors, his pungent, salacious replies to the Fascist officials, his natural intimacy with the humble, good and intractable reality of the body, of elementary physical life; the devoutness exercised by this kindly and sharp-tongued parish priest was above all else a lack of concern for "what others think", that religious open-mindedness that is often the antithesis of the spirit of the laity.

The publisher of his "pleasantries" advised that they should not be read by "persons of delicate conscience" who may well have been scandalized by his witticisms or his story of the accident he had during a pilgrimage to Lourdes when, getting out of his bed because of a spasm in his leg, he slipped on the floor and banged his head twice as he fell.

Small, thin and unkempt, with a sharp face that could be a portrait of the Piedmontese land and its wine, Don Girotto was worthy of his parishioners, those inhabitants of Revigliasco who are described by Casalis, in his *Historical – Geographical Dictionary*, as "robust and strong, well-built, healthy, long-living, well-behaved and industrious". Poet of human existence and a born master of the difficult art of keeping cheerful, the archpriest of Revigliasco was truly a shepherd to his flock throughout those tormented and tumultuous years of social transformation. He was as simple as a dove, but was also as shrewd and sharp as a serpent, because the shepherd, in order to defend his flock, must know that the weak and the poor find themselves in the world as sheep in the midst of wolves, and therefore he must be able to recognize the wolves and must know how to give them, whenever necessary, a good hiding. The villagers remember not only his generosity, but also the paradoxical discretion with which he would disappear when harvest-time came, so that those working the parish land could steal without feeling embarrassed.

Philosopher, Latinist, Oenologist: his secret perhaps lies in these three words. Even today, in the oratory that carries his name, the shelves and counters bear various bottles of the epic Piedmontese red wines. Probably the *trait d'union* between the three terms, the link that holds them together, is the word which the ingenious and anonymous author of the plaque placed quite rightly in the middle: Latinist. Latin, for the archpriest, was the scholarly *latinorum* of the seminary, the language that called the faithful to worship and sent them home at the end of the service; it was above all classic clarity, the syntax that gives a hierarchy to the inchoate dust of the world and puts everything in its right place, the subject in the nominative and the object in the accusative; it was the logical and moral order that classifies, identifies, defines, judges, distinguishes venial sins from mortal sins, vague, shadowy notions from definite intentions, actions from ghosts. In that symmetry there was a place for everything, for the revealed truths and for the vintage bottles, for the passing of the seasons and for the mutation of habits and morals, for the edifying episodes in the lives of the saints and for the epic hidden in the kernel of grain of wheat that ripens, for the crystalline geometric structure of a snowflake and its dissolution into nothing.

That centuries-dead language was also the language of irony, of that which exists only in the word itself and excites love and respect for its gratuitous and pompous unreality, which makes us smile affectionately. The Latinist oenologist probably realized that the smooth surface of that Latin was like the taste of Barbera and Dolcetto, so quick to slide into the glass and down the throat and worthy of all the care and competence that he dedicated to the gifts of the grape, with a symbiosis of theology and oenology that is not rare among these hills, given that already in times long past the theologian Allasia had obtained a royal warrant that gave his wine exclusive access to Piazza Carlina.

Another unrepentant Piedmontese, the Germanist Giovanni Vittorio Amoretti, used to recount how he completed his secondary education in a private boarding school run by the Scolopi Fathers where only Latin was spoken and a rigid discipline prevailed, although this he eluded by lowering himself out of the window with a sheet to go chasing girls. One evening as he was on his way back, the Father Guardian heard him; in vain he hid behind a bush but he had to come out at the peremptory summons: *Amorette, veni foras!* On being quizzed – in Latin – by the Father Superior, he fluffed everything because he couldn't remember the word for "sheet" in the Roman tongue and so the Father Superior inflicted a small punishment on him, not for his escapade – deplorable, but not inexcusable, given his age – but rather for not knowing the Latin name for a sheet, on which his little romp had literally depended: praying is also paying attention to objects, gratitude for created things.

For Don Girotto the science of Latin and the science of wine became philosophical knowledge, the art of making a genial passage across the planet as a guest. He used to write couplets celebrating the village of his birth, Orbassano, and its polenta; the arcades of Latin syntax, beneath which the realities of life in all their absurdity came together in mischievous innocence, were not unlike the composed, the ineffable objectivity with which Don Cuniberti, Don Girotto's biographer, wrote his small learned treatise recording the centuries-old rivalry between Revigliasco and neighbouring Pecetto. "This hatred between the two villages," as the reverend gently put it, "exploded dutifully on the holiest day of the year: after the office of Good Friday the young lads left their respective parish churches and took to the two banks of the Gariglia, where the traditional stone-throwing took place; cuts and contusions resulted on both sides."

Oenology and love of Latin, thoughtful charity for others and awareness of the comicality of existence, faith and disenchantment came together in an amiable and robust philosophy. Don Girotto's "pleasantries" reveal the free spirit of a person who has understood how the differences in greatness or intelligence among men, between a universal genius and a poor devil appear vast, but are in fact tiny in the face of death, of pain, of war and of the fact that even a genius is incapable of predicting and preventing these things, not to mention insomnia, misery, toothache. Faced with the simple reality of living one's life, the exceptional performance of a genius is like the jump of the proverbial flea compared to the Himalayas.

With such a philosophy looking death in the face is less arduous. His successor, evidently more inclined to Hamlet and the Baroque, loved the admonitory skull in the garden next to the oratory, which carried this written message for the visitor: "I was like you, you will be like me." In quite another spirit the eighty-six-year-old Don Girotto, celebrating Mass on All Souls not long before he died, said: "It's my turn now," adding however, "but I won't be offended if anyone wants to go ahead of me."

According to its panegyrist Don Nicola Cuniberti, the air in Pecetto, the most famous village on the Collina (the sweetest clime, the most salubrious air, delightful location, purest sky, most fertile soil, the tastiest and the most abundant fruits), guarantees not only a "robust constitution", but an "open mind" as well. In the atrium of Villa Veglio, now the village hall, the lecturer, as he waits for the others, is reading the timetable for the harvesting of the truffles (black and white). He is too much a follower of logic to hope that one night spent there might be enough to have attained that openness of mind to which all intellectuals aspire. He indeed had only spent one night in the village, although for years he was registered as being officially resident in that white house at 56 Via Mogna, a road named after the Mayor who had taken Giolitti's advice and populated Pecetto's hill with its famous cherry trees. But the hagiographer of the place assures us that even the faces of the holiday visitors, the people who spend a few days here in the year, "are pictures of gaiety and loyal friendship" – so there is hope.

The lanes and the roads of the Collina lead towards the void of the horizon, but the topiarist's art, for which Pecetto is justly famous, invites one to linger happily beneath those pergolas and those arbours and to proceed with the crossing. The dark falls more quickly than one expects and every now and then someone drops behind, too far behind, perhaps they hear the voices calling but it is late, and something of everyone remains with those who do not come back. The last to go, when the time comes, won't find it too much of a struggle to leave – they will be as light as a feather, after having buried so many pieces of themselves. But the ranks remain intact, the names are all there, for ever, indeed they grow; the friends, as it should be, haven't stood twiddling their thumbs throughout all these years, but they have made sure that the shape of a face, a look, an inimitable gesture or the sound of a voice are not lost but are transmitted for God's greater glory and for the pleasure of future generations.

With the passing of the years the farewell gun salutes are fired ever more often; it is all a drumroll and one no longer knows whether it's New Year or a funeral; anyway, in Pecetto even the cemetery is cheerful and neat and its graves, assures Vittorio Benedetto, the theologian, "are much sought after by the new holiday visitors and outsiders."

*

The wolves, we are told by another of the village's bards, Colonel Capello, disappeared from Pecetto at the beginning of the century; the bears, the deer and boar long before that and, the Colonel continues, the mastodons earlier still. For thousands of years ancient peoples – Celtic – Ligurian, Taurini, Bagienni, Statielli, Eburiati – have been strata of the earth. History is among other things a list of names, peoples and cities, sovereigns and rebels; even the names of wines ring glorious and evanescent like those of ancient dynasties – Cascarolo, Brazolata, Guernazza, Mostoso, Cario, Manzanetto, Avanale, Mausano, Castagnazzo. During the Revolution, when Branda Lucioni arrived in this area to wipe out the Jacobins with his "Christian clout", he set up a cross, took Communion, requisitioned foodstuffs left and right and then got drunk.

Marocco, like Baruffi, underlines the merits of this misfortune, "so beneficial for everyone, but above all for the princes." The latter, however, seem to benefit little from it, or perhaps in order to benefit more they continue to pile it on, spreading war and death. Sometimes it seems strange that death, cultivated with such care and passion, should not have had the last word. Life gives the lie to all the forecasts and every announcement of death, just as it has obviously confounded the smug statement issued by a cleric in 1740 observing that in Pecetto, "the youngsters have completely renounced the practice of lovemaking."

Clerics and parish priests above all others have sung the glories of Pecetto and the Collina in general, but anticlerical Piedmont has not repaid them in kind. The priests tried as hard as they could, but with little success. Don Perlo, for example, who in 1870 is attacked by a drunk with a pistol; he forgives the man and embraces him, and the drunk goes away but then on second thoughts comes back and has another shot at him – evidently without much success since ten years later Don Perlo, passing by the cemetery in his trap, gets another thirty bullets.

The *Theatrum Statuum Regiae Celsitudinis Sabaudiae Ducis*, commissioned by Charles Emmanuel II and printed in Amsterdam in 1682, displays the imposing castle at Pecetto, towering above the village, in an illustration by Giovanni Tomaso Borgonio. The castle, however, was never built and this disparity between reality and its catalogue-entry does not displease those who – coming from that "nowhere" which, in the words of the Hapsburg traveller Hermann Bahr, is Trieste – love things that are not there and, in the tradition of Svevo, find their own destiny in absence. But the Collina, it has been said and said again, is a landscape that gives a sense of physical support and moral certainty and so puts flirtations with the void peremptorily in their place, inviting one not to mistrust reality and the perception that grasps it. Irritated by the uncertainty over the date of construction of the church of Saint Sebastian, Vittorio Benedetto, the priest already mentioned as connoisseur of the holiday visitors' physiognomies, knows that all uncertainties are contagious, and hastens to ensure that it does not end up jeopardizing the very existence of the venerable building: "It is a fact," he writes, "that the church of Saint Sebastian at Pecetto Torinese exists, and, at least for as long as the external senses remain the criteria on which truth is based, we can and we must conclude that it was built. As to its existence, therefore, there is no doubt. The great question that is begged regards the precise period in which it was built. . . ."

It is best to affirm the objectivity of what is real, in a century of Pirandellian doubt, otherwise things go wrong. Felice Genero, whose name was given to a villa that has become a splendid public park on the Collina, was a banker and member of parliament; he became involved with counterfeiters, pretended to be mad and fetched up in a lunatic asylum. Objects are, thanks be to God; the church is there, in front of one's eyes, confirmation of the world of created things, like the robust vines grown into the walls of the villas, or like the seductive Lodovica Pasta, whose beauty made the reputation of the Piciotta Fountain at the foot of the Collina, for it was by that fountain that passers-by had the pleasure of catching sight of her.

The Collina, with its University of Vermouth-makers and Confectioners, is a good school of reality. The unbeliever enters the church of Saint Sebastian, touches the marble of the holy-water stoup and is obliged to change his mind, like Doubting Thomas. In the fresco of the *Washing of the Feet*, which is fading, there is the face of a woman – beautiful and enigmatic; the mystery is in the reality, in the things that are there, in that unforgettable, unknown face.

Villa Talucchi is on the left on the way up from San Pietro to Pecetto. The door is submerged in ivy and virginia creeper, in the garden there are palms and magnolias, dominated by a gigantic cedar of Lebanon. Come with me from Lebanon, my spouse. How beautiful are thy feet with shoes, O prince's daughter! Thy navel is like a round goblet, thy belly like an heap of wheat, thy two breasts are like two young roes that are twins . . . The darkness lightens, the darkness of the paths and the years, at the end there is a face, her face that has not darkened in the presence of death, advancing like a rising dawn – fair as the moon, bright as the sun, terrible as an army in battle – side by side for ever and more than ever; the night that falls, that has fallen for some time now, can do nothing against that smile, which pervades it like a light, the darkness is very soft, arms tighten against the breast, dark and laughing eyes in which to sink . . .

It was worse for Silvio Pellico; sickly as he was he used to come up from his Villa Barolo near Moncalieri, to pay court in vain under that cedar to the actress la Gegia, when she came to stay with her cousin Carlotta Marchionni. She was the leading lady with the Royal Sardinian Company, which created a stir with its productions of Pellico's *Francesca da Rimini*, and *Gismonda*. But the author of *My Prisons* took no pride in these literary successes; those poems, those tragic gestures, those books that had fired the spirit of liberal patriotism now appeared to him empty or to no purpose, written by another hand. Now he was fleeing from that agitation, he was seeking refuge in the shadows of churches and in prayer that might dowse his heart and his passions, already so weak that to extinguish them required only the draught that came in through the church door, slightly ajar. He was indifferent to the echoes of his fame that crossed the oceans, and perhaps he was even indifferent to la Gegia's rejections. He enjoyed courting her shyly, but she would have unnerved him had she said yes – a wind too strong for his candle. He felt well when he managed to forget himself reciting the Rosary or annotating entries for his majordomo's expenses.

Norberto Bobbio writes that there is the tragedy of the strong and the tragedy of the weak, indicating Pavese as an example of the latter. There is perhaps another one, less straightforward, the one that comes to a final reckoning with one's own radical weakness, with one's own inadequacy in the face of life and History, fighting to transform helplessness into dignity; tragedy of silence, of oblivion, of whoever – after having lived a compelling, vital moment – is forced, by others or by himself, to eliminate it and eliminate his own self, dulling it into a lifeless grey, which becomes a refuge.

Pellico's last years are a moderate and camouflaged version of that empty, reeling self-dismissal. Pellico could not and would not have anything to do with History and with his ego that had once contributed to the making of it; he worked at the nullification of himself. Perhaps his tepid courtship of la Gegia was a small distraction from this terrible task – like the stroll with which Kafka stretched his legs between chapters of *The Trial*.

The villas are often associated with the pastimes of Eros: Madama Reale's affaires in the Vigna, the cruelties with which Annie Vivanti, when she was writing *Naja tripudians* at Villa Bergalli, used to torment her secretary-lover Maniscalchi (who enjoyed being tormented), the adroitness with which Cardinal Maurizio di Savoia – who abandoned the purple for reasons of state – used to keep Ludovica, his thirteen-year-old niece and bride in the Queen's villa. The villas of the Collina have been loved above all by the Germanists: Barbara Allason's near the Eremo, Arturo Graf's on the Fenestrelle road, Arturo Farinelli and Leonello Vincenti's at Cavoretto.

Italian German studies are at home, indeed were born, amidst these hills and the university at their foot. Arturo Graf nurtured his poetry and his teaching from German sources, Paolo Raffaele Troiano warned, before the event, that Nietzsche worship would take particular hold in Turin. An enthusiastic young Gramsci, just before the First World War, attended lessons given by Farinelli, the founder of German studies in Italy. Although Gramsci later rejected Farinelli's lyrical rhetoric, at the time the Germanist appeared to him to be like a volcano, an enthusiastic explorer of new cultural continents, leading his pupils to their discovery.

Farinelli was a slovenly genius, rich in that indomitable vitality which is a priceless gift in life but is often the bane, too, of other people's lives and of thought itself, when it is induced to deny itself emphatically in the name of thoughtless worldly wisdom. He held the first Italian chair of German literature and had a gift for sweeping through the literary landscape, communicating a sense of the universality of the world of letters, although he was concerned less with philological rigour than he was with his own legend. He once pretended, for example, during an official visit to an Italian Institute somewhere abroad, that he had distractedly thrown his gold watch into the water as he was pensively skimming stones across a lake, so as to have an anecdote to pass down to his descendants.

A temperament like Farinelli's was not one to resist the blandishments of Fascism; but out of his school came some of the greatest Italian Germanists, above all Leonello Vincenti, who lived – probably without being too pleased about the fact – alongside him on the Collina, at Cavoretto.

It is no coincidence that German literature and culture should have been for the most part discovered and transmitted to Italy through Turin. German literature, with its symbiosis of poetry and philosophy, has set itself the most radical questions regarding the individual in modern society, regarding the possibility or impossibility of the individual's fully realizing himself, of finding a place in the workings of social mechanisms that are ever more complex and depersonalized, mechanisms capable of providing a firm anchorage for the individual in History or of crushing him, a mirage of salvation and the spectre of Medusa. German literature has been unique in taking up the epoch-making character of the modern, its radical transformation of man and the world and what this means for the journey towards the Promised Land or for its disintegration as it comes into sight, for the quest and the exile of real life. Turin – "the modern city of the peninsula" in Gramsci's words – has been at the core of this modernity and has created a culture rooted in politics, but not subordinated to politics.

This culture saw its own destiny bound, for better or for worse, with the new industrial reality and its proletariat – the proletariat of Turin, the Italian Detroit or Leningrad – which in Gramsci's, but also in Gobetti's view, was supposed to become the class which, as a result of the industrial realities and its own struggles would be the general harbinger of universality.

To be a Germanist in Turin meant coming to terms with modernity as destiny, with a Germany which had been the cradle of Marxism, the historical and ideological scenario displaying the strengths and the weaknesses of its Utopia. The dream of a Marx who reads Hölderlin – as Thomas Mann put it – or rather the reconciliation of the prose of the world, freed from alienation, and the poetry of the heart, this is a lynchpin of modern German literature and in Turin's culture the dream has been lived to the full. In Giulio Bollati's opinion such a culture was already dead in the Fifties – crushed by the weight of a historical evolution that differed from the forecasts. If this is true, then its light, which has continued to shine for a long time, is like the light that arrives, aeons later, from a dead star, but Bollati himself – another friend whose absence makes our steps more uncertain – still keeps that light alive with his book that formulates the diagnosis and thus demonstrates that the culture is not necessarily dead after all.

The present, certainly, seems to have crushed Gobetti's and Slataper's hopes of a real life that one carries tucked away in one's baggage. Utopias that fall, Gates of Eden that everywhere close behind you – ever more, everywhere; so many Adams and Eves who do nothing else but eat the wrong apples and get themselves thrown out of earthly paradises or even out of halfway decent places.

The double inheritance of Trieste and Turin and their unfulfilled promises can be a heavy one. But, as Frédéric Moreau said, even though in reference only to the waiting room in a brothel, it is the best we've had. And so, in spite of everything, one carries on along this road. And anyway the Germanists, notwithstanding those often brick-like tomes they carry about with them, also know how to apply a light touch when required – take Giovanni Vittorio Amoretti for example, also from this area. Susceptible to excessive beauty, frequently exuberant and not particularly controlled in his essays, Amoretti had always improved with the passage of time and, having written for *La Stampa* in the Twenties, at the age of ninety he became a regular contributor to the *Gazzetta di Parma*. At ninety-six he was admitted to the Molinette hospital in Turin and wrote a note to a younger, though no longer all that young colleague: "Would I be too forward to ask you, should it prove necessary, for a couple of lines by way of adieu for the *Corriere*?"

A few days later those lines appeared in the *Corriere*. In any case, although facing up to the eventuality that then occurred, that letter showed no sign of distress over death: the conclusion was, "We shall see." Perhaps those are the words needed when there is too much pathos around regarding an irrevocable end – even the end of Gobetti's and Gramsci's dreams, definitively consigned to the tomb. We shall see.

The Piedmontese made Italy. But nature – wrote Cesare Balbo in 1855, six years before unification – made them "as non-Italian as was possible" and they have found themselves "wishing, wanting, believing [. . .] that we must be, that we are Italian." All identities, especially national identities, which vaunt themselves as immutable facts of nature, are acts of will, as heroic and artificial as any other peremptory moral imperative. Giovanni Cena spoke of an "Italian mission that we Piedmontese must carry out."

If identity is the product of a will, it is the negation of one's self because it is a gesture made by someone who wants to be something that he evidently is not and who therefore wants to be different from himself, to make himself unnatural, to pollute himself. In Carlo Alberto's day, Tommaso Vallauri proposed to him that there should be an illustrated version of the literary glories of the "Piedmontese nation", misunderstood by the "foreign" historiographers such as the Italian Tiraboschi. But Piedmontese identity is no less ideological and precarious than the Italian; each identity is an aggregate and there is little sense in dismantling it so as to reach the supposed indivisible atom. Even to maintain that it is enough to be Piedmontese to be immune from rhetoric, as Thovez suggested, might be an exaggeration.

The true Piedmontese, from Alfieri onwards – as Carlo Dionisotti reminds us – are those who have been capable of stepping outside of this Piedmontese identity. This capacity to transcend one's own roots, however much beloved, is also part of that sense of history, of liberty and of Europe that made Piedmont a bastion of anti-Fascism and led Natalino Sapegno more or less to identify Piedmont with anti-Fascism. Today – after so much rhetoric about the Resistance, but also in the face of a suspect revisionism that seeks not so much to re-evaluate myths, reveal truths and understand and respect the enemy, as to place everything on an equal footing, the executioners of Auschwitz and their victims – today we cannot fail to call ourselves Piedmontese. The Collina is also Pian del Lòt, where on 2 April, 1944 twenty-seven people were massacred by the Fascists.

Baldissero, Pavarolo, Bardassano, Sciolze. The leaves are red and yellow, and behind half-closed eyelids everything is red against the sun; the red advances, extends and darkens, the strident chirping of the cicadas fades into the far-off whine of a trimmer, the geometrical squares of the yellow and brown fields, yet to be harvested or already reaped, shine in the limpid air, heraldic devices on a large shield.

"The variety of sites to be found in this hilly region is inexpressible." Davide Bertolotti, 1840. One could even travel around on one's own; the hills themselves would provide sufficient company, the locust trees that are crowding out the sweet chestnuts and the young oaks, the cypresses that invite one into a perfectly sociable solitude, benevolently open to chatting with whomever one meets along the lanes buried in the green, in the underwater light of the foliage.

Azure vineyards, yellow and rust-coloured splashes of the fields, which gave Casorati, in his house at Pavarolo, the hues for his paintings. The Collina is a feast of colour. In the 1700s Monsieur de Saussure, of the Turin Academy, who studied mathematics so as to learn the language of reality, had invented the cyanometer, in order to measure the different shades of blue in the sky. On the Maddalena it is intense, almost violet, higher up it fades into a pale sky-blue, the colour of distance, degrees of absence, of that which is missing. A man from Baldissero, who lived near the well, said that there should also be a cyanometer for the colour of eyes, but no one ever did anything about it.

Bardassano is quiet and sun-drenched. The grass flowers among the tight joints of the fortress, at once masculine and gentle, with its bulwarks high and red in the solitude. The village is empty; two old women appear at a window, they ask something we cannot catch, then disappear.

They say that the Magistrate lived in one of these quiet houses with his sister who every morning would take him to Turin and in the evening would go to collect him and bring him back to Bardassano. The Magistrate – this at least was the name by which this diligent and kindly man was universally known – used to wander the streets of Turin at all seasons, and especially the corridors of the university, in his over-coat with its leather collar and carrying his bag always bursting with documents. He was always busy, discreet but inexorable, keeping everybody up to date on the workings of the World Committee and the constant thorny problems it was forever resolving happily by general consensus and always for the common good.

Above all the Magistrate hung around the lecture theatres and the offices of the university. At first he was not noticed amidst the confusion and the crowds, because of his obsequious politeness and reluctance to disturb. Often, as one dashed into the German department to pick up a book needed for a tutorial, one would find him sitting at the lecturer's place, hunched over the typewriter, but he would always stand up at once, offer a deferential greeting and vacate the chair. He used the desk and the typewriter regularly, but he always left everything tidy and never touched the papers.

The Magistrate had founded the World Committee and always kept the lecturers informed – at least those he felt he could trust – on the progress of the work that he chaired with much tact and without any tendency towards authoritarianism. The serene and ordered rhythm of the universe depended on this work. He used to meet Johnson, Brezhnev, Mao Tse Tung, the unions, the British prime minister, the anarchists, the Churches, the president of the university principals, underground groups, the boards of directors of many companies, students' representatives, ministers, news vendors, political parties, sporting groups. The Committee – presumably in permanent session – resolved crises in the Middle East, the war in Vietnam, the proliferation of nuclear arms, the overcrowding in the universities, the postal strikes, the shortage of lecture halls, the chaos of the traffic.

The Magistrate was always calm, happy and perfectly at ease in the reality of his Committee; its ideal harmony was never disturbed by the acrid presence of any other reality, the reality in which others lived, where those who wield power never meet unless it is to study the possibility of unleashing a fatal blow on the other; in which there are not enough lecture halls, the traffic is gridlocked and men are tearing one another apart. In the straightforward reality of the Committee, everything was in its axis, was smoothed, was resolved; everyone was fraternally united and evil did not exist. In this harmonious reality the Magistrate did not grow old, he remained ever the same; with his black hair he could have been seventy, or even forty-five, he never had a cold or a bad back, the nervous disorders that thwart and upset the existence of ordinary mortals.

The Committee had at its disposal, obviously, a World Police Force. But this was simply a superfluous precaution, a mere formality, because, said the Magistrate, it was not necessary. During lessons he would open the door and look in for a few seconds, respectful and reassuring, telling the lecturer that the World Police were ready for any eventuality, but nobody need worry because all was in order and there was no reason to call them in. Unlike so many of his predecessors, who dreamed of universal domination so as to keep an iron grip on a world peopled (in their view) with ne'er-do-wells in need of stiff, tyrannical control, the Magistrate lived in a world populated entirely by men of good will, motivated by the best of intentions.

The World Committee limited itself to providing sensible advice, with a good-natured and paternal authority deriving from experience and certainly not from spiritual or ideological superiority; the others listened and explained themselves and then decisions were taken for the best. Often he would recount with pained insistence how the World Committee was opposed to the indiscriminate criticism levelled at modern youth – "Come along, we were all young once" – or at the unions' claims or the iniquity of the times. Rather, during the high school diploma examinations, he would visit all the schools – perhaps being taken for some inspector from the ministry – and sing the praises of the examiners for their attentiveness, the students for their diligence, the school janitors for their zeal.

Gradually he took *de facto* control of the German noticeboard, which thus carried his proclamations alongside the lecturer's notes regarding exam dates or office hours. In these publications he "warmly greeted the entire", nay the "universal ranks of educators", or the "university–universal–educators body"; he nominated committees of honour and was especially concerned with protecting freedom, or rather freedoms, like a true disciple of de Tocqueville. Indeed, in his proclamations, which often rambled into interminable parades of enigmatic acronyms or incomprehensible sequences of syllables, he sustained "uninter-ference", the abolition of "underminers", the "conjugation of rights, safe, legitimate, generousitive cohabitation, and safeguarding from "remotisms", "equifiscalization", "educatorialists' serenity", the "gerund of the dialogue", "universal accessibleness".

These cyclostyled proclamations went the rounds of the lecture halls and the corridors. When the Magistrate spoke in the fiery student assemblies of the Seventies, his tranquil voice, rich in terms that suited the lexis of that period (committees, social surrogation, structuralization), took control of the auditorium for some minutes until the inevitable adjective "lunaceous", proffered sweetly but firmly, disconcerted his listeners.

He abhorred all forms of insult and all militancy, but was also firm in his rejection of any excessive criticism of them and even expounded his reasoning. All was well with the world, all it needed was a little indulgence in its ordering and above all it needed someone who would say that everything was alright; thus, when he stood in the middle of the road to help in thinning out the traffic or when at the entrance to the theatre he invited the audience to take their seats, he did it above all to soothe the spirit and calm everyone down. He was stern, regretfully stern, only with the alarmists: one newspaper had reported on the crisis in the university, with the exception of one faculty, "the only island of happiness", and he replied, in a letter, that "all the university, all the world, is an island of happiness".

These were the years of lead, of terrorism, of blood in the streets. The Magistrate even addressed a leaflet to the Red Brigade, calling them "O propounders of eternal preludes", but he felt it was not necessary to call in the World Police, given his reluctance to use force of any kind. Indeed, he refrained from using violence even when he was beaten up by some thugs and then, when asked how he was, he immediately launched into a speech about the Committee with the dignity of one who has no time to concern himself with his own personal condition.

Who was it who said that in the rationality of Turin there was a hidden element of delirium, and that the checkerboard of her streets favoured the dream of Total Institutions? When all's said and done that Committee was scarcely more unreal than the United Nations or any other high-ranking organization. Certainly the Magistrate, too, had his prejudices: during a session of the Committee he once observed that there was room for everyone, for Russians and Americans, for Generals and hippies, but, he regretfully added, "If at all possible, basically, we'd prefer to do without the semiotics."

It is almost night, even though the embers of the sunset light up the Collina with a glow that appears inextinguishable. "The day, he said, can never die," thus sang D'Annunzio: but the day does indeed die, even a glorious day, and he knew perfectly well, he had understood everything, the death and the prostitution of beauty, the seduction and the vanity of that rape. When Senator Giovanni Agnelli, owner of FIAT, asked him to use his Muse to christen the *Winged Victory* statue he'd had built on the heights of the Maddelena, the poet who had created the impossible and immortal language of *Undulna* promptly delivered the most trite of banalities, "Fiat lux", as the epigraph says, well knowing that no one would have dared to scrape away that crust of the sublime and to cry out that the king was naked – to have done so would have been in no one's interests. Money buys poetry, but poetry shows money its rear end.

And so the day ends – Marisa always knew, but without being afraid of it – and almost everyone goes; beyond Sciolze the Collina drops to the plain. It is time to hurry up, supper must be almost ready and if it's not too chilly we'll eat out in the garden. Our hostess will probably already have laid the table under the big trees, she knows the lecturer's preferences, she knows how much he likes those trees, he's been coming here to eat for many years – but what does that mean, many years, they are always so few, it has all barely started.

Someone wanted to stop for a moment at Superga, out of respect for the usual Collina itinerary. But it is not worth arriving late for supper for the sake of that cold and monumental pomp, erected by Victor Amadeus II in thanksgiving for his victory. If one really has to think of that sovereign, it is better to think of him as a miserable old man, a prisoner of his son in the castle at Moncalieri, after losing his throne and his life, rather than as the victor on the hill. As with all victories that victorious basilica is appropriate for death, and there are too many *memento mori*. It is certainly true that the Torino team whose plane crashed into the Superga would beat any of today's football clubs. Even the geometry of that basilica, whose curves are praised as being in harmony with those of the Collina, is a monument to Reason, and Reason, we know, often has a disturbing underside. Baruffi recommended that on arriving at Superga one should admire the surrounding view with one's head down, between one's open legs. The World is widely known, the Province, however, very little, wrote Amedeo Grossi, Architect, Geometer, and Surveyor, at the end of the eighteenth century, and perhaps for this reason Baruffi sought unusual perspectives for the province, but even the universe, at least every now and then, should be observed from that position.

Apsyrtides

Nino is always telling the story of Palazzo Petrina, on Lussingrande, and it is difficult to remember when one heard it for the first time. The story of the palace, but more importantly the story of Captain Pietro, who had it built, and gave it the old family name, which had already been steeped in glory for some time thanks to the services rendered to the Serenissima on the high seas. Pietro Petrina defeated the Algerian pirate Haggi Bechir in the waters off Cyprus, chasing him all the way to the coast of Carmania, suffering little damage in the process – the mainsail riven, the foresail riven. That was how he earned himself the title of Knight of Saint Mark, a gold medal and other coin that went towards the construction of the palace, where he slept just one night. Indeed, he was off again immediately on the *Grazia Divina*, the same ship that had brought him victory in the battle with Bechir, off to meet death by shipwreck on the Scillies, where the seas foam and seethe on the rocks, one of the most wretched places on earth, where even the ablest sailor can soon come to grief. And the waves had carried the ship's figurehead off to the other side, to leeward, and it beached on the coast of Tresco, with its violet-blue irises and lilies, where the water breaks white and blue on the granite and shines like gold. But immediately after Captain Pietro the story goes on to speak of his grandson or great-grandson Marco, who lived and died in the same palace, ownership of which in the meantime had passed to the town council, which had turned it into a public almshouse.

Whenever it was first told, Nino often tells the tale at home, too, in Trieste, and certainly does so every time the boat comes within sight of Lussingrande, having left behind, to starboard, the two islands of Oriule, Greater and Lesser, with their red soil and the fig trees and the night-blue water breaking as white as snow on the rocks. He points his finger towards the belltower of the church on the shore, a great mast standing in the wind, and he indicates the palace, hidden as it is by the houses from which in truth it can barely be distinguished for all its high-flown name.

It may well be, at least in some moments, that for Nino the story alludes not only to the inconstancy of fortune in general but also, more specifically, to the destiny of the Italians who lived for centuries on these islands: boat-owners who had acquired the habit of bullying the Croats. At the end of the Second World War they were chased out of these lands which the Slavs in their vengeful uprising tore from the Italian defeat. The exodus crushed and dispersed them in their thousands – like Nino who left his home, his boat and all the rest – while those few who remained at home, which was no longer their home, were harassed and intimidated.

But every time one comes to the archipelago – rarely by sea, in a boat, but more often by car, catching the ferry at Brestova, on the eastern coast of Istria and disembarking at Porozine, on the island of Cherso – every reference to a History that is present in still-tender scars evaporates, disappears like mist in the reflection of the sun on the sea and the light-coloured Cyclopean ridges to the sides of the road – an epic, Homeric landscape in which there is no place for tortuous psychology and resentment. History is absorbed, like the rain or the hail in the cracks of the rock of the Karst, in that larger and incorruptible time of the summer light, of those blinding white stones; the wounds and the scars of History never become infected, they dry and heal, like scratches on the sole of a bare foot that lands on the island, stepping onto those sharp stones.

The slopes of the mountain, aflame with flowering broom and covered with blue sage that ripples in the wind, drop steep into the Gulf of Quarnero. The cliff leans over the sea and its trees give shade to the waters, "silvis aequor inumbrat" sang Lucan, aware though he was of the rigours of the winter and the Bora, which assorted better with the civil war between Caesar and Pompey, which was also fought on these waters. Everything seems clear on the road that leads to Cherso, the capital which gives the island its name, between the two seas and beneath the cliffs on either side – on the one hand Istria and on the other the island of Veglia and, beyond that, the Croatian coast. Smell of sage, of myrtle and pine, salt on one's skin, the wind dry on one's face, the strident, ceaseless trill of the cicadas, changeless as the yellow noonday light, the honey and the bronze of summer – memory of a childhood more ancient than any already lived or any still to come reaches us from the sea, memory or portent of a grandiose, regal world in which one is at home, like the Knight of Saint Mark in his palace. "Looking at that shifting landscape of bitterness and enchantment, as though in a mirror, it was myself I discovered," wrote Marisa Madieri in *Water-green* on seeing the land of her birth for the first time in adulthood and finding in it not a lost, inexistent past, but rather the place of happiness in which to live in the world, that during childhood exists as a promise.

The promise remains for ever unfulfilled and yet is never disowned, because it is nurtured deep down and is everyone's deepest truth, everyone's truest face, the face of childhood not yet stripped of all that life tears away. That face re-emerges from the mirror of the sea: those bays, those waves, the profiles of those ridges are the features of an uncorrupted face that reappears as the rough, patched-up mask of the years dissolves: "I turned and I saw my smile on her lips," continued Marisa Madieri, reflecting and finding herself in that landscape, as described by Riobaldo in the *Grande Sertão* by Guimarães Rosa.

Whoever looks in the mirror of that sea beholds the child of a king and cannot say whether he was unaware of the fact or had simply forgotten it. The high summer inflicts wounds; that gaping horizon holds everything and everything, too, that has ever been lost and all that will continue to be lost. It is so easy – even if there before the sea you cannot understand how it might possibly happen – it is easy to forget you are the child of kings and to go wandering about the world knocking like beggars at strangers' doors. Even Captain Petrina must have forgotten that the Palace was his; he probably felt like an intruder and immediately slipped away, ending up on the bitter, inhospitable sea.

Nino, too, the first few times he had set foot again on the island after years of resentful absence, found it absurd to have to show a passport in order to obtain permission to visit his home. Then he became used to feeling like an exile and a foreigner, even there, and therefore everywhere. Sometimes, on returning to the island, one is left thinking that perhaps death, too, is the product of this habit of forgetfulness, that perhaps we die because we forget we are immortal. As the Bull of the Zodiac in Kipling's story (yoked to the plough and having just been stung by the Scorpion), says to Leo, who is even more afraid of death, "I had forgotten too, but I remember now. . . . I forgot that I was a God. . . . And you, brother?" But it is too late to remember and to shake off the yoke. Perhaps the yoke is appropriate, perhaps it is a just punishment for the crime of having known or even simply foretold love and happiness and for having forgotten them; for having held the whole kingdom and yet not realized it. Perhaps the exile that has made foreigners of Nino and his people is a harsh punishment for having initially behaved like foreigners towards those who lived alongside them, those who now live in their turn as conquerors, that is as foreigners, in their own home.

Cherso is one of the thousand islands in the eastern Adriatic, scrupulously counted by Pliny. As late as 1771 Fortis, the abbot, an enlightened traveller who believed in progress though not without some reservations, defined it as a single island together with Lussino, despite the narrow channel dividing them at Ossero, opened up in the remote past of the first protohistoric settlements. Cherso and Lussino divide the Quarnero vertically and form its heart; beyond the small islands that form a crown on their southern extremity – Ilovik, San Piero in Nembi, the two Oriule – a different sea, another world opens up. The Quarnero is the reflective familiarity of white houses on the shore, it is a conjunction of Venetian levity and *Mitteleuropa* gravity, the latter flowing out into the Adriatic at Fiume. Beyond the Quarnero wider spaces begin, rocky, marine solitudes or more luxurious vegetation, an East and a South that are more verdant, less temperate than the awkward northern asperity that still resides in the light and the rocks of Istria and the islands of the Quarnero.

Even the Ossero channel is a lesser threshold between differing landscapes. Cherso is barer, scored by the Bora and the karstic crevasses. Its flowers are sage and broom, its buildings are small and light-coloured fishermen's houses on the shore or, in town, narrow and decorous Venetian-style buildings. On Lussino there are agaves and palms, purple bougainvilleas and light-coloured yuccas, orange- and lemon-trees, almond trees that blossom as early as January, Austro-Hungarian villas and gardens such as those of the Archduke Charles Stephen of Hapsburg, a Riviera sweetness that once – we learn from Giacomo Scotti in his erratic guide to these islands – was Venus's preferred wintering place. At the end of the nineteenth century it was a favourite resort of aristocrats and *haute bourgeoisie* from Vienna and Budapest.

The goddess of love is unimaginable without the sea from which she was born, fertilized from the genitals of Uranus, who was castrated with a scythe by his son Cronus. It would be nice to think, succumbing to an overly relaxed etymology, that it is Time, Chronos, who mutilates the Sky, the Infinite, making a fragment of it fall into the sea, which together with love is an echo of the infinite and a challenge to time. The etymology is false, because Cronus, the divinity who dethrones his father Uranus, has nothing to do with Chronos, but every now and then it is pleasing to lift a shell to one's ear and to pretend that the murmur heard in that emptiness is the sea. And after all it is not so empty, all it takes is to lift your eyes up and the sea is there in front of you, inexhaustible and unexplainable. Marisa comes out of the water – the first time, the hundredth time; each summer is unique and unrepeatable, one after another they come like the beads of a rosary, time rounds them like pebbles on the beach, between one and the next an infinity opens up.

On Cherso the rich – the Petrises, the Patrizis – owned fields; on Lussino – where the celebrated Nautical Schools produced the long-haul captains who soon became masters of all the oceans, the Premudas, the Gladulichs, the Ragusins – the maritime families lorded it, the Cosulichs, the Martinolichs, owners of merchant ships and cutters known in the most distant ports of the world. Cherso has an ancient and illustrious history – a Roman colony and a city of Saint Mark. Lussino – which soon superseded its neighbour – emerged much later and displays, together with the Venetian and Croatian mark, that of the Austro-Hungarian twin-headed eagle, much less apparent on Cherso.

Over the centuries and under various dominations – from Venice to Austria, from Italy to Tito's Yugoslavia – the two islands have maintained their own particular plural identity and their links with Istria. Tudjman's regime seeks to break this identity and these ties, creating administrative bridges between the islands and various provinces on the mainland, which are historically and culturally unrelated to them. All this to weaken the Adriatic islands' democratic autonomy, mistrustful as they are of the authoritarian and oppressive centralism of the Croatian government. "The Italian Fascists never managed to wring our necks, and now this lot won't manage it either," says Ivo, a Croatian who in his time gave the Blackshirts a run for their money, as he fills his guest's glass in his inn on a bay opposite Susak – Sansego, the only sandy island in these seas, perhaps made of the silt brought here over millennia by the Po or by mythical underground rivers.

Ivo empties his glass, fills his customer's once again. This gesture, repeated every now and then, is the only chore he has; the others – cooking, washing dishes, doing the shopping in Lussino, mending the nets – are all entrusted to his wife. What does he think of Tudjman? "Ah, I'd slaughter 'im," he replies calmly, with the air of one who quietly considers the work to be done.

Cherso, Crepsa, Crexa, Chersinium, Kres, Cres – Latin, Illyrian, Slav, Italian names. The vain search for ethnic purity reaches down to the most ancient roots, brawling over etymologies and writing systems, in a fever to establish the racial origin of the foot that first stepped on the white beach and grazed itself on the thorns of the thick Mediterranean vegetation, as though this were proof of greater authenticity and guaranteed the right to possess these turquoise waters and these perfumes in the wind.

The journey down never reaches a point of arrival or departure, the Origin is never identified. Scratch an Italianized surname and out comes the Slav layer, a Bussani is a Bussanich, but if one continues then sometimes an even more ancient layer appears, a name from the other side of the Adriatic or elsewhere; the names bounce from one shore and from one writing system to another, the ground gives way, the waters of life are a yielding, promiscuous swamp. Losinj is the Croatian rendering of Lussino, or rather of the Venetian Lussin, which perhaps derives from *luscinius*, "nightingale", and perhaps from the Croatian *luzina*, "undergrowth", or *loše*, "nasty", a reference to the rough soil covered with impenetrable bushes, and according to others it comes from *loza*, "vine".

Colchidians, Greeks, Romans, Istrians and Liburnians and other Illyrians, Goths, Franks, Byzantines, Slavs, Venetians, Saracens, Croats; the jail at Nerezine named in honour of Lepanto, the Hungarian king Bela who gave his name to Beli when he landed there while fleeing from the Tartars, the people of Cherso who demonstrated in the streets when the flag of the Serenissima was hauled down. French, Austrians, Italians, Germans and Yugoslavs – men and peoples are grain ready to be milled by history, and it hurts at the time and there are bloodstains left on the floor, but then it all dries and the resulting bread is good. The wave that arrives every now and then is a storm that wrecks everything, the annals are numbered in forays, in raids; Ossero was devastated by Saracens, Normans, Uskoks and Genoese. The rumble of one thunderstorm is lost in the next and the sea washes the blood from the shores, but in the shadow someone is keeping the tally and will present the account at the proper time.

In charting these seas, everyone has his own personal toponymy, from the intransigent nationalist who enunciates every name in Italian or in Croatian, implicitly affirming a compact ethnic homogeneity in that world while denying the existence of the others who form part of it, to the inexperienced reporter from Italy who would never dream of saying "London" for "Londra" or "Beograd" for "Belgrado", but says Rijeka instead of Fiume out of ignorance or fear of being taken for a revanchist. That mosaic is already full of variety and everyone composes the pieces in a way that corresponds to his own experience of that world – saying Ossero instead of Osor or Miholaščica rather than San Michele according to whether, in essence, a place has meant for him a meeting with one civilization or another. "But me, why do I speak Italian?" asks a woman on Cherso, in Italian, unaware of where those words that issue from her lips come from, because for her they are part and parcel with everything else. She is confident that the lecturer from Trieste, who is lodged in her house by the Italian community's club, will have an answer for her.

The combination of names in the different writing systems and pronunciations is a labyrinth of destinies. A Sintich, at Miholaščica, defies the Croatian nationalist parish priest who will have no truck with Italian being sung in his church; he strikes up with the hymn "Mira il tuo popolo", and then asks a guest in the nearby pension the meaning of one or two of the words. Fascism imposed the Italianization of surnames and back then at Lubenizze, perched up high in the mountains of Cherso and buffeted by the wind, the mayor – recounts Livio Isaak Sirovich, as he rummages through old papers – informed the Prefect, in an Italian that was not quite Tuscan, that a certain Dlacich, unlike the various Kral who became Re [King] and Smerdel [*merda*, shit] who became Odoroso [Smelly], would not hear of changing his surname, "and he always *will* be Dlacich," he told me angrily, "and you, I don't care what you do."

So, Miholaščica, rather than San Michele. Anywhere can be the centre of the world. There is almost nothing at Miholaščica; perhaps it is for this reason that someone can feel it to be the heart of this world made up of great voids and openings, wind and light, violet horizons in which the evening rises slowly like a tide to submerge the profiles of a few islands. The world, in any case, is just a few steps away, in Martinščica, a beguiling place, with its harbour where the white yachts still moor, and the Albanians from Macedonia arrive every year with the fine weather, bringing all that's necessary to make their popular ice-creams, along with their women who are always kept locked up in the hotel room or at the most are taken out for a walk at dawn, when there's no one yet around.

In Miholaščica the houses and people serve to ennoble the horizon; rather than arrogantly taking up position in the centre or occupying all of it, they keep themselves to one side, ancillary figures in the grand scenario of clouds and seasons – a boat moored at a jetty, another one immobile out at sea, the changing colours of a sail in the glare. History is eroded and burnished by the water, the summers rise and fall on the beach, superimposed one on the other, mixing over the years like the smooth, white pebbles. Sitting on a stone, Tania plays with the surf that always brings her ball back to her; she's already almost a girl, a dark, surly roe deer. "Mismo stari," we're old, grumbles her uncle, the oldest of her father's six brothers and sisters, old enough to be her grandfather, as he drinks his early-morning slivovitz. He doesn't pay much attention to Mr Babić, just arrived from Carlovaz, he too with his slivovitz, as he comments with a satisfied air on one of Tito's speeches. Francesco and Paolo are on the shore; their childhood is familiarity with this world.

A few houses, which in the summer fill up with holiday-makers and relatives and friends, an inn, a small church kept open on a rota by the neighbours and by the innkeeper; inside there is a painting of Saint Michael, the town's patron, finishing off the fallen dragon. The archangel's sword enters the dragon's jaws, Heaven's final victory seems certain, but in the meantime the dragon spouts fire and it would be all too easy to get caught in its fangs; in the sea, too, there are fierce jaws that devour smaller fish, each one in the jaws of someone or something, but in his fall the dragon carried with him a piece of heaven – this bay and these incorruptible waters, as they close over silent catastrophes.

All told there are but two or three surnames in the town – Kučić or

Saganić. A neighbour tells of how her grandmother gave birth to eighteen children and brought them up, working nights at the loom after putting them to bed. A few decades later the total number of Miholaščica's inhabitants is much smaller than the number of their descendants. The years come and go like tides. Francesco and Paolo, who for many summers no longer came to Miholaščica with us, start coming back and they too start building a life with those stones on the shore. The wave flows back, and Tania's ball, thanks to the slivovitz, has outlived her uncle, but Barbara, Tania's daughter, is less interested in the ball than in a grasshopper she has saved from the sea and holds in her hand. One of the insect's wings is broken but she is still proud of it – It's mine and it knows me, she says to Gussar, who has no home and sleeps in the bays, in his untidy boat which he uses for fishing for squid and ferrying the odd tourist about. When a gust of wind carries the grasshopper off and it disappears in the water, the girl starts crying, protesting that it was hers and she wants that one and no other.

My grasshopper, my wave, that very one, with its jagged edge and its white foam, the one at that angle, with the impetus that makes it curve – there is a wave that ought never to break, a face that must never disappear from these waters in which it seems to have always been reflected, from time immemorial and dilated like the summer, embracing all of a shared life. Mrs Babić's daughters run to the sea, beautiful *djevojke* laughing and showing their white teeth, they dive into the water, white gulls and spray of foam, the waves break, the girl's crying is already mixed up with the backwash and then comes Tania's voice calling her daughter: it's lunchtime.

No, that doesn't figure, it's easy to get the summers mixed up, with the never-changing light; they must be her granddaughters, because when Nadia, Tania's sister, celebrated her sixteenth birthday and her father got a bit drunk and started hitting the wrong young man – not the one who was unceremoniously courting his daughter, but another one who had nothing to do with it – that summer the house to the back, behind the mulberry tree with its fruit that the children would eat, staining their faces and their arms with the blood-like juice, that house wasn't there yet; now his daughter uses it for parties with her friends and her boyfriend who has come back from the war in Krajina. Never mind whether it's mother, daughter or granddaughter, what counts is that a woman should be like this and this, says Jure, who has been Barbara's husband for years, as he sketches in the air large breasts and a narrow waist . . . otherwise, ppprrr, and he concludes with a sort of raspberry, rubbing the back of his hand against his mouth, while Tonko, his neighbour, who came over when he saw we were roasting a lamb on the spit, protests that the rear end shouldn't be neglected either.

Maria, Mrs Gliha's mother, who arrives in May with her husband and children from Zagreb and opens up the house where they spend the summers, up until a few months previously had never moved from St Ivan, the small village just down the road. But now she has just come back from New York, where she had been to visit one of her children. Does she like New York? Yes, she replies, graciously, after having had the question repeated because she is hard of hearing . . . yes, nice, but a bit out of date with those carriages and the horses, and then so few telephones. If you're out and you have to call someone you have to hunt all over, whereas here in St Ivan there's a telephone just there in the shop. But it's a nice city all the same, she repeats, benevolently, even if a bit old fashioned. And she is silent again, paying attention to no one, her eyes fixed somewhere in the evening, which is dark by this time.

At St Ivan there is the cemetery that also takes in the people of Miholaščica and Martinščica. Among the gravestones is one belonging to Velemir Dugina, "Prof. Violine", who died at the age of twenty-nine. The photograph shows a handsome, open face. Velemir loved these places, he came whenever he could. He composed beautiful songs, one of which is about the sea-green waters of Miholaščica. On coming back from a journey to a distant continent, where he had gone to visit his mother who hadn't been living with them for some time, he killed himself in a hotel in a big city, leaving a note asking that he be buried not in Trieste, where he lived, but at St Ivan. When they ask her if she knew him, old Maria replies, listlessly, yes.

The evening has fallen, as it has to; so many evenings meld one into the other, the same but different in the flames of the summers and in the faces that are a little more time-worn. The lamb is browning on the fire; Mr Babić, turning the spit and basting with oil, praises the policy of the Croatian government in the war in Bosnia, and Toni the innkeeper throws him a look without saying anything, the same look his dog Max has when studying the hens that he knows he cannot touch. "We *fjumanke* don't know much about politics," says Mrs Gliha, trying to change the subject. The wine is strong and dark, the lamb tender and crisp. "Poor mamma," says Mrs Gliha, "who knows why she always preferred her lamb without rosemary, but why, Mamma, I was always asking her and she would never tell me why . . . as stubborn as they come she was." Jure and Tonko sing *tamo daleko, daleko kraj mora*, "far away, near the sea", then they stop. From the garden across the road comes Teodoro, wearing a helmet and a topi on top of that, a stick in his hand and a scythe over his shoulder. Every now and then, for months at a time, he fails to recognize anyone and pisses against the church wall – but not out of contempt, Jure explains, it's just that he doesn't think. "The gravy's finished!" shouts Teodoro as he comes out of the darkness, as the flames reflect brightly on his scythe. And so the fact is that Miholaščica has everything, even the fool who speaks the truth.

Paolo from Canidole has had his day too, and its memory has been preserved among the people of the islands in the stories that hand down his little history, always with the same sentences and in the same words. Canidole – in Croatian Vele Srakane – is an increasingly deserted island covered with cane-brakes, just a few kilometres to the west of Lussino. Some decades ago there were still one hundred and fifty people, who in a few years were reduced to twelve, almost all of them elderly; in the summer, at least back when the terrible Yugoslav war was not threatening to spread to the Quarnero as well, some emigrants from the mainland or America would return to visit relatives, and a few tourist boats would moor for an hour or two.

The other islands around Canidole are either deserted or truly inhabited – they either live the immemorial life of the sea, of the surf and the tides, or they live the holiday season, of hotels and cafés open from May to September. On the other islands either no one lives or, for some months or for the whole year, they are inhabited by people who mesh, like everyone else, into the chain of the material, ordinary world. Canidole has remained out of all this, living its ancient, immutable life, which is burning out. There are no hotels, bars, tourists; the school built some decades ago is in ruin and on the classroom walls, written in Italian and in Croatian by erstwhile pupils, one may read scurrilous names or declarations of love. There are many cane-brakes on Canidole, some fig trees, a few sheep and the odd vine, just enough for the island's few inhabitants; in the winter, when the Bora blows strong across the Quarnero, they can be cut off from Lussino, the mother island and capital, for two or three weeks at a time, waiting for calm weather and for fresh bread.

The short distance that separates the people of Canidole from Lussino is greater than the hundreds or thousands of kilometres that lie between Lussino and Munich or New York, because this shorter distance involves a temporal remoteness that will soon be wiped out altogether by the total extinction of the island's inhabitants. Already the neighbouring island, Canidole Piccola (Male Srakane), is deserted.

Death will make Canidole an island like the others – wonderful for the indescribable colour of its sea, a tourists' stopping-off point for a few hours, an island with its place in the organization of the world and of the summer season.

Levrera is the island off Miholaščica, so called because of its invisible wild rabbits, and one July, back in the time of Yugoslavia, during the ferry trip there, a loquacious and sententious boatman told Paolo's story. In the early Fifties the Federal Republic of Yugoslavia, which had recently become mistress of these islands that had previously belonged to Italy, called Paolo up for military service. Paolo provided his widowed mother's only form of support and he already considered the four years spent on the front during the Second World War a form of abuse practised on him for the dubious glory of the Duce and the Empire, thanks to whose initiatives his island had changed flag. He refused to report to the Yugoslav military authorities and stayed at home, helping his elderly mother. The police, when they came to arrest him, drew a blank because he had gone into hiding; and so an army squad came and in vain searched the island's 1.2 square kilometres while Paolo, submerged in the sea up to his eyes – in December – watched the fruitless operation from the rocks.

The village observed the manhunt in silence, with the instinctive hostility of wild game towards hunters. The primary-school teacher, on being questioned, replied that if he was a teacher then he couldn't be a policeman as well and this risposte is still quoted, on the islands, with philological precision. On returning to base, the leader of the squad reported that Paolo was not to be found on Canidole, but Paolo sent word to say that he *was* on the island. Later, but the story gets a little confused at this point, the Yugoslav military authorities, with benevolent sagacity and thanks to the good offices of an understanding lieutenant, came to an honourable compromise with their antagonist, who agreed to a brief period of conscription.

Paolo had stymied the police and the army, an army that had given
the Germans a hard time. It was only natural, after hearing his story, to
go and call on him a few days later with the first available boat for
Canidole. The island was devoid of the usual sounds of life – children's
voices, noises of work. The crumbling houses and their walled-up
windows were like tombs. An old man sat immobile on a chair, a flower
in his hand; the eyes in his wrinkled face were two oblique fissures,
as though they had been screwed up against the sun for many years.
On the ground in the shade of a wall a maimed person of indefinable
sex sat watching the sea, the arrival and the departure of the odd boat,
and responded to a greeting with a whine, waving two deformed arms,
and with a grimace which, under the dribble, was a kindly and indeed
serene smile. Imperturbable and mythical like the rock of the island,
those men were lords compared to the banal visitors, who felt embarrassed in their swimming costumes, in their privilege, in their vacuity.

None of us was wearing a uniform and so it wasn't difficult to find
Paolo among the scattering of houses and people. He was old, much
older than his age; he had not shaved for some time and his body
trembled and kept shaking; he had only one eye behind his spectacles
and with a constant, uncertain gesture he cleaned the weeping from
the empty socket. He was kind, contented and indifferent. He told
his story in the same words as the boatman, including the famous
declaration by the schoolmaster as though he too had heard it from
that source and had learned it by heart.

Enveloped in the aura of that remoteness and before that incorruptible sea, one could believe that one was still a god, immortal. In the
meantime the hero of Canidole, racked by his trembling, recounted
how he had lost his glass eye among the canes and how the sight in his
real eye was fading. When asked if he was diabetic, Paolo replied in an
encouraging tone, pleased by the shrewd diagnosis: "Yes, that's it, well
done . . . diabetes, right, well done." And he reverted to speaking about

the fig tree whose roots had damaged the water cistern and which should be cut down.

The hero of Canidole was waiting stolidly for death, and before that blindness would probably come because there was nobody on the island who could give him the necessary insulin injections. An anonymous euthanasia, slow and steady, was taking care of the erstwhile hero, now superfluous. Looking at this old man who had challenged an army and now could not even shave himself, it was easy to understand how we must inevitably forget we were once gods.

But in his listless resignation to dissolution, there was something regal – the tranquillity. On the frightened face of his wife – she kept well out of the way and offered a jug of fresh water almost in fear and trembling – all that was to be seen was an age-old acceptance of the burden, the blows of life, a kindness all fractured, the wan resignation of a person who has not had her day, who has never had anything at all. A face to belie the harmony of the sea, the perfection of the sky.

She told of a son who died in infancy; she added only, with a touch of pride, that she had brothers and sisters in America, who every now and then sent some dollars. She had the air of someone who apologises for existing, but she perked up a little as she listened to one of the visitors, who spoke to her with an affectionate and respectful concern, for which, on Judgment Day, much will be forgiven. She was withering alongside her man, the vanquished and fragile hero, placid as a trunk of wood, still majestic as he peacefully faded away. But perhaps the truer crown sat, unseen, on the head of the woman who had no name and no story, because the weight she had carried was more taxing than that of being hunted by an army and the kindness that her face had known how to preserve betokened a majesty even more exalted than that of Paolo, the hero of Canidole.

*

Cherso and Lussino, with their archipelago, were also called Absyrtides or Apsyrtides, from the name of Medea's brother whom the sorceress, out of love for Jason, had lured into a fatal trap in these waters; the islands were born of the pieces of his body that were thrown into the sea. The Argonauts, fleeing from Colchis with the purloined Golden Fleece, had made their way up the Danube, the Sava and other rivers, carrying the vessel on their shoulders until they reached the Adriatic in the Gulf of Quarnero, where the fleet sent by Colchis to chase them was waiting. It was led by Apsyrtus, subsequently killed in treachery at Ossero . . . Apsirtos . . . Apsaros.

The sea is a place of treachery and death and it is on the sea once again that deceit, crime and the help of a woman save Jason, the great thief and great seducer, the uncertain hero who keeps a low profile and almost seems not to be there. We know that he is less valiant than his Argonauts – less skilful than Meleager with the javelin and Phalerus with the bow – but he is very good at setting up the heroic feat, myth and self-advertisement, and very good at seduction, at letting himself be trapped with candid bad faith between the arms of emotional, frenzied women who solve all his problems and sacrifice themselves for him and whom he subsequently abandons with the contrite air of the good boy who fails to understand how such things can happen, but simply surrenders to the contradictions in life and in the heart.

Myth, with its floodlights and its coloured filters, needs victims, and women, Jason immediately decides, exist for this purpose; he knows how to exploit them to the very bone; in all of her roles, those played on these shores too, Medea is crushed to the point of blood. Tradition has the *Argo*, the ship, sail across various seas, from the Mediterranean to the Cronian or White Sea to the great western waters of the ocean where the Golden Fleece is the evening glow, but the most convincing mythographers are those who have it sail in the Quarnero, among these islands on which the unbearable otherness of the sea is at thesame time the entirely familiar, the landscape of every return.

And here is where Robert Graves locates the isle of Circe: "The island is now named Lussino." The shadow of the laurel darkens the sea purple in front of the goddess's cave, dogs and pigs root about through the bushes, the trill of the cicadas makes the air tremble through the pine needles, as filaments of light shine, and the goddess weaves her immortal web. Graves loved to succumb to Circe's power, she who capriciously transformed man into a beast to be ridden or to be made to sit at heel, and perhaps his identification of the island of Eea with Lussino derives from Pseudo Skylax who, in his fourth-century BC *Periplus*, describes Lussino as an island on which women governed men as they pleased and mated with slaves, turning all of their mates into slaves. Bitter-sweet serfdom of Eros, an animal liberty that Circe's bed restores to lovers; go down to the sea and climb into the goddess's bed.

The legend that has the Danube flow into the Adriatic is an expression of the longing to dissolve the dregs of fear, obsessions, inhibitions, defensive deliriums – with which the continent crossed by the river is so laden – in the great persuasion of the sea, an extended self-abandonment, the pure present moment of life that is enough in itself and does not tire itself out in the rush towards goals to be reached, the anxiety of doing, or of having already done and already lived; rather it is happiness with no object, no torment, the eternity and the self-sufficiency of the moment. The sea runs in the veins, the original water of the species and of the individual, who in the first dawn of existence learns to breathe like a fish and to swim before he walks. Perhaps it is this essential familiarity with the sea that often makes the coastal peoples more open, kinder, more receptive towards the foreigner and to the Other, and on those peoples' faces it prints a

candour and clarity that is so often seen in the eyes of those who come
from these islands.

Around the lamb as it turns on the spit, Miro – back from Arbe where
he had taken some tourists on his boat – tells a story that for a long
time now has popped up each year, with slight variations: the alleged
return in tourist guise of one of the torturers from the concentration
camp set up during the Second World War on Arbe, not far from the
bay at Kampor. The camp was built by the Italians under General
Roatta with the supervision of German officers; many Slavs and Jews,
including children, died there.

   Every summer, on Arbe, someone maintains he recognizes in some
tourist – almost always German – one of the torturers from those
days. Others agree or disagree and after a while all the conjecture boils
away into nothing. Time is an expert in *maquillage*, straightening and
touching up features and expressions, and after so many years it is
difficult to recognize a face that looked down from above on someone
lying on the ground while his or her nails were being ripped off.
And murderers generally have an ordinary type of face, they look like
anyone else.

   This year's variation focuses on a German couple staying in a pension
kept by two of Miro's friends, a place he often recommends for a
night's stay to the people he takes around the islands. She was a young,
inexpressive girl, always barefoot and with a rosy complexion that was
prone to sunburn, he was over sixty with close-cropped hair cut very
high at the back and with thin blue eyes behind his almost always
half-closed lids. The two of them spent their time on the beach or in
the wood; it was a hot, fierce summer, the cicadas scratching the air
as though it were glass. They said that every now and then he went
for a walk to the Remembrance Cemetery, built where the camp had
been; certainly he liked to stretch his legs a lot.

Once, apparently, he went to buy cigarettes at the supermarket and old Mrs Smilka, who had seen her husband taken to the camp, from which he never returned alive, looked the German in the eyes, which he screwed up, as she gave him his change. "Two slits on an idol's head," had commented another of the guests at the pension, Professor Ebner, from Gorizia, who happened to be in the supermarket at that moment. Old Smilka had a strange feeling; she stopped to look at him, while he stared back impassive, just a little tensed, like a cat getting ready to pounce – she thought there was something familiar, and something strange, but at that moment everything around her was strange, even the pink and red oleanders, immobile under the sun at its zenith in the still air: large, unfamiliar blooms, enormous, fleshy and obscene, and she shook herself; she had no taste for the bizarre, nor for strange ideas and so she finished giving him his change and he left in silence, smoking.

When he was with the girl the man spoke very little, she would laugh and he would caress her naked feet and he sometimes slipped a hand under her bathing costume without worrying that there were other people around. Often he got up and signalled to her to come back with him to the room, to the point where Mrs Mila, who kept the pension, said jokingly to her husband that he could learn a lot from their mature yet sprightly guest. But Professor Ebner, they said, had observed that the man, as he petted the girl on the beach, never kissed her on the mouth.

Once again on Canidole, two years later, to visit Paolo. In the meantime the story of the first meeting had appeared on the features pages of the *Corriere della sera*. Paolo had been back at home for just a few days after a long stay in the hospital in Lussino; he was a bit older and much the worse for wear, talking about a barley plant that had sprung up by chance and had been pecked at by the birds and was a little suffocated by the stones, just as in the New Testament parable. At a certain point, proudly, he said that he "had appeared in the newspaper". Evidently some tourists had read the feature and from curiosity had sought him out, bringing the cutting for him. "A fine story . . . lovely," said Paolo, ever so pleased, and once again he recounted his famous adventure, but this time using the very words and rhythms as he had read them in the *Corriere*. The journalist had listened closely and had noted his linguistic idiosyncrasies – a predilection for complicated adverbs and dubious shifts of logic; a fine story, repeated Paolo, praising the article. Eventually the feature writer gave in to vanity and told him that he had actually written the piece. "Bravo, bravo," replied Paolo, indifferently, and continued the story. He was not struck by the news at all, no more than the author of the article would have been struck on discovering the name of the person at the newspaper who had laid out his copy. The story was his, Paolo's, because in the world, in reality, he was the one to have written it with his own existence, and it did not really matter who had transcribed it. Ulysses cries at Alcinous's table when he hears the bard singing of his feats, which no longer belong to him. Paolo was happy, because on Canidole even an old *Corriere* is something, and he certainly had no fear that that crumpled sheet of paper might purloin his story, his life.

Capital of the two islands until 1806 and inhabited since the Stone Age – as the Neolithic tools and the Bronze-Age pottery with its cinnabar-red rims confirm – Ossero has been virtually deserted for some time. There are about a hundred people there now, but in the past it was almost a metropolis with 25,000 inhabitants in Roman times and in the Bronze Age the canal was an important point in the amber and tin trades, thanks to which came traffic, riches, distant peoples who in myth became the Argonauts. The amber came down from the Baltic along the Vistula, the Oder and the Danube, reaching the Adriatic at the latitude of Aquileia and through Ossero it went on towards the Aegean and the Mediterranean, to cure fevers and earaches, to bring good luck and for adornment.

Condensed into a brief tract of the town, between large oleanders that brighten up the narrow streets in white and pink cascades, we find layers of several ancient, important cities. In the clarity of the piazza, where once stood the Roman forum, the cathedral now stands, built in light-coloured stone; it has three naves, a Virgin flanked by San Gaudenzio, the town's patron, by Titian, an Annunciation by Palma the Younger, a tabernacle attributed to Bernini and the Treasury rich in sacred tapestries, illuminated codexes, monstrances, crosses borne in procession for centuries. In the adjacent mediaeval Town Hall, where on 1 June 1797 the municipal Council of the Serenissima met for the last time, what is to be found, rather, are gravestones, inscriptions, jars, coins, statues.

What remains concealed in the easy charm of a town in which one tends simply to look at the sea and feel the wind fresh and dry on one's face is Antiquity in concentrated form. The remains of over twenty churches, the fifteenth-century bishop's palace, the early-Christian basilica with its seven naves, a wonder of the world in the sixth century, and from its ruins sprang the church of Santa Maria degli Angeli, ruins of old convents that passed from one order to another, the ruins of a castle and traces of a ducal palace, remains of a Roman theatre and the intersection of the Roman arterial roads, north–south and east–west, remains of a Romanesque basilica that cover those of a Palaeo-Christian church that in its turn stands on the vestiges of a pagan temple – ruins grow on ruins like the ivy on the walls, and the oleanders, opening up like fireworks, pay homage to time.

Layers of walls everywhere: megalithic, Illyrian, Roman, Venetian, with a lion of Saint Mark at the western gate and another at the eastern one. The walls say that history and life are above all else a defence and often they perish because they are absorbed and consumed by this obsession with defence. Above all else fortresses and walls rise only to fall – whether demolished or eroded; when it is necessary to build them as protection against some threat it is already too late, meaning that the menace is already too strong to be contained.

The walls not only failed to protect Ossero from malaria and the plague, but also from the Saracens, the Genoese and the Uskoks, Serbo-Croat refugees who devastated the city in 1544, in 1573, in 1575, in 1606. The story goes, at least along the Adriatic coast, that it was during these attacks that the Uskoks made clothes out of the hides of their skinned victims and coloured their bread with blood, just as when they cut off Cristoforo Veniero's head under the Morlacca, urged on by vicious words from their women.

The small town of Ossero is alive, Ossero the city is dead; perhaps every metropolis is a necropolis – trade, ships, temples, forums, palaces, merchants and soldiers are an emblem of mortality, like the hundred elephants that Kipling's white cobra remembers and vaunts underground amid the buried treasure in the jungle. Over every great city death rises up, on its clouds ride the Horsemen of the Apocalypse. Of Ossero's glories too, as of the great cities sung by Brecht, all that remains is the wind blowing through its narrow streets. But that wind comes off the sea, it is fresh and young like the oleanders. Pestilence, wars, massacres – death and history, once they have passed on, no longer hurt. Ossero remains, airy and light, a white filigree suspended between the two islands, in the great milky blue of the summer.

Marco told the story of his war during a night's fishing, after a leisurely day's sail, setting just a bit of canvas out of respect for the gentle puff of Mistral which served well enough to give the sense of a little breeze on one's face rather than for propelling the heavy boat. It had set out from Lussino, from the deep-green anchorage at Vallescura, and had wandered easily, following no precise course, towards Ossero and then towards Punta Croce, the extreme rocky point of Cherso, where the anchor had been dropped about midday in a bay of blinding light, of merciless colours: the emerald band along the shore, the turquoise meadows on the white sand and gravel bed with splashes of indigo and violet, and then out to sea the remoteness of the deep blue, the smile of the foam crests. In the water the sun's rays shivered and broke like lances. The Greeks said that when the gods in play cross swords and beat on their shields, one can behold the blaze of their game and their weapons.

Then the boat had turned back south, because Marco Radossich, a fisherman, knew precisely where he could and should pay out his big trawling nets. He wanted to pass in front of Oriule, with its red soil, the fig trees, the olive trees and the big brown and gold spiders that wrap them in their vast gossamer webs, imprisoning the island in an enchanted stillness. In the summer, up until a few years ago, old Mr Jovani used to sit outside the only house on Oriule – a corpulent and beaming Silenus who spent his time eating the odd fleshy fig, drinking from a jug of acrid Sansego wine and watching the young women who, every now and then, would arrive by boat and strip off for a few hours to sunbathe. Mr Jovani's time was marked by these arrivals and departures, the women who undressed, dived, climbed back on the boat and disappeared were the hands of his clock; he watched them arrive and leave while dabbing away the fig juice from his mouth, gluttonous and satisfied but above all imperturbable, as indifferent to the passing of the hours as the sea there before him. "Were the figs good?" he would ask, deadpan, whenever he saw someone creeping out from behind the house, where his big tree was. That year they had ripened a trifle earlier, and they dissolved sweetly in one's mouth.

Marco Radossich is no youngster himself, being almost seventy-five, but for him the sea is not a place of peaceful idleness, it carries the rhythm of work, attention to winds and currents, an eye which does not lose itself in the eternal, but watches the water for sandbanks and rocks, for the right place to anchor or to throw out the nets. His beard and hair are white, his eyes light-coloured and peaceful, the eyes of one who is self-reliant and independent on all fronts; effortlessly he would lift the heavy anchor that others struggled to move. Helped by a Bosnian deckhand, who had difficulty understanding the Venetian sailor's terms that are used identically in Croatian, Marco threw the nets carefully, sinking down to trawl the seabed and to be brought up much later, around midnight.

The hours passed by slowly, emptily, time was simply the rising and the setting of the stars, the trajectory of the heavenly bodies that changed the light of the afternoon and the evening. Seagulls hovered about the boat, every now and then swooping down on the water, breaking its surface like sudden gusts of wind. Cormorants swam, lifting up their black necks like the periscope of a submarine, and when the boat came near them they dived underwater, surfacing far off. There were terns, too, snowflakes with their heads stained dark; there were many more of them than the previous year and someone tried to remember in which summers they had seen more and in which less, because the years can be told apart thanks to a graduation, an illness, a death or the abundance or scarcity of a particular animal. Marco decided to land, for half an hour, on a low, circular island, literally at sea level, with a small barrier of stones, soil and canes that made it seem like an atoll. There were scattered bushes of myrtle, tufts of mugwort and wild garlic, strong and good to chew, and its reek tightened one's mouth and immediately made one want to chew another clove. The sea was as transparent as the air, its floor limpid, an invitation to swim underwater, mouth open, as though to drink it all.

Back on board, we waited for the moment when the nets were to be pulled in. The wood was still warm underfoot, the good feeling of contact with things, with what there is beneath us. Splitting open a water melon that spurted red on the deck, Marco chatted away in his Venetian dialect, and he himself could not say whether it was an Italianized Croatian or a Croatianized Italian. What he did know was that his father had been a Croatian patriot, but following the Second World War he was thought of as the enemy because he owned a small factory and so he decided to leave the island, which had become Yugoslav, and opted for Italy. But to do this he had to declare that his mother tongue was Italian, like that of his neighbours who were also leaving, and since then he had never been quite sure of what his place was in the world. Marco had stayed behind, even though deep down he had good memories of Italy, despite the war, the war he had fought as an Italian sailor in the Mediterranean. But he hadn't been afraid of the war, nor the mines, the torpedoes, the death. He had been afraid of just one thing, which gave pace to his story like a refrain – hunger.

Conscripted in wartime, Marco had tried to avoid the navy, which was offering itself up to the British radar like a sacrificial lamb. And so, reporting for duty at Genoa, he claimed to be a farmhand who had never set eyes on the sea, and added that, as a farmhand, he was used to eating eggs, milk, meat, cheese and fruit every day. Despite this he was assigned to the navy where he deliberately rowed incorrectly during a regatta, even snapping an oar, to try to convince his superiors of his seamanly ineptitude, but all he earned was a few days in solitary confinement on bread and water, much to his distaste, in spite of his protests that he was used to eating eggs, meat, milk fresh from the cow, and cheese. He was then assigned to a destroyer that patrolled between Sicily and Africa. In his story aerial attacks and naval battles faded into the background – a little spot of bother, that was all – while the really painful note regarded the food even though the captain, an understanding Sicilian, had given him double rations.

One day the destroyer was struck by a torpedo, which hit the ammu-nition store. Marco said he remembered nothing of the explosion; all

he knew was that he found himself in the sea – one of three survivors –
hanging on to a wooden plank. Nearby a shipmate was treading water
in desperation, his leg injured – "They amputated it, but not now, later
at the hospital, but I haven't reached that point yet, I'll tell that bit
later," he said, thus solving the demanding epic problems of narrated
time and storytelling time. Marco had grabbed hold of his shipmate,
letting him share the slender plank and keeping hold of him for a whole
day, without worrying too much about the sharks, until they were
picked up by an Italian ship. At the hospital in Palermo, disappointed at
not being injured and thus obliged to return to active service, Marco
had pretended to have strong pains in one leg, and moaned loudly;
but when he saw the large syringe with which the nurse intended to
administer a painkiller, the sight frightened him more than the bombs
and the shipwreck and he hurriedly declared himself fit.

   After Italy's about-turn and the end of the war, Marco had returned
to Lussino, Yugoslav by that time, where a letter he was carrying for
the family of an exiled fellow islander had led the police to arrest him as
a spy. And here Marco recounts those terrible months in that terrible
period – the threats, the beatings, and one particular occasion when
he thought they were about to shoot him and he crossed himself, for
which they slapped him and so he promptly blasphemed to gain a bit
of credit. But the most terrible thing was the hunger. "No eggs, milk,
meat, not even cheese." One day the police let him go, telling him,
however, that he had to keep his ear to the ground and report anyone who complained against the regime. "Stuff like that, Christ, I'd
never done anything like that," but the idea of being free. . . . And he
found a solution: every Saturday he sneaked off to the police and
scrupulously named all those who used swear words, those who
complained that it never stopped raining or that there weren't enough
fish, or those who were quarrelling with their mother-in-law, and
those in whose opinion life was brutish and nasty. After a few weeks

of these reports, the police gave up on their clueless informer and Marco returned to his life's work, fishing.

His story had been rambling, digressive, constantly breaking off before picking up the thread, all tangled up in non-sequiturs, forward leaps and flashbacks. In the meantime night had fallen, the big reddish moon had turned white some time previously, the wake of the boat was dark silver. Marco gave the order to haul in the nets. The sound of the winch engine blended with the lapping of the waves. Soon the first nets emerged, emptying onto the deck shovelsful of livid, pulsating fish on the wet wood, piles of hake, countless scampi cautiously moving their claws then suddenly banging their heads two or three times in a frenzy before lying motionless. The lantern wavered over the deck, over dying fish and crustaceans in strange vitreous colours, momentarily transforming the heaving pile into an enormous serpentine Gorgon's head.

Many of the fish were already dead, their swollen eyes protruding. A few crabs ran towards the bulwarks, but they almost always stopped, dead, before reaching them. As they collected the nets Marco and the boy continually used their feet to recompose the formless heap which tended to spread, pushing the creatures that slipped away back towards the centre. Sometimes, inadvertently, their booted feet would crush a fish or a crab and a little slime would run over the deck, clots of what had once been life, wretched, repulsive yet appetising, like flesh that suffers and dies, that rots and yet provokes longing and excites the tastebuds when it ends up between our teeth, the stuff of procreation, of eating and dying. The fish came up from the deep, the prosecution's witnesses to the perfidy of the universe, to the evil and the pain of killing and dying, but soon they became strangely familiar; in the hand their scales looked like the skin of the fingers that held them, stung by the salt spray and refreshed by the water. Holding them and touching them, one is ashamed to recall the instinctive revulsion with which one sometimes brushes off an insect that lands on one's arm.

After a few hours' work the boat turns towards Lussino, to lose no time in selling the fish. Pulling out some *pecorino*, sheep's-milk cheese from Pago, together with some wine, Marco resumes his story and brings it to an end. Some years after the war the Yugoslav army had called him up again for a brief exercise, a march from Lussinpiccolo to Čunski, a town some ten kilometres away. Marco had worse memories of that modest march, in August, than he had of the war. He had no faith in army rations, so he asked his wife to prepare some pancakes with cheese and told her to bring them to him nice and warm, in a thermos container, in time for lunch. And so his wife had set off an hour or two after him and had followed the route taken by the battalion, arriving at midday and delivering the pancakes. Just at that moment they were ordered to fall in for an hour's political instruction. Rather than waste his wife's efforts, eating the pancakes later and there-fore cold, Marco had continued his meal, and so arrived late and earned himself a small punishment. "They were really good, those pancakes," he said, the boat now within sight of the harbour, "good and warm, and then that cheese . . . cheese as it used to be, not like the cheese you get today."

"The sea, the sea . . . the eye of man, o disciples, this is the sea: visible things are the rage of this sea. Of him who has gone beyond the raging waves of visible things, of him, o disciples, is it said: he is a Brahman, who in his internal space has crossed the sea of the eye with its waves, with its swell, with its depths, its monsters."

Thus speaks Buddha to his followers. If the desire to live is the cause of evil and pain, the sea is devastating because it intensifies the joy in and the thirst for life, its seduction lies in its infinite repetition and regeneration. In the sea's light visible things acquire an absolute intensity, too intense for the senses that perceive them, an unbearable epiphany – Apollo flaying Marsyas. More than the abyss or the leviathan of the deep, it is the surface of the sea that shows us glimpses of annihilation, it is its transparency of the void, its reflection that blinds the senses with their need for shade, for halftones, for mediocrity. The purely visible is a flame that burns, says another of the Buddha's sermons, and the sea is the realm of the purely visible. On Levrera, opposite Miholaščica, there are moments when the summer, as it stops suddenly and remains suspended, is a burning bush.

The sea is a great trial of the spirit. In their "journey to paradise" on the shores of the Adriatic, the two lovers in Musil's *The Man without Qualities* in the end cannot bear its tension, a happiness that hurts. The sea wears, corrodes, consumes. "The sea is defeating us," says 'Ntoni during the storm in Verga's *The Malavoglia*. But the epic nature of the sea teaches the freedom to recognize oneself as having been vanquished, while still fighting; it frees us from the longing for affirmation and victory that is the mark of an obsession with impotence. And this splendour that is sometimes too intense is also an invitation to abandon oneself, to sleep; the great expanse of water quenches thirst, it helps us understand that if the surf wipes out the footprint in the sand, the fact is not too tragic. Love of the sea and love for death, as Thomas Mann had it? Whatever, in its swell one learns one's own insignificance and this helps placate the fury of the waves that Buddha spoke of.

The brochures recommend a stop at Goli Otok, "the island of peace, its shores lapped by extraordinarily pure water, an immaculate environment steeped in silence, an island of absolute freedom." Goli Otok, the Naked Island, near Arbe, was the final berth in a tragic odyssey undertaken by some of History's rejects. After the Second World War, while some three hundred thousand Italians abandoned Istria, Fiume and Dalmatia, now occupied by Yugoslavia, some two thousand Italian workers from Monfalcone and other towns along the Isonzo river and in lower Friuli decided to move, with their families, to Yugoslavia. Their purpose was to contribute to the construction of socialism in the country that had freed itself from the Fascism of the Nazis and was now the closest example of the advent of Communism, which was to mark the end of exploitation, of injustice, of oppression. Many of them had been militant anti-Fascists, had fought in Spain, and had been prisoners in the German camps. Cooperating in the construction of socialism was for them more important than belonging to a state or a nation, more important than the upset of leaving one's own land and facing real hardship; the socialist, or the human, cause was worth the sacrifice of so many personal situations and feelings.

What the *Monfalconesi*, as they were called, brought to Yugoslavia, a country devastated by the war, by the backwardness inherited from the monarchic regime, by the errors of the new economic policy, was their enthusiasm and their skills as workers and technicians in the shipyards and other industrial sectors. Most of them went to work in Fiume, others in the arsenal and shipyards of Pola and in various places in the heart of the country. Unlike almost all men, even their new mates and colleagues, they worked not to survive, rather they lived to work at the construction of a new order.

In the mines of Arsa or in the shipyards at Fiume, the Monfalconesi spared neither strength nor stamina. In 1948, at the time of Tito's rift with Stalin, they remained faithful to the USSR, to the country and the party leader that represented the orthodoxy of the faith that had given them the strength to face Fascism and Nazism fearlessly, and to undergo imprisonment and torture in the German camps, to forsake all things in choosing Communist Yugoslavia. In the words of Djilas, who would later become a symbol of libertarian dissidence, was it not true that without Stalin the sun would never even be able to shine as it does? Now, in their view, Yugoslavia was betraying the world revolution while they themselves were foreigners and traitors in the eyes of the Yugoslav regime.

The match, on the chessboard of world history, was a matter of life and death and Titoist Yugoslavia, which has the undeniable merit of being the first to dare to make a significant break with Stalinist barbarism, fought the threat with means that were in their turn barbaric. Fearful of conspiracies and internal coups, the regime persecuted the Stalinists using Stalinist methods, in the process arresting many others who were not involved in any way. They created their own camps in various places throughout the country and even used old prison and extermination camps set up during the monarchists' and the Ustashi's war against Tito's Communists. The worst and most notorious were created by Ranković, the ruthless Interior Minister, at Goli Otok and nearby Sveti Grgur, two desert islands, nothing but rock of a burnt and blinding white.

These camps were the final destination (together with Yugoslav Stalinists, Ustashis, war criminals and run-of-the-mill criminals), of those Monfalconesi who were not lucky enough to be expelled and who remained, as almost all of them did, faithful to their credo. Goli Otok and Sveti Grgur were hell – solitary confinement, starvation, beatings, heads down the toilet, exposure to the frost, relentless forced labour, "self-incrimination" sessions whereby one repented of one's heresy and had to demonstrate one's conversion by inflicting blows and torture on those companions who were more reluctant to reform.

Ligio Zanini recounts in his autobiographical novel, *Martin Muma*, how as they arrived on the island, the deported had to pass through a corridor formed by the other internees, who were required to beat the new arrivals while singing the praises of Tito and the party: "Tito – Partija! Tito – Partija!" Those who refused were sent into *boikot*, into total solitary, fair game for the most gratuitous violence. Zanini was born and raised in Rovigno and had been enthusiastic in greeting the annexation of his land by Yugoslavia, convinced that the advent of Communism meant justice for all, even for Istrian Italians like himself. His courage led him to Goli Otok and he had enough of it in reserve to preserve his morale in the midst of so much humiliation. Later he declined to return to Italy, because it did not seem right to him to start eating once more from the plate into which he had spat, and the remainder of his blameless, courageous life was spent on the sea as a fisherman, conversing in his Rovignese dialect poems with the seagull Fileipo.

The names of the deported are a chorus from the Day of Judgment; names that also appeared in the lists at Buchenwald, in the files of the Fascist Special Courts, in the annals of the Resistance and the war in Spain. The mark of infamy that stamped them as enemies of the people also marked their relatives, depriving them of every social and legal protection and leaving them a prey to poverty. Djilas, who visited Goli Otok and called it, "the most shameful stain on Yugoslav Communism," says that the party leaders were unaware of the worst cruelties inflicted by common criminals whose violence was unleashed by the mechanisms of persecution set in motion by the authorities; they were in the end beyond any possible control. Other Titoist leaders, like Kardelj, sought to justify Goli Otok, citing the exigencies of the moment, the need to stamp out any potential nucleus of Stalinist subversion. It is undeniable that subsequently the Yugoslav regime did generally pursue a policy of progressive, notable expansion of freedom.

Everyone was silent about this tragedy and this disgrace: Yugoslavia for obvious reasons, the Soviet Union and its satellites – while throwing every possible slander at Tito – so as not to draw attention to its own camps, the West so as not to weaken Tito in his revolt against Stalin, and Italy because, as usual, the country had other things on its mind, as Giacomo Noventa says in a poem of his. In the meantime the Monfalconesi resisted, in Stalin's name. Those who some years later returned to Monfalcone found themselves, as Communists, open to intimidation and sometimes aggression from Italian ultranationalists. The police regarded them with suspicion, while the Italian Communist Party sought to sweep them under the carpet because with their unfailing loyalty they were unwanted evidence of the party's one-time Stalinist and anti-Titoist policy, which was now a source of shame and embarrassment. During their absence some of the homes of the survivors of Goli Otok had been assigned to Istrian refugees who had lost everything with the Yugoslav occupation – a harsh symbol of a two-fold, double-crossed exile.

Thus these people found themselves always on the wrong side at the wrong time, out of place in History and in politics, fighting – with indelible dignity and courage – for a cause which, had it prevailed, would have seen the birth of many more slave-camps in the world, created to crush free men like themselves. To pluck this bloody footnote of world history from oblivion means saving the moral inheritance of that strength and the spirit of sacrifice that allowed the Monfalconesi and their companions in misfortune to resist annihilation, even if that resistance came from faith in a cause that was worse than the cause that persecuted them. This moral inheritance ought to be garnered up even by those who did not march behind the Monfalconesi's banner; it would be terrible if, when faith in "the god that failed" collapsed, those human qualities were to disappear with it – dedication to a public good, loyalty, courage – qualities which that very faith had helped to forge. No one sings "Tito – Partija!" any longer; but on the other hand someone, on leave from the war in Slavonia or Bosnia, recounts horrors so much worse than those of Goli Otok, while the brochures are still applied, like sticking plasters on sores, all over the surface of the world.

Lubenizze is high above the sea and often bears the brunt of a powerful Bora; it is almost deserted and among the inhabited houses, surrounded by rubble and unsafe walls, elderly women predominate. Rosarija lives in a neat little house in the midst of the ruins of other, dilapidated, homes. She lives alone; every now and then a sister comes from Cherso with a little something, to supplement her paltry pension. On the walls there are many photographs of her father, who died very old not many years ago, and who always lived with her when he was not at sea; together with the precise nomenclature and chronology of the village's clergy, he is the only object in her life and her memories.

Rosarija is proud that Lubenizze has bred so many priests, relatively speaking – three of them – and she is happy to look after the church, to change the water for the flowers, to light the candles. She is also proud of the cards that some tourists, who once came all the way up here, send her every Christmas. Her myopic eyes laugh cheekily in her wrinkled face, she moves quickly. She is petite, light; none of life's gravity pulls her down. When the time comes she will go to heaven on a puff of air, like a feather.

At Lubenizze there is wine, cheese, strings of garlic and sheepskins for sale; there is a Golden Fleece hanging from almost every door, even the women dressed in black wear one and in the small square they offer them for sale. An old woman – black headscarf, shawl, skirt, stockings, and a thick and woolly golden fleece under her arm – disappears under a tumbledown portico: a solitary, ancient Medea, unreachable in the mute pain and alienation to which she has been condemned for centuries by Jason's masculine arrogance.

Paolo from Canidole is, to the last, a witness in defence of Tito's Yugoslavia. One summer Paolo was much debilitated and completely disheartened; he still had his pride, but seemed to be actually frightened. After much hesitation, almost ashamed to reveal that he was in trouble, he explained how during the weeks when they were cut off over the winter his neighbour, a younger, sturdier man, had started taking pleasure in tormenting him and his wife, often threatening him and even giving him a severe beating. Rina, his wife, kept quiet; it was clear she was afraid, perhaps exaggeratedly so, but for her it was all a terrible ordeal. A solitary island, an Eden on earth, can become a concentration camp for those who find themselves exposed to brutality with no means of defence.

Paolo was asked what might be done to help, whether he preferred that his aggressor be confronted or that an admonitory letter be sent from some bigwig in Zagreb. He thought about it for a long time, his head in his hands, and finally the fascination and the authority of the written word won him over and he replied, "No, the letter's best."

Thus a letter was written, in which a precise list of the violence inflicted on Paolo, indicating dates and times, was blended together with a vaguely sinister threat, hinting at the idea of an authority which, though remote, was aware of all transgressions committed in every far-flung corner of the empire and was determined to punish them without recourse. This letter, addressed to the aggressive neighbour, advised him to desist from any further acts of violence, which he could not hope to maintain concealed, if he did not want to be severely punished. The letter was translated into Croatian and sent to a friend, a writer and teacher in Zagreb.

Although approaching its ever more liberal sunset, the Party still existed and Tito's portrait still looked out, from all public offices and every shop and café, over the unity and order of Yugoslavia. The friend in Zagreb, after having garnished the letter with stamps, official endorsements and symbols of the Party, transforming it into a message from Authority, signed it and sent it by registered mail to Paolo's grim persecutor, to whom it was delivered one winter afternoon, and had the dramatic effect of an unusual event for the island. Apparently that winter, Paolo's last, was a quiet one for the elderly couple, protected as they were by the power which the hero of Canidole had disobeyed so long before, even though that power itself was unaware of the fact.

Paolo died some years ago. Over past summers, since the beginning of the war between Croatia and Serbia, there has been no news of Rina, perhaps she has gone to live with her sister, in America.

Eufemia, Nino's wet nurse, was very old when she died in the hospice on Lussingrande. On 8 March of the previous year, International Women's Day, she had paid homage to the Director of the hospice with an address, in which she invoked Saint Anthony, venerated in the cathedral by the sea that bears his name. She expressed her hope that Saint Anthony might grant the Director sufficient grace to be able always to provide prompt assistance and to call in the doctors quickly, "God look after they all," and here she named the others who lived with her in the hospice, "and that theys don't fall ill." She had excluded herself, generously, from the list of those who might be in need.

And so, for her funeral, Nino set foot once again in his ancestral palace, thinking that after all things had not changed so much with that reverse of fortune centuries before, because this is where Eufemia had died, as would certainly have happened if that home had still been the family palace, and seeing those bright rooms, with the oleanders and the laurel through the windows, and those old men and women, somewhat befuddled but happy enough, he felt a little as though he were at home, for the first time since the brutal days of the exodus, and the thought crossed his mind that perhaps it might even be a good thing, everything belonging to everyone in common. But the thought evaporated immediately and in fact during the funeral Nino lost his temper when an acquaintance told him that another lion of Saint Mark had been torn down and the Italian school had been given a hard time.

Anyway, the palace was well kept, clean and bright and besides, dying did not seem to be such a sad thing. Goodbye, mate, safe journey, say the people on Cherso when a funeral passes through the lanes. Nino is not a church-going man, quite the contrary, but for whoever is born and brought up on the sea every departure is not only the sadness of the farewell, but carries the thought of the return as well. The Lussinians who named the most beautiful bay of their island Čikat, in Italian Cigale, knew this fact; the name comes from the Croatian verb *čekati*, which means to wait, to wait for relatives who have departed in a boat or on board a ship.

Cigale is a breast that opens up to the sea and at the same time it encloses the sea, arms that open and close, a circle of the horizon, music of disappearing and reappearing; verses full of sunsets and returns, sang Gottfried Benn, the evanescence of the individual and the permanence of being – eras and millennia that reappear again in words and in the pebbles smoothed by the sea. The shards on the beach are smooth, but the sharp point was rounded recently, perhaps some ten generations ago; the megalithic and Liburnian peoples have disappeared like the light the sea slowly drinks, the sand stirred up by the surf mingles ancient bones. A young foot steps on a shell, the shell breaks and the foot hurts itself on the sharp fragments; it is the blood of life, "Love is like a little walnut / if you don't break it, you can't eat it," goes a song from these islands. The shell is on the beach, open and wounded; the water washes it and wipes out the footprint, the centuries pass on like tides, the shards become rounded, they give way gently beneath another naked foot. A boat comes back into the bay, it is pulled up onto the shore; someone is returning home.

On Levrera: myrtle, rosemary, a tangle of bushes block the way, yellow sea poppies on the shore, and behind them the blue deep as the night, and sparkling with light. Behind the barrier of rocks on the beach, the water that has washed over it during the days of wind and breaking waves stagnates in a soft warm mud, teeming with dark germinal life into which the foot happily sinks and wallows. In May, in the nests among the rocks, the seagulls' eggs hatch. The young, little grey things, run towards the water or hide in the scrub. The gulls hover over the nests, screeching interminably, a deafening and shocking noise in the abounding light; when they dart threateningly alongside the visitor who gets too close to the nest, there is a mean, fixed look in their eye.

A gull lies on the ground; beating its wings in an attempt to raise itself, it collapses exhausted. The sick bird trembles, soft and fragile between the hands that pick it up. In the beauty of the world, writes Simone Weil, brute necessity becomes an object of love; in the folds that the force of gravity imprints on the waves, which nevertheless swallow up ships and shipwrecked sailors, there is the beauty of obedience to a law. The beauty on Levrera is perfect, but it seeks to be only happiness, freedom from every force of gravity, the wind dissolving the torrid heat and the closeness. Is this absolute beauty harmony with a law or a pardon wrested from every law? Placed on the water, the gull immediately reassumes the dignified position of a bird of its species floating on the waves, its neck held high and its head directed straight out towards the open sea, while the current takes it from the shore. A few minutes later it is already far away, indistinguishable from the other gulls rocking on the water.

Antholz

Go easy on those who balance. It is not a binding rule, but is rather a question of style, of gentlemanly conduct which a player of *cotecio* must always live up to. A real player that is, not one of those good only at dumping or jettisoning their dangerous cards willy-nilly. A player balances when, even though he is in a position to get away with a low card, he plays a high one, thus picking up everything on the table to his own detriment, sacrificing himself, but at the same time preventing another player from twisting. Such a player balances the general situation and pulls the others out of trouble, too, because everybody would lose a point if that twist succeeded. Thus it is a moral obligation to go easy on players who balance, and to avoid dumping on them the worst cards one has in one's hand.

In the *Stube*, the lounge of the Herberhof hotel in Antholz Mittertal, the local patrons, their faces as though carved from ruddy wood, generally concentrate on other games more appropriate to a land which Charles V, referring to the entire county of Tyrol, defined as being vital to the German nation. There is nothing strange in the fact that every year for many years now Hans, sitting with the others at that table near the big tiled stove, decorated with green motifs on an ochre background, has shyly proposed a game of *watten*. Even the twelve apostles painted on the pine-panelled walls of the *Stube* support Hans's suggestion, and just behind the table there is even a tabernacle housing a bottle of Riesling. A German game would be more the thing than a Venetian one in this hotel, which is mentioned in the chronicles from ancient times and which over the centuries has been extended while still preserving its original nucleus. The *cotecio* of Oderzo or Trieste, so Latin in its expertise in History's deceit and so aware of the fact that all cards pass from hand to hand, *cotecio* is a game unbecoming to the *deutsche Treue*, to German trustworthiness.

But Hans, who arrives from Vienna between Christmas and New Year, is in a minority in this company, and does not insist. Beneath the portrait of the mustachioed and now defunct Mr Mairgunter, erstwhile landlord of the hotel and father of the seven children who gradually, over those decades, have distanced themselves from the gravitational force of the Herberhof like planets pursuing ever wider orbits – it may well be that unbeknown to the players (themselves the playthings of History's cunning) the decades of *cotecio* played at that table constitute an involuntary if marginal chapter in the attempt to Italianize the Südtirol–Alto Adige and to contribute to the transformation of Antholz Mittertal into Anterselva di Mezzo. Or rather, the *cotecio* players who grow old agreeably at that table represent – at any rate during the days spent in the *Stube* with the cards in their hands, approximately between Christmas and Epiphany – again unbeknown to themselves, a rearguard action in Italy's hobbled imperialism. In the progressive Italian retreat from those valleys they too are withdrawing, but they hang on with the odd spot of twisting and perhaps even, when required, dumping.

Indeed, in playing *cotecio*, the winner – the one who amasses most cards and earns most points – is the loser. For this reason too, says Toni, the game imitates life, in that it often deceives most when it adds to one's pile, even attractive things like the ace of diamonds or the king of spades; they seem so light but sooner or later they begin to weigh a ton and drag one down. Unless a win comes every time, gathering up everything, as when one twists, breaking the bank of probability and all the calculations that have existed for ever in the web in the mind of God or in the space–time continuum, in order to ensure that people lose.

Someone like Toni, for example – even the laws of statistics and Sod's law find him a tough nut to crack – can easily manage a twist. Even before he pulls the card out you can see it in his eyes, narrowing and imperceptibly grinning and glinting, turning slantwise to the faces of the other players, to the apostle Andrew painted on the wall, the cards spread over the table, the glasses of Terlaner or Fol, in any case always a golden white wine, the same colour as the sand in an hourglass. While the card falls, those eyes look out of the window of the *Stube* for a moment, into the dark and empty evening, and returning to the table they slide over Lisa's face, as she stands at the door waiting for someone to order another bottle. That dry, chiselled face, which could belong to a thirty-year-old as it could belong to one of fifty, also carries the bottomless dark of the evening. Toni's eyes descend into that darkness, for a moment they illuminate it like a candle lit in an empty church; Lisa laughs for no reason, her mouth is young between the early wrinkles and she lights a cigarette, ignoring the drunk who mumbles something as he leans on the bar, opposite the portrait of Mr Mairgunter, father not only to her and her six brothers and sisters, but also to another two children from his first marriage.

But Isidor Thaler is used to being ignored and doesn't take it amiss; although his legs can barely hold him, he bows respectfully to Lisa. Every year the alcohol adds another red blotch, just like the circles in the trunk of a tree, but it does not alter the nobility of his face nor the lightness of his loose-limbed gait. He learned some time ago to be ignored, whether in a crowd or alone in his house, a little lower down in the valley in the direction of Anterselva di Sotto, almost opposite the Riepenlift ski-lift, a fine house on three floors with the balconies facing the sun and a fresco depicting the flight into Egypt, all that remains of a much larger patrimony that has passed into other hands. In the summer he works in the reservoirs and in the winter they lay him off, but it makes little difference as far as the solitude goes, and it's alright that way. To be ignored is a kindness of fate. Mrs Mairgunter, too, from the other side of the bar, her hair combed like a little silver crown and her serious spectacles, pays little heed to him; if he speaks to her she smiles dutifully and looks at Lisa.

When Jakob, the youngest of the children, comes in and whispers something in Lisa's ear, Mrs Mairgunter turns her eyes the other way, drums nervously on the bar with her pale, slender fingers, and nods goodbye to Isidor Thaler. He, too, takes his leave and goes out into the night, kindly and silent though unsteady on his feet, while at the *cotecio* table everyone has dropped a point and Marisa deals again. Her hand is sweet and firm, like her smile, outside it is cold and the dark comes not only at night, but she gives to each his own, as she does at home when she ladles the soup into the plates. Let not your heart be troubled, it is written.

Irene and Angela were so sleepy they'd started whingeing and Barbara has just sent them to bed, after promising to take them onto the lake tomorrow with the sledge, because they are too young to ski and she says "refo", "I redo", because at the beginning of each hand, if one finds oneself with bad cards, one can ask the others to redo, or to shuffle and deal the cards again. But one has to be careful because if instead of saying "refo" Barbara says "mi referìa", "I might just redo", then it could simply be a ploy to see whether the others have good or bad cards and it gives her the right, after considering their reactions, to change her mind and stick with the cards she has.

The *Stube* is the heart of the Herberhof, as this last is the heart of Antholz Mittertal just as the village in its turn is the heart of the entire Anterselva valley, severely cut off from the rest of the world. To the north it is bounded by the Riesenferner chain and the Stalle pass, always closed in the winter, to the east and the west it nestles between mountains that rise abruptly and to the south there is the clearly defined entrance, a sort of door through which one enters as if the valley were a fortress, through a pass between high golden walls, arranged in several rows to block any advance. A sign saying Holzhof SAS/KG informs that behind that wall is the storeyard of a timber mill. The planks are piled in fixed and regular order, the tawny phalanx shines in the freezing air; the smell of the wood is good and dry, sharp as snow, a light wind scatters a handful of golden dust from freshly sawn trunks.

The road, through the timber, is reached by turning left if coming from Brunico, right if coming from Dobbiaco – in any case one is already in Pusteria, and the Antholzer Tal, with its villages that rise up it towards the pass and the lake – Niederrasen, Oberrasen, Salomonsbrunnen, Antholz Niedertal, Mittertal, Obertal – is a lateral valley of Pusteria, a concentrate on a reduced scale. Pusteria's original name, Pustrissa, is Slav, but, especially during the years of most bitter conflict with the Italian state, it proved to be a relentless and sometimes ferocious custodian of Tyrolean Germanness, of the uncontaminated *Heimat* among the mountains. The ancient name might refer to an ethnic substratum, claiming an at least partial Slav character for the territory, but since it means empty and deserted, it might also bring to mind (with some rancour) the devastation that followed the wars with the Slavs, who arrived in that land with the Avars at their heels.

Closure and intermingling, frontiers marked out and crossed. The

Tyrol vaunts an ethnic virginity that is protected by the mountains, a closed endogamy, a family concern, a Germanic pearl locked away in a chest, but it is also a crossing and transit, a bridge between the Latin and the German world. The great Roman road that led to Aquileia came through here on its way to the Brenner and later the Alemannic road, travelled by mediaeval merchants. According to primary school teacher Hubert Müller, historiographer and exhaustive cosmographer of Antholz, as well as frequent patron of the Herberhof, before the great flood there was a road providing a direct link along the summits of the mountain.

Prehistory favours the peaks, while history prefers the valley floors, carved out by the glaciers over time immemorial. Now we are down there and the most we manage is to climb up as far as the Pietra Nera, the Black Stone, an erratic rock thus christened one day by the *cotecio* players because it stands out dark in the snowfield below the Antholzer Scharte. Since then, because its nomenclator became truly obsessed by it, not only has it become an obligatory destination for a walk between Christmas and New Year (and it has to be reached, even when at each step one sinks into snow up to one's knees), but it has also entered, albeit unofficially, the local toponymy thanks to the debriefings held by its conquerors on their return to the *Stube*. For some time now we have all been down here, on the valley floor; even whoever it was who brandished the stone axe found on the right bank of the Antholz stream, near the ruins of the Neurasen fort, or the Iron-Age bowls and knives found in 1961 in a necropolis at Niederrasen, even those peoples were used to looking at the world more or less from our height, from below.

The river erodes and consumes its bed, history carves the rock and descends ever further, like a blade cutting the furrowed sphere that rotates in space; one fine day the cuts will reach the centre of the earth and each slice of the water melon will fly off on its own. The detritus of

time, which fertilizes the valleys and the pastures where the shepherd
lives for months with his animals, are ancient bones reconciled together
in the humus that melds them, Carantanian Slavs, the Duke of Tassilo's
Bavarians, Franks, Longobards and before them remote peoples,
Ligurians, Illyrians, Celts, Rhaeti and others who are pure names,
Venosti, Saevantes, Laianci, names that perhaps indicate the same
people and their conflicts, their mingling, their destruction and their
extinction. At Rasen, writes Müller in his *Antholz Village Chronicle*,
which deals with each and every farm and reconstructs the genealogy
of their owners, the ethnic substratum is a Germanic–Romance–Slav
mix, while Antholz is an "unsullied German settlement".

There are borders running everywhere and one crosses them without realizing: the ancient one between Rhaetia and Noricum, the
frontier between Bavarians and Alemanni, between Germans and
Latins. All the Tyrol is a frontier, dividing and uniting; the Brenner
separates two states and yet lies at the centre of a land that is felt to
be a single entity. Names, too, change their meaning. Once Südtirol, a
term that appeared only in 1839, indicated Trentino, and the Tyrol was
a land that vaunted three nations: German, Italian and Ladin. But the
Brenner, geography tells us, is the watershed between the Adriatic and
the Black Sea, between the waters that with the Adige run into the
sea of every persuasion and those that through the Drava flow into
the Danube. Adriatic and Danube, the sea and continental *Mitteleuropa*, life's two opposing and complementary scenarios; the border
that separates them, and which in the course of a day trip one crosses
without realizing it, is a small black hole leading from one universe
to another.

The car that heads for Antholz every year in the days immediately
after Christmas comes from the direction of Dobbiaco, and so it enters
the valley turning to the right; the front wheel, as it turns, flattens
the neat parallel lines at the edge of the road traced by the skis of

someone who has come this far down – their trail is clearly visible on the snow – sliding the whole length of the valley.

The weeks spent at Antholz, which over the years add up to a period of respectable length, are made up only of December and January days, fused together into a single, collected uninterrupted time containing all the faces of the winter: the frosts, the avalanches, the snowfalls, the sharp icicles hanging from the roof and dripping when the Scirocco is in the air. The valley is winter, a place for wintering; sleep and hibernation in which life, freed from the inhibitions and the stress of our usual enforced wakefulness, comes to and relaxes. The Tyrol, said the Emperor Maximilian, whose throne was his saddle, is a rough coat but it keeps one warm. The body stretches under the soft snow jacket, one's face turns to the sun with eyes half closed and cheeks braced by the fresh snow, worries fly away like birds from a field, chased off by the laughter that in the *Stube* runs from one to another like wine; sex awakens in a vigorous flux, in the room under the pitched roof the heavy complicated layers of woollen underwear and pullovers come off more easily than jackets and ties.

Under the snow, weeks and years distil into a single present that preserves them all and from which they reappear like objects returned by the thaw. Time crystallizes in a perennial snowfield, the layers of snow fallen over different years touch each other and are superimposed, one on top of another. Behind the Herberhof, on the nursery slope, Marisa's hair is dark, on the terrace of the Wildgall hotel near the lake, under the mountain that gives it its name, the white streaks in her hair do not come from the snow, but the painter who has added that new colour comes from a good school and that little touch is the mark of a skilful hand.

It is curious to know a valley and a life covered with snow, at the most some tuft of withered grass revealed by a wet thaw on a warm day, together with cow dung and mud. The striations of the frozen lake, the trembling of the rigid water that streak it now green now blue, according to its depth and its exposure to the sun, these are the object of an experimental science learned over years of observation: the shadow of the Wildgall that lengthens rapidly over the lake in the early afternoon, darkening the bright sky-blue into a violet blue; the crested edge of the pistes that cut into the lake, frozen lacework in the evening. In the summer those waters are turquoise, at least so suggest the postcards to be found at the bar. Angela is writing one to her boyfriend who has stayed behind in town, while Francesco and Paolo, already at the door with Marianna, tell her to hurry up if she wants to come with them to the firemen's ball in the Kulturhaus, an institution which bears the name of Haward von Antholz, a mediaeval troubadour from these parts.

On entering the valley the first village is Niederrasen – Rasun di Sotto – and all the guide books point out that the dialect spoken here carries small but obvious differences, especially in pronunciation, compared with the dialect spoken twelve kilometres away in Antholz. At the village limits, which the car leaves behind and to the right on its way to Antholz, a small monument takes one back to a familiar space – time nexus. A chapel, decorated with images of San Rocco and San Sebastiano, commemorates the year of the plague, 1636. The world of the Danube, which begins just beyond the watershed, is dotted with plague markers, those columns of the Most Holy Trinity erected to the glory and the wretchedness of Creation during times of pestilence; radiating out from the one standing in the Graben in Vienna, they multiply repeatedly throughout *Mitteleuropa*, right up to its eastern and southern extremities, and give these regions a unifying seal.

The chapel rather than a column is a trifle irritating, like those small deviations from the mealtime ritual that upset Kant, but the link between the plague and Counter-Reformation compassion is anyway confirmation of an expectation, a habitual reassurance. Nevertheless, *Mitteleuropa* is Catholic and Jewish and when one of these two elements is missing it is lopsided; the Jewish part is absent in the mountains of the German Tyrol – that symbiosis of restless melancholy and irrepressible vitality which makes the Majesty of the empire and the world picaresque and in its solemn incense gives a hint of the acrid smell of the back alley.

The Germans without Jews are a body deficient in a substance necessary for the organism; the Jews are more self-sufficient, but in almost every Jew there is something Germanic. Ethnic purity leads to rickets and goitre. Nazism, like all barbarism, was also idiotic and self-destructive; in exterminating millions of Jews it mutilated German civilization and destroyed, perhaps for ever, the civilization of *Mitteleuropa*.

Gestorben – "dead", someone says, tracing a cross over Beppino's last stake, and having lost that one too, he is out of the game. Beppino stands, picks up his anorak and his leather cap to go for a walk. Jakob is back from the stable and smiles a cunning smile, a look of greed in his eye. The stable is his realm, like the pastures in the summer; in the division of labour within the family, he has been entrusted with the job of dealing with the animals, while the others attend to the humans. He milks, grooms, pitches hay with the big fork, empties sacks of steaming manure, which once upon a time in winter the village children would try to get hold of to warm their bare frozen feet in the muck. Jakob is the one who, when the time comes, takes the calf off to the slaughterhouse; he strokes it behind its ears, gives it some moist hay to eat, which is the tastiest type, and pulls it behind him by its halter, whistling contentedly.

Jakob disappears into the kitchen to eat the left-over soup which has been kept for him. Lisa smokes, watching the streetlamp out in the dark road. Before vanishing into the kitchen, Jakob moves closer to her and tells her something with a chuckle, but she makes no answer. "It's only gone ten, time never ends," says Lisa to Beppino as he passes in front of her on his way out. Everything's changing, have you seen Joseph's hotel, the one he started when he went into business on his own? A bit of change is a good thing, but not too much. I've been to France, Mum took me to the station at Olang, past Niederrasen, hours and hours we had to wait for the train, but at least there, in the station, nothing changed and I was happy to be there with Mum. I was in Paris for two months. Mum came to pick me up at Olang when I came back as well, the train stopped and lots of people got off . . . lots, too many. Lisa looks at Beppino and her eyes burn with a black fire. Why is there all that running about and shouting in the streets? Outside there is not a soul, the night is empty. From one of the rooms upstairs comes the sound of a newborn baby crying. Lisa climbs the stairs, while in the *Stube* the man who works with the snowmobile on the lake sniggers, a bit drunk and drowsy.

Beppino goes out, looks up, recognizes Orion. *Gestorben*, as Toni used to say it so well, happily tracing the cross on the others' stakes, because it never happened to him. Once Baron Mattia challenged him to a game of *cotecio*, their respective living room and dining room at stake: the next day Toni sent a truck to the baron's villa to load everything up.

> *In a brothel not far from here,*
> *I saw the Baron Mattia,*
> *With his dick in his handy*
> *He looked anything but randy*
> *And out of one eye rolled a tear*

Toni used to recite this, a doggerel rhyme thought up by an imaginative local rhymester who spent his time in the pubs watching and commenting on the players and their game.

The stars hang in the sky like snowflakes on a Christmas tree, many large twinkling stars, little candles and glass balls lit up among dark branches. One lifts one's head and at first there is a great blackness powdered with luminous dots, then more and more appear, a dust and a whiteness that flower in the dark, flowers of ice on the windows of the night, ever clearer, ever whiter. A car passes and you move to the edge of the road; you lean over the kerb and disappear in the shining darkness, you fall into the Milky Way, you are already in the midst of its black waters and its white foam.

Betelgeuse passes through the meridian at midnight exactly on 21 December and its diameter varies in strict relationship with the oscillations in its luminosity. Up there or down here, angles, distances and orbits are rigorously prescribed, one cannot get the game wrong, nor can one change it. Who knows whether the cancer that wrote Toni out of the game, *gestorben*, is part of the mandatory rules, as in *cotecio* there is *padre Gorna ciapa e torna*, "Father Gorna picks up and returns," picks up and replies with the same suit, so that it will be the other who has to pick up and then fetches up with more points. With Toni Father Gorna's law never failed. That really was a priest's joke, which is to say a bad joke, to leave them all in the lurch. Laughter, now, comes a little bit more difficult and laughter is everything; luckily there was a lot of laughter in that *Stube*, for many years, a capital investment that continues to produce interest, and one laughs again, especially when one thinks about him.

The barracks to the left of the road are closed, the rolls of barbed wire keep no one out now. The Südtirol bombs no longer explode: pylons, monuments and people are no longer blown sky-high for the liberation of the Tyrol. Antholz always has been quiet, not that this prevented the carabinieri, in 1964, from beating up a few card-carrying members of the Volkspartei in the course of some interrogations and searches. A little farther on, again on the lefthand side of the road, not even the night manages to hide the camouflaged bunkers on the mountainside, the so-called "I don't trust them" line built by Mussolini along the frontier with his disconcerting German ally.

Those papier mâché bunkers are the wings, part of the stage set for a comedy of misunderstandings, for the initially haughty and later servile relationship between Fascism and Nazism. In Alto Adige the misunderstanding reached its most grotesque level. Fascism had sought to strip the German population of its sense of nationality and yet it submitted itself to the Reich, which promulgated German domination of the world. The majority of the Südtirolese would have chosen Fascism, would have been glad of Fascist protection against the Bolsheviks, had not Fascism afflicted them, as Germans, with its Italian nationalism. Thus they were often driven to becoming Nazi supporters, in spite of their traditional Catholicism which made them mistrust Hitler's pagan proclivities. Even at the time of the Axis, recalls Claus Gatterer, in Südtirol the children played at Germans against Italians and, during the Ethiopian campaign, they supported the Negus, the emperor of Ethiopia.

Hitler, the Führer of the German people and therefore also the guarantor of their Germanness, sacrificed the Südtirol to the alliance with Mussolini; they reached agreement with the famous 1939 operation. Following this the Südtirolese, so tenaciously attached to the unity of their own land and stock, had to accept that precisely land and stock were to be sundered, they had to choose between joining the Italians to remain on their land, or to remain Germans, uprooting themselves from the land and transplanting themselves to Germany; indeed some plans even envisaged their being moved still farther away, to places yet to be incorporated into the Reich, the Crimea for example. The outcome of the Second World War compensated them for this ordeal, since even those few who had left have rightly returned to their homes, where now if anything it is the

Italian minority that finds itself in trouble. The abandoned bunkers are still there, an effective stage set for the absurd theatre of the world.

Another few metres along the road, leaving to one side those mournful and garish relics, we reach the pine tree, it too on the left on the way up the valley, the symbolic limit of Anterselva di Mezzo. Every evening, before going to sleep, one takes a stroll to embrace its trunk. During the first years it was easy, thin as it was. Now the arms that wrap around it cannot join up on the other side. It is good to feel the rough bark on one's cheek. From the end of the road come voices, a familiar high-pitched laugh, and one can just make out a slender and intrepid figure, someone else a bit behind in the darkness. Beppino buttons up his trousers before the others reach him, spits into the snow the piece of bark that he had in his mouth, sharp and bitter, and goes down to meet them.

The twelve kilometres between the fork on the road for Brunico and Antholz Mittertal are long, they cross years; the car that travels along them penetrates invisible walls of time. Niederrasen is a hybrid town; the vestiges of its history have been absorbed by the style of the tourism there, a style which as nearby as Oberrasen, Rasun di Sopra, almost disappears, sucked into the long and slow rhythms of the *genius loci*. The houses are clean and well looked after; the church, rebuilt in 1822 but dating back a thousand years, is decorated inside in a flesh-coloured Baroque marble and has intricately carved wooden pews. Near the entrance there is a female saint in a blue mantle severely applying the scourge to her own body; opposite her, a male saint prays with ecstatic fervour, but he spares himself the flagellation. Even in the exercise of their devotions men have an easier time of it. In the dark green of the Christmas fir-tree, next to the altar and adorned with small red apples, shine stars of light-coloured hay, cottage lights in the dark of the wood, to which we are drawn like lost children.

Opposite the church, the rectory with its weather vanes gathering the wind from the Taurus Mountains. From the seventeenth century it was the seat of the Gericht, the tribunal that had been housed up till then in the castle of Altrasen that had fallen into ruin. Its jurisdiction bordered on that of the Antholz tribunal, which the counts of Pustertal had entrusted in the eleventh century to the bishops of Bressanone; these administered justice by means of their judges from Brunico, until secularization in 1803. Like the ski tracks on the snow, ancient borders of territorial competence and various powers intersect over the land, splitting the geopolitical atom of the small, closed valley into an erratic fractal multiplicity, into the tortuous plurality of all feudal macro- or microcosms.

The foot that moves forward in the snow and the automobile that ascends the valley are the simulation of a Jacobin advance, the battalions of General Broussier on the heels of the Tyrolean patriots in 1809 following the Battle of Brunico. Those who come from the city or the plain unwittingly bring a Napoleonic code with them, along with their skiing gear. But the foot sinks, the car skids; in the *maso*, that family concern on the side of the mountain, the hereditary succession follows other laws, rooted in centuries of difference and mediaeval tradition rather than in the universal equality of Reason. We are not in the world, but in Tyrol, and as the old saying proudly goes, if the world betrays, the Land, the country, holds good.

Like the *maso* and the valley, the Tyrol vaunts its closure, the compact identity of an "us" to the exclusion of all others. "The Viennese, the Czechs and the other Jews," Claus Gatterer's godfather used to say contemptuously, including in the list other treacherous outsiders such as the Hapsburgs, the socialists, exponents of international finance, the Hungarians, the Slavs in general, priests (except for those from his valley), the Bolsheviks and the Italian police. Ethnic purity, like all purities, is the result of a subtraction and it is as rigorous as subtraction is radical – true purity would be nothing, absolute zero obtained from a total subtraction.

Tyrolean autonomous identity, which first asserted itself in 1254 and reappeared in 1919 with a plan for an independent state, has often been based on exclusion. The Tyrol's fatal dates are those when, time and time again, that autonomy came unstuck: 1363, when the Tyrol became Hapsburg following Margareta Maultasch and lost for ever its chance of becoming a Switzerland; 1806, the Bavarian occupation; 1809, the French invasion; 1918, the separation of the Südtirol annexed by Italy; 1939, the choice between Germany and Italy that left the Südtirolese warped and divided.

Never realized at the political level, autonomy survives in local prerogatives and idiosyncrasies, in the fabric of existence that lies beneath History, and which at that depth moves more slowly than the dynamic surface, like a geological stratum that remains in place even when the earth above is moved and shovelled away. The key to the Tyrol is the ancient right – sanctioned in 1511 by the Emperor Maximilian's *Landlibell* – to use its own territorial militia, the *Landwehr* and the *Landsturm*, only within its territory, for the Tyrol and not for any larger nation. The region, not the State – ethnicity, not nationality.

Up until a few years ago, the standards and the pennants waved by the *Schützen* seemed to be pathetic old junk, stuffed birds or stags' antlers nailed to the wall. Now the rosy napes and thighs that stand out between the feathered hats and the leather shorts are a guaranteed hallmark of ethnic purity which, in this Europe of local specialities and chauvinisms, are appreciated once more. History gives the rudder a shove, great empires are undone, the boroughs are called into the limelight; the closed *maso* survives the Napoleonic prefects and the Communist *Internationale*, it claims to represent the here and now and the immediate future. In all Europe the fever of local nationalisms is raging, the cult of diversities that are no longer loved as so many concrete expressions of human universality, but rather are idolized now as absolute values, each one rabidly at odds with the rest.

"Refo," is what an exponent of the Enlightenment would like to say, knowing that the cards will be shuffled again and the universals of politics, now eclipsed in the postmodern Middle Ages, will sooner or later return to govern a greater game. And thinking of the episode in 1910 when startled horses were about to involve Francis Ferdinand in a fatal accident as they pulled his carriage along the valley, one speculates on what might have come to pass if the accident had happened, thus avoiding Sarajevo and heaven knows what else. But the *cotecio*-playing exponent of the Enlightenment, perfectly aware of how varied and unpredictable the plot of life is, finds himself in considerable difficulty because of the twist events have taken. What's more, he knows that even the perfunctory faith in progress, in history and the universals, has much to answer for. Anything but enthusiastic about the cards he has in his hand, he is not so sure he will receive anything better from a future deal, so he lets the others decide – cock-sure and impassioned as they are – whether to redo or not, as indeed is his right under the rules of *cotecio*: "Indifferent," he says.

They'll end up getting cross, Helga, the big sister, says to Lisa, pointing at Konrad as he nips about on all fours between and under the tables, tugging at the guests' trousers. Lisa looks at her son, she doesn't smile but something on her thin lips dissolves, as if she had been kissed. Konrad has curly hair, he has a sweet, intelligent look and when he vanishes under the chairs to escape from those who try to catch him, his laugh is seductive and irresistible. One Christmas there was the sound of a baby crying coming from somewhere; Mrs Mairgunter shook her head, Marisa told her to bring him out so everyone could see him. What do father and mother matter? When a boy is born he is the one who counts; shepherds and kings came to welcome him

and never asked a thing, even the ox and the ass set to work warming
the newborn in the hay with their breath and they paid no attention to
Joseph, nor to Mary.

Konrad stops, looks at the cat lying near the window. The cat is grey,
but its paws have white marks. The snow outside is white too. In the
glass there's another cat, with whiskers too, and two of his uncles have
whiskers as well. *Muine, ps, ps.* Francesco wants to teach him how to
say, "kitty kitty", but Konrad laughs. He knows Italian, but cats are
addressed in the dialect of the valley. Sheep, too, *Pampa, lock, lock.* There
are many ways of saying sheep, *Görre* if it's a female that has already
lambed, *Tulle* if it's a ram, *Gstraun* if it's been castrated and *Killpole* if
it's a young female. Konrad laughs, does some acrobatics and blows a
kiss towards the window. Lisa almost smiles.

Uncle Jakob gives him a sweet, strokes his head, Lisa stands and goes
to pick the boy up in her arms. Jakob drinks, laughs at a joke cracked
by a man sitting in the *Stube* and gets ready to go to sleep, holding a
blanket under his arm. He has a room, but he likes to sleep wherever,
even on the bench in the laundry next to the cellar, it's always nice and
warm. It's good in winter, he says, his voice a bit thick, even before
and after the holidays when no one comes, only the drunks from the
village. There isn't much to do and the evenings are long. Even if
we often quarrel, especially when we've had a bit to drink, we brothers
and sisters are all very close. You mustn't think Lisa's rude. Lisa's a
good sort. And tears come to his eyes as he chuckles.

Just once a year the car enters the valley taking a left turn, coming from
Brunico, or rather from Schönhuber's, where we go in the afternoon,
Christmas after Christmas, to expand, piece by piece, the Meissen porcelain dinner service. Meissen porcelain, the Zwiebelmuster, is white
and cobalt blue. Azure is the colour of the stained glass in churches, high
in the nave and far back in the apse; remote heaven of seas and skies

above the people kneeling, pushing, praying and growing old in the pews during Mass. Heaven is azure because it is far away. The blue of those plates, tureens, coffee cups and salad bowls is a bit more accessible.

Each return from Anterselva brings a piece or two more – a cake slice, a vegetable dish. Anniversaries, birthdays of the son of God or of Granny Pia; laying the table is a dress rehearsal for the Promised Land, Marisa dips the ladle into the tureen, and the cobalt flowers sink into the leek *velouté* while the wine drains from one's glass. A year later her hand makes the same gesture, simple and unfathomable; there is a new square serving dish and a cheese platter, in partial compensation for someone who has left the table once and for all and as a welcome for the latest arrival who sleeps in the arms of the nearest aunt to hand.

The Meissen service, calendar and reckoning of the years. We started off with the basic plates, dinner and soup, way back when Paolo first went to nursery school; then, twelve place settings having been reached, came the serving dishes, or at least the essential ones, circular and oval in two sizes; then the triangular vegetable plates – confirmations, a good mark in Latin, the coffee set for twelve with milk jug and sugar pot; the first girls start coming to the house, the sauce boat: before managing to complete the service for sixteen, the Soviet Union has time enough to disappear. Between the purchase of the oval serving dish and a triple candlestick one loses the tempo of the music a couple of times and those inadvertently muffed beats continue to produce, now and then, a few false notes that spoil the party.

Momentous meals, the wine ordered at Collalbrigo or Isola d'Asti, with due respect to the Mairgunters who always put the wines of the Kalterer See on their table. The film with which food and bottles cloud reality is a benevolent one, it does not remove things from sight, nor the upset they generate, but through it they arrive a little muffled, like noises in the snow, subdued just as much as is necessary to let everyone continue telling stories, sometimes even coarse ones.

That buzz of words and laughter does not slow down the rush of time,
rather it transcribes its brusque dissonance into a score that is a touch
more fluid and listenable:

> *Everybody says I'm blonde*
> *But I'm not blonde at all*
> *I wear my hair black*
> *Black in making love to you*

The lunch is over, the table is cleared and the Meissen plates are
replaced in the Biedermeier dresser – table, bridal-chamber and tomb.

The car returns to Antholz with the fruit-salad bowls bought earlier
from Schönhuber. As the evening falls the snow at the sides of the
road begins to acquire the colour of the swords and the blue pome-
granates on the porcelain. At one bend, near a fallen tree, the tracks
left that morning by Donatella's skis can be seen clearly, fixed by
the cold. She turned sharply just there, to avoid hitting that trunk, and
dug deeper grooves in the snow. At Oberrasen, Francesco and Irene,
their skis over their shoulders, are waiting for the bus to return to
Antholz for supper. Perhaps Beppino is right to grumble about Irene,
saying that she shouldn't ski; she's already in her fourth month and
has decided to call her unborn daughter Stella Giulia. But Barbara, who
does not know the meaning of fear, replies that the slope is so gentle
that to fall over would take all of Beppino's rare skill coupled with
those twenty-year-old planks he insists on wearing on his feet.

The Heufler stands out on the right, at the same level as Oberrasen,
an improbable castle with its sloping four-sided roof, towers at each
corner and iron grilles at the windows. Built in 1580, it is a hotel
now and the bar is in the big dark room where the *speck* used to
be smoked; the ceiling and the walls have been blackened by the
centuries, condensed in an ancient smell of ham. On the first floor,
in the *Hearrnstube*, the hexagonal Renaissance ceiling dominates inlaid

tabernacles, columns that end in beehive shapes, a splendid stove in green ceramic tiles, and doors with a design that reproduces the entire room, a heraldic algorithm. The furniture is perfectly preserved, but there are signs of woodworm at work. "Allah alone conquers" is written on the walls of the Alhambra, and He, the Inscrutable, can take the form of the worm gnawing away at that precious wood, making it disappear in his black and winding tunnel, the empty riverbed of time.

The Heufler is a glossy illustration of the Tyrol, evoking family crests, tournaments and manor houses, that mixture of dreamy fantasy and clumsy heaviness that goes to make up German civilization which in the Tyrol advances towards the Latin world. Heufler is the Tyrol to the nth degree and therefore artificial, it is too real and therefore seems false; it already seemed familiar thanks to some animated cartoon and so for years one walked past it without stopping, believing it to be a kitsch reconstruction. Only on learning that the fake castle is real does one go to take a look at it, in homage to learning and history. Perhaps even the woodworm would lose his poignancy if he were inexorably consuming a mere imitation.

At Bagni di Salomone, Bad Salomonsbrunn, the pine trees are thick and healthy, rich in cones, and they surround the chapel that invokes the Ave Maria, as also the thermal springs celebrated over the centuries for their therapeutic virtues, especially against female sterility. The springs run mild through the snow and the lukewarm moss, like Carducci's celebrated Clitumno, although in a poorer, German version.

On these fields Inge, the ski instructor, taught Maïthé to ski, when Toni brought her into the valley for the first time. A few years later she taught Marianna, since that visit was prolonged into an indissoluble marriage till death them do part, and for the past year now she has been teaching Stella Giulia. A little higher up, which is already Antholz Niedertal, is the Obermair farm, with its wooden balcony turned towards the sun, concealing a story worthy of Céline. In May 1945 five French Pétainistes who had been condemned to death were hiding there: a journalist and writer, one of the marshal's bodyguards, an important functionary from the Vichy government's propaganda ministry, a woman and a young man of eighteen, who was discovered and shot. They lived hidden away, one in Obermair and others on nearby farms, Unterhauter and Pallhuber and traded jewels for foodstuff. Hunted as they were like wild beasts, they had not made a bad choice for a hideaway in this valley, where people hoped for the Reich's victory and where there had been no shortage of volunteers for the Wehrmacht and even the SS. If Pétain and his government had sought refuge in the unreal castle at Sigmaringen, these refugees had ended up in a Sigmaringen in miniature, with bales of hay and piles of wood in place of antique gold.

One of them, for fun, even wrote a book on the Antholz valley and its customs and traditions. Writing has this function, too, it takes one's mind off death. Pastures, hillocks and slopes are dotted with small-holdings; even the life of all this timber scattered down the mountainsides has its all-encompassing historiographers, warring with time as they record every detail, without neglecting the least old cabin as it slowly rots away. In the footsteps of the first comprehensive chronicler of the valley, the Redemptorist priest Lorenz Leitgeb who described it in meticulous detail in his seminal *Mei Hoamat* of 1909, Hubert Müller, in recent years, has reconstructed the story of every farm, of the marriages, deaths and successions that have kept them in the family or passed them on into other hands, of the inns and the genealogy of the innkeepers, of old Bruggerwirt by the stream, of Sonnenwirt who sold Mesnerwirt part of the Maishof, and the venerable age that the innkeepers' widows generally reach (ninety-eight for Rauter-Mütterlein and ninety-seven for Zieles-Barbele), of past unpunished crimes and purported judicial errors, such as the death penalty by strangulation, passed in 1880 on Josef Steiner, owner of the Innersiesslhof; he had been accused (unjustly in the people's view) of murder and died in jail in Bohemia after having his sentence commuted.

Müller's *Antholz Village Chronicle* is a universal history condensed in a small valley; perhaps the most effective strategy for avoiding the pain of living is to dedicate oneself to exhuming other people's lives, thus forgetting one's own, and Hubert Müller, moving between the *Stube* of the Herberhof and the parish library close by, found his way in the cadenced rhythm of the time that was assigned to him. Under the scholar's patient gaze, cramped space dilates, the atom splits into a mobile plurality, into a kaleidoscope of names and events: the three Germans on the run in 1945 who throw a crate full of money into the lake; the winter in which a horse sinks into the same lake because the ice gives way under its weight; the first parish priest in 1220 and the first teacher, Johann Messner, in 1832 who, as well as teaching, was also a clockmaker, umbrella repairer, broom-tier, toothpuller, turner, carpenter, and the postmaster.

Hubert Müller spends his life putting down on paper real events and names, those names that all narrators find it difficult to relinquish, even when discretion and diplomacy require that reality be touched up. Storytelling is a guerrilla war against and a connivance with oblivion; if death did not exist perhaps no one would tell stories. The more humble – physically closer to the earth, *humus* – the subject of a story is, the more one is aware of the relationship with death. The ups and downs of men, famous and unknown, flow once more into those of the seasons with their rains and snowfalls, into those of the animals and the plants, into the ups and downs of objects as they endure, as they are consumed.

The annals of Antholz are a grand history, because they recount the species rather than individuals or peoples, and the species includes the entire landscape in which the species moves. The annals mention not only the Russian prisoner found dead at Niedertal and those who returned from the Second World War, but also the changes in the signs that announce the arrival of bad weather; the last bear in the valley, killed in 1790, the last wolf hunted down in 1812, the last lynx perhaps in 1824, the twenty-five-kilogram trout in the lake, the lightning bolt of 2 August, 1712 that hit the belltower and killed a girl, the hailstorm in 1828 and the flood in 1879; the great number of eggs gathered through-out the village by the Reverend Galler on 13 May, 1908, so as to break and beat them and spread them over the burns suffered by a charcoal burner, Konrad De Colli. The arrival of the Italian troops in 1919 is recorded alongside the great snowfall of the same year.

History slowly seeps into Geography, into deciphering the tracks and the furrows dug in the soil. The landscape slowly crumbles, the play-house flats slide about almost as though hit by a small earthquake; close-ups recede and monuments shake, other things pop up and move forward – tools, jackets left hanging in the abandoned farm buildings, crowns painted in the family crests.

Geographical time is as rectilinear as historical time, because the mountains and the seas are born and die, but its timescale is so big that it curves, like a line traced on the surface of the earth, and establishes a different relationship with space; places are bobbins, where time is wound up upon itself. To write is to unravel these bobbins, to undo, like Penelope, the fabric of history. So it is perhaps not a complete waste of time to try to write something down while sitting in the *Stube* at the Herberhof, even if Lisa might be right to pull a face as she says, "What . . . writing again? Always writing, writing . . . that's no use. A little bit, yes, but too much, no. You'd be better off writing a bit less and thinking a bit more."

Antholz has produced more than the peasants who on 15 April, 1916 mistook the first aeroplane to pass over the valley for a big kite or a buzzard; it has also produced two personages from the big world of politics – a revolutionary and a rebel. Peter Passler, one of the leaders of the 1525 peasant revolt, was born and raised in the Altenfischer house in Anterselva di Mezzo. His father had already been expelled from the village for his ideas on religious and social reform. Peter assumed the leadership of groups of peasants linked to the movement led by Michel Gaismair, the great Tyrolean revolutionary whose back was stooped as a result of nights spent reading and studying, and whom he met at Antholz in 1526. Passler and his men took on princes, bishops and prelates, preaching and fighting for religious freedom, the destruction of ecclesiastical power, the destruction of the walls of all cities, which were to become villages, the collectivization of craftsmen's work, Anabaptism and price control.

Jailed, then freed by his followers, he fought fiercely in these valleys, as ready to wield the scythe in battle as in the harvest. He went on to take refuge in Venetian territory, but was betrayed and killed by one of his followers who cut off his head and sent it to the government at Innsbruck, obtaining in exchange an amnesty and a reward. Gaismair, too, fetched up assassinated with forty-two stab wounds, after extracting considerable concessions from Archduke Ferdinand, who went back on his word as soon as the revolutionary movement began to lose strength.

While their peasants continued to believe in the legitimacy of the sovereign even during the struggle, attributing the injustices to the perfidy of some individual counsellors, Gaismair and Passler sought to create a new social order. They cannot be reduced to any cramped local framework, being two tragic figures of German and European history and of the contradiction that marks modern life. The modern, in radically changing the world, carries within itself the need for an even more radical change, of Messianic redemption, and at the same time it suffocates at birth the Utopia of social redemption through the very force of its development. The failed peasant revolt, which took place at the beginning of the violent and vital modern transformation, is the mark of this ambivalent destiny of modernity, particularly fatal for Germany; the "German misery", the political immaturity that was to produce so many catastrophes, was born of this schism between religious and social freedom. Faust, the symbol of the new man, is an apolitical hero; the remoteness of this individual Titan from the German peasant revolt of the 1500s is a symbol of this laceration.

For centuries the defeat of the peasants and the restoration effected by Ferdinand II made the Tyrol the land of bigoted and conservative loyalism, celebrated bulwark of tradition against modernity (and of the customs and privileges sanctioned by that tradition), against the principles of 1789, the Napoleonic code, liberalism and socialism. In keeping with this approach, the Tyrol, which was devoted to the Hapsburgs (whose fiefdom it was from 1665), opposed the enlightened reforms of Maria Theresa and Joseph II, defending the privileges of the estates and the entire social order against the modernization proposed by the Hapsburg sovereigns, and resisted their great effort to overcome reactionary feudalism while avoiding revolution.

Not far from the Altenfischer house is the Wegerhof, whose landlord for a certain time was Josef Leitgeb, the rebel, the martyr – like Andreas Hofer – in the struggle against the French and the Bavarians who invaded the Tyrol in 1809. Leitgeb was shot on 8 January, 1810, at the entrance to the valley, where he is commemorated now in a small niche with an effigy of Jesus. Like Andreas Hofer, Peter Mayr and other patriots – and unlike Gaismair or Passler – Leitgeb was not a revolutionary who subverted the law so as to lay down a new one, but a rebel whose opposition to the new usurping power merely sought to restore the old order. He is a martyr of tradition attacked by the universalism of reason, of ethnicity menaced by the Nation-State.

Like almost all true rebels, the Tyrolean rebels were betrayed by the princes they fought for and who sacrificed them to reasons of state;

it was the armistice of Znaim, concluded by Emperor Francis I of Hapsburg following the defeat at Wagram, that left Hofer, a guerrilla fighter now deprived of all legitimacy, in the hands of the French and Bavarians. Great-power politics penalizes the Tyrol, but then it was for the Tyrol, not for the house of Austria, that Hofer and Leitgeb died. Or rather it was for a part of it, the German part, excluding the Welschtirol or the part which – according to the centuries-old nomenclature, only superseded in recent times – is properly the Südtirol. The champions of Tyrolean freedom sanctioned the division of ancient Tyrol and its unity, which dated back to 1254 and whose cultural fulcrum was in the southern part until the fifteenth century, after which it moved to Innsbruck. The patriots of 1809 split the unity of the Tyrol, separating the German component from its Latin counterpart and were then abandoned or annihilated by the German nation powers, respectively by Austria or Bavaria. As late as the Sixties Südtirolese terrorism would be marked by the contradiction between separatist nationalism and the tie with Austria or Germany.

Leitgeb fought for ancient liberties, but also for ancient privileges and servitude, against the introduction of the principles of equality and a social mobility capable of offering individuals new possibilities of emancipation. But the Napoleonic model of modernity that invaded the valley of Antholz with General Broussier's troops was also a totalitarian and levelling violence, which brutally destroyed diversity; in the reactionary resistance of Hofer and Leitgeb, which became the symbol of an uncompromisingly conservative ideology in the Tyrol, there is also the defence of real freedoms threatened by tyrannical projects. Leitgeb is an extra in the drama of modern history that seeks to balance Scylla with Charybdis, the violence of the part and the violence of the uniform whole, an unresolved impasse that still torments Europe and explains many of the ghastly centralizing modernisations and many of the visceral barbaric regressions.

When Leitgeb died, the third route towards a modern world, the route that the Enlightenment had attempted, was already closed – the enlightened absolutism of Theresa and Joseph, sensitive to diversity even in their projects for unity and respectful of tradition even in their impulse towards innovation; this third road had been vaguely marked out to avoid the Terror and the unbridled accumulation of early capitalism. But the Tyrol rejected Maria Theresa and Joseph II and embraced Kaiser Franz – he who had abandoned Andreas Hofer to his destiny – or in other words the reactionary Hapsburg restoration, antithetic to Theresa's innovations and responsible for so much of the Tyrol's ethical–political backwardness. Napoleon, the invader who had for a moment thought of creating a Swiss–Tyrolean confederation or of integrating the Tyrol into the kingdom of Italy, granting it substantial autonomy, had understood the particular nature of the country, even though the borders he imposed are those that divided it, briefly, in the most radical manner.

Leitgeb is also the name of the sawmill at the beginning of Antholz Mittertal, near the Gruber Stöckl – a little chapel in a greenish colour that makes one think of the sea. The walls are covered with the classic stereotyped images of the Via Crucis, the same first seen in the church of the Sacred Heart in Trieste. The wooden and brachycephalic Christ hanging on the cross is a man from these valleys, his features marked by generations of poverty and inbreeding. The days at Anterselva begin, on the first evening, before this crucifix in the dark and empty chapel; the past year is deposited beneath that wood, like a bunch of flowers or a rucksack taken from one's shoulders.

Behind the sawmill the road climbs steeply; from on high one can see the church, dedicated to Saint George, and all the village, with its new houses and roads that have grown clumsily around the *Kulturhaus* that bears the name of the mediaeval poet. The village is small, but during the evening stroll it dilates in the dark, it loosens into a yielding space. Space, too, not only time, is elastic, it expands and contracts according to what it is holding, because it is time coagulated, like people's lives. Between the two shops, the one that is also called Leitgeb and Handlung at the end of the village, the snow keeps and restores years and events, layers of time. All straight journeys, with a precise point of arrival, are brief, a few hours by train between Trieste and Milan, or by plane between Milan and New York. The evening stroll with no precise destination loses itself, caught up on half-buried wrecks that trip one up, sends one down paths that have been erased. It is like looking into a face, sinking into the waters of someone's eyes, being sucked into a mouth. The name Antholz, according to some perhaps debatable etymologies, may mean, "beyond the wood", the place on the other side of the great woods. Those dark deserted roads in the evening are beyond a forest, the one crossed leaving pieces of oneself among the branches, the thorny bushes, the rotting tree-trunks.

In 1856, not far from the Gruber chapel, in a house which is now a mere ruin, Lorenz Leitgeb, the Herodotus of the valley, was born. The priesthood took him far away. In the Austrian monasteries and in his frequent journeys as a missionary, Father Leitgeb was homesick for Antholz, but his superiors wanted him elsewhere. Finally he was able to return to the village of his birth thanks to a soporific sermon given by the Antholz parish priest. One evening, while the latter was preaching, a villager fell asleep and on waking up found himself locked inside the deserted church; to get out he had to let himself down from the belltower holding on to the bellrope, accidentally stopping the clock. Thus the parishioners asked for a preacher who was at least able to keep his congregation awake, and Father Leitgeb, known for his eloquence, was sent for. He spoke from the pulpit with great spirit and enjoyed his return home.

*

There is a funeral reception at the Herberhof; one of the valley's important livestock traders has died, father of ten children and holder of every possible degree of kinship. In the kitchen preparations are underway for lunch, following the set menu for these occasions: broth with sliced beef, wine and water; in the big dining room the tables are being laid. Jakob lords it from behind the bar. He is the master of the hotel, he always has been; even when he was out in the stable, the hand that gripped the pail full of manure kept all his brothers and sisters in order. Two or three of his siblings have gone, one never sees them at the Herberhof. When it came to it he simply left the stable and took his rightful place.

Exercising his domination openly, rather than in secret, has done him good. He continues to laugh often, but his quiet chuckle has opened up into an affable cheerfulness, into the *bonhomie* that suits a hotelier; even his movements are more composed, more self-assured. He adds up the bill with exceptional speed, pulling his pencil out from behind his ear. He sleeps in a fine room, with a woman who is from Romania. Lisa has nothing to say, when he speaks to her about it she shrugs. Konrad is almost off to do his military service and Jakob slips him some money, gives him a pat on the back, too, but he pays less attention to him now than he did before, now he makes sure that everything works as it should, especially during the high season. Only some evenings, when his sisters and brothers have already disappeared to their rooms under the stairs, he waits for a while, behind the bar, alone, a glass in his hand and a moist look in his eye. Sooner or later the Romanian will have to go, says Helga, either Jakob marries her or a foreigner can't stay for ever, and she's not even Italian, the police wouldn't allow it. Or perhaps they would? Anyway, it wouldn't be right.

The bells toll for the funeral, the coffin – nestling among fir branches and preceded by a big blue and gold standard – arrives from Niedertal on a cart drawn by a horse. There is quite a crowd, the deceased was an important man and death has no power to correct social hierarchies. *In Deiner grossen Barmherzigkeit tilge meine Schuld*, sing the three priests, "In Your great mercy free me from my guilt." The bellringer's sharp face looks out from the belltower, a boy from a painting by Brueghel or Bosch; behind him, way up there, another two or three wooden faces look hungrily at the crowd. Brachycephalic and hyperbrachycephalic Tyroleans, says the old illustrated encyclopaedia of the Hapsburg monarchy sponsored by the Archduke Rudolph – goitre and pellagra handed down through the generations.

Beyond the windows of the belltower, the sun illuminates the ice on the mountains, gold and blue tongues of fire. The bellringer leans out even more, the body that stretches and bends is the hooked beak of a bird of prey; beneath him the shadow of the big hand of the clock is projected onto the wall like a sundial and it moves slowly, at its tip it is slightly curved, a little scythe. The coffin crosses the cemetery that surrounds the church, wrought iron railings round the tombs, among many German surnames three Italian ones – Scanso, Benato and Amelio. Alois Niederkofler lived for a few hours or a few minutes, he died the same day he was born; Aloisia, his younger sister, was a little girl when she fell into the stream and drowned, 9 June, 1951.

The hymns and the prayers echo in the church. On the ceiling the dragon lanced by Saint George lies gasping with its tongue hanging out, a dog panting in the heat. Opposite the church is the Wegerhof hotel, which belongs to a Niederkofler. A building adjacent to it, the Weger-Keller, used to connect the hotel directly to the church; now reaching the Weger-Keller is more difficult, by means of a rickety stairway that takes one over wooden trunks and logs. In 1696 the innkeeper Andreas Gruber had the walls frescoed with a Dance of Death. The participants are the Emperor, the peasant, the soldier, the priest, the Pope, the maid, the lawyer, and Death and each one has his or her own line to say: I govern you all, I feed you all, I fight for you all, I pray for you all, I absolve you all, I seduce you all, I defend you all, I make off with you all.

The room is full of old tools – frying-pans, broken saws, rusty scythes, wooden yokes. No one, says another inscription, knows when this thief will come. Even in this modest reproduction of a stereotype the greatness of the Baroque resounds, its objective sense of the majesty and the nakedness of creation, that universality which recent European culture has made a mess of in the psychological–sentimental miseries of the vain little ego. In that Dance of Death there is the humility and the glory of a common destiny – being born, living and dying. The girl who announces, "I seduce you all," proclaims the absolute, the vanity of desire, and ignores all bourgeois squeamishness, the erotic Machiavellism, libertine cynicism and the sentimental rhetoric with which – according to his epoch and his social class – the individual who has lost the absolute seeks to replace it with remedies dreamed up out of his own private squalor.

In that unassuming Dance of Death there is an echo of Baroque music and its broad embrace; we who pass in front of it, skis on our shoulders or books tucked under our arms, we all have parts in the opera and we have to sing, each in our own way according to the whims of ideology or states of mind, some bravura to express the exceptional nature of our hearts. For the Baroque, the world is theatre, we go to the theatre to enjoy ourselves or to receive applause. Broch lamented that for the bourgeoisie the theatre had replaced the cathedral, but the worst thing is that it has also replaced the inn. Or perhaps it comes to the same thing, given that the inn, too, serves bread and wine.

A few metres farther on, towards Obertal, near Leitgeb's shop, there is a wood-inlayer's workshop. Outside the door there is a trunk with a monstrous excrescence, on the other side of which is a crib full of

Madonnas, Saint Josephs, animals, a religious humility in wood which domesticates even that evil protuberance. Woodcarving, which reached its height in the sixteenth century, is typical of the Tyrol and it knows nothing of rigid distinctions between sculptor, inlayer and craftsman – art is simply the hand that does a good job.

There are many guests at the funeral reception; it is all a general greeting and reunion, people have come from the various hamlets in the valley, they have not seen one another for years and they exchange news on families, comings and goings, admissions to hospital, and they sow seeds for a few good deals. Death does not dissolve, rather it binds; it is a rite of social cohesion, a centripetal force. A man who dies is a small star that implodes, acquiring density and mass and attracting to itself other bodies from society. Here and there one can see the centuries-old faces of the valley, cheeks ruddy with wine and toothless gums, but generally the features testify to a settled and continuous civilization, the faces are no longer those of the crowd who scorn Christ in the old altar panels of the valleys, rather they are the faces of a civilized and developed well-being.

Isidor Thaler moves softly among the tables like a leopard; he is drunk and cannot speak, but he smiles and bows civilly, slipping into the crowd without hurting anyone and without spilling the glass of wine he holds in his unsteady hand. All the village is here and even people from other villages in the valley. Here too is Rudi, with Elisabeth, his pretty wife. Rudi is a postman. As dark as a gipsy, crisp and fast-moving, he was the Adonis of the valley; a southern seductiveness made him irresistible to the pale and rosy little German girls and only his taciturn sobriety, which made him all the more attractive, kept him from taking too much advantage, from becoming a little Faust of Antholz – the joy and heartbreak of too many Marguerites.

He has been married for a few years now and is becoming ever thinner and more drawn. Elisabeth, his wife, has been filling out, her double chin deforms her pouting little mouth into a snout, but then her mouth widens into a look of insolent satisfaction, her eyes shrink between her red apple-cheeks, good enough to eat, her breasts have grown and droop negligently, her puffy hand is imperious as it orders Rudi to go and get her a glass of wine, to fetch her shawl, which she has left in the car, or to take her home. Rudi obeys and keeps his mouth shut; an empty and listless silence, different from the silence there once was. He stares straight ahead, empties his glass without listening to what others say to him, he gets up and follows his wife.

At the bar Huber, the baker, he too with a level of alcohol in his blood that is clearly over the limit, leans gallantly towards Viviana and tells her that next year Antholz won't be in Italy any more. In Austria? What do you mean, Austria? In Bavaria. And he fails to pick up on Maria's provocation when she butts in – ignoring his flattery – and asks if it will therefore be necessary to dig a tunnel running underneath Austria. The most anti-Italian of the Südtirolese look to Bavaria, even though, in the popular comedies that are performed almost everywhere in the valleys – in Niederrasen too – and which celebrate the indivisible nature of the *maso*, the cheat who pretends to love the beautiful land-owning widow often comes from Munich, the metropolis or the heart of big-city corruption, and in the end he is unmasked by a faithful young man who truly loves the widow and ties the knot, thus uniting the ace of hearts with the ace of diamonds and above all else saving the integrity of the land from the speculative clutches of the immoral financial capital.

Relations between the Tyrol and Bavaria have always been marked by ambivalence. It was the Bavarians, in the struggles against the Slavs between the sixth and seventh centuries, who definitively guaranteed the Germanness of the Tyrol – even though to the west it is the Alemannic element that prevails – of which their Duke Tassilo III is the first suzerain. Nevertheless, Meinhard, the count of the Tyrol to

whom the country owes in large part its particular character, resisted
the Bavarians with all his strength and turned to the Hapsburgs. This
clash recurred in the time of Margareta Maultasch and concluded with
a victory for the Austrians, which indeed signalled the end of Tyrolean
independence.

Generally it has anyway been the Bavarians who have been considered the foreigner to be fought off: in 1704 the Tyrolean peasants rose
up successfully against the invading Bavarian army, which had been
welcomed by the nobility; if the cosmopolitan aristocracy was therefore untrustworthy and pro-Bavarian, which at that moment meant
pro-French, the common people defended the soul and the soil of
the Tyrol. Andreas Hofer himself fought against the French and the
Bavarians – once again it was the peasant element that took up arms
for the Tyrol, the Vendée of the Germanic world.

The Bavarian constitution introduced into the Tyrol in 1808 set up
the dominion of the State-machine created in Munich by the minister
Montgelas, an enlightened and modernizing absolutism which aimed
to level the diversities and privileges of the mediaeval heritage. Hofer
and Leitgeb defended "their ancient right" against the universality of
Reason, which legislated under a unified code, and against Bavaria,
which represented French-style Reason. Things change slowly over
the following decades, which witnessed the progressive symbiosis of
modernizing authoritarianism and popular Bavarian tradition; from
this compromise the political cohesion of Bavaria was born, and Bavaria
gradually presented itself to the Tyroleans no longer as the invading
enemy, but as a sympathetic supporter of the Tyrol – even the terrorists
and the extremists, like Dr Burger, for example, given life imprisonment
in Italy for his activities yet acquitted in 1970 by a Munich court. In
any case, today Bavaria's charm centres above all on the Deutschemark
and for some years now Giuliano, in the *Stube*, has no longer been able
to say to the Tyrolean nationalists that if they want to be annexed by

Germany, then they should simply have themselves incorporated into East Germany.

There is a *jus loci* that has been in force for more than twenty years which guarantees that even on days when the entire establishment is reserved for a wake, there is a table for *cotecio*. "I'm going on to the end," says Sergio, worried that Traudl might block his twist. On winning four consecutive hands one has the right to attempt a twist, but with the risk of losing, or to decline the right to a twist and so render that game void. Going on to the end is not necessarily a mark of cowardice, of a lack of love for risk-taking; it is a guerrilla war with time, deferring so as to prolong the game and to put off the final outcome, which anyway is still an ending. Hapsburg civilization always went on to the end, procrastinating and putting off in order to survive. Gradually the wake comes to its end, people begin to leave, they wait behind a while to talk, to say goodbye, to empty a glass. There is no fuss, neither is there any disorder, everyone is composed and calm. It's not right, it's really not right, says Lisa. There was a time when the meals after a funeral were great – everyone cheerful, laughing and making a racket, singing, telling jokes. It really was fun . . . a party, even more so than New Year, not at all like this, I really don't know, I don't understand why. . . .

Heinz S., too, having drunk one last glass to the eternal health of the deceased, leaves the premises. He is one of the twenty-five young men who left on 25 November, 1939 for Germany, having opted to leave – together with the vast majority of the valley's inhabitants – cutting the umbilical cord between blood and land. He came back in 1941, others in '48 and in '56. In fact relatively few left and most of them returned, but the figure of the *Dableiber*, of those who at that time had opted to stay – renouncing German nationality – is a disconcerting shadow, the ghost of a foreigner. Literature has not ignored the option, but it has not been up to dealing with that laceration which is at once age-old and ultramodern, one of the many artificial and violent movements of frontiers in our century. It has featured in two plays, by Pircher and Riedmann and even, many years ago, in 1941–42, by Joseph Raffeiner, a writer destined to a sad fate: after witnessing the drama, with its element of power and protest, he became a Volkspartei and then a Heimatpartei politician, in other words a spokesman for officialdom.

It would be interesting to talk with Heinz about all this, but he is silent on the topic and his silence is fitting for the wound. A veritable *eingeklemmt*, a man stuck and blocked in – to quote Norbert G. Kaser, the writer who studiedly embodied this blockage in his own life. The most vibrant Tyrolean literature has assimilated this self-accusation, dressing up in it as evidence of authenticity and transforming it into a mocking and aggressive celebration. Tyrolean writers enjoy an enviable advantage – a petty political–cultural establishment which, in pro-claiming the pure, untarnished virtues of the *Heimat* and its tradition, involuntarily confers importance and authenticity on every deviation from this model, even banal albeit liberating deviations. Thanks to the often retrograde conservatism of official Südtirolese culture, it is easy to be the persecuted writer and to earn high regard thanks to the over-bearing hostility of the conformists. In a different cultural context such literary posing would be considered adolescent or pathetic, but in Alto Adige it still has a value as protest.

An obvious symptom of this backwardness is the posthumous canonization of Kaser: the sensitive, rebellious young man, unem-ployed alcoholic, Capuchin friar and militant Communist, suffering and sneering, a man who died very young after declining to complete any of his books, expressing himself rather in glosses and fragments, is not a bad writer, but the legend that has taken hold of him, a true hagiography of dissent, is the reverse side of the *Heimatliteratur* and its liturgies, which are certainly lacking in the land's real drama.

Tyrolean writers are obsessed by the frontier – by the need to cross
it and the difficulties involved in crossing it – and by identity, and they
search for this in a denial of the very compact identity that is so dear
to the cultural establishment of their country. With the painful but
facile, overdone rhetoric frequently found among frontier writers
(for example writers from Trieste), they are too willing to take up a
position on the other side as well – distressed and yet also delighted to
feel themselves Italian among the Germans and German among the
Italians, eagerly awaiting the brutal onslaught of the custodians of
the homeland's memory so as to be able to say, with ringing sincerity,
that the pain is in not knowing to which world they belong.

All this is literature, often good. As long as the angry, pugnacious
ideology of the Heimat exists in all its potency, there are bound to
be poets like Kaser who want to serve up the Tyrolean eagle roasted.
These writers are certainly the true heirs of that eagle, because Tyrolean
literature, even without going back to the mediaeval giants such as
Oswald von Wolkenstein, has by no means been lacking in voices
harshly critical of the gut instinct, the social exclusiveness of its own
world, as in the plays of Schönherr or Kranewitter and their desolate
pictures of peasant brutality. But now it is time for the Tyrolean eagle
to be roasted, eaten and digested once and for all, with no further
need to spit on its bones as well; indeed it is time to shake off the
polemical obsession with the border, to stop considering it a peculiarly
Tyrolean or Triestine problem and to realize that it can concern a
Milanese no less than an inhabitant of Antholz or the Karst. In their
scornful protest, many Tyrolean writers display sentiments that are too
benign, they espouse ideals of liberty, protest, deterritorialization,
Niemandsland. Praiseworthy sentiments and ideals, unlike those of
their detractors, but not really the stuff of poetry. It is no coincidence
that an author of the first rank like Franz Tumler went through a truly
horrendous ordeal, his youthful support of the Nazis, which he later

overcame, and which – obviously only because he had got over it – allowed him fully to grasp the nature of the Südtirol and the demonic link that might exist between a sense of the frontier and a sympathy for the *Anschluss*.

Südtirolese writers should be a bit – just a bit – less Südtirolese or rather less anti-Südtirolese and forget their umbilical cords. The new magazines – *Arunda, Der fahrende Skolast, Distel, Sturzflüge* – have tried to bring in some fresh air, but the photomontage of Andreas Hofer naked on the cover of *Sturzflüge* still smacks of Tyrolean infantilism. Solutions, however, certainly can neither be prescribed nor proscribed. Perhaps in taking his own life Klaus Menapace died of Tyrolean pain. His poetry, extraordinary vignettes of the charm and the pain of living, transforms the actual landscape of shimmering snow and woods, into landscapes of the soul, into a winter scene that evokes the places in which those images were born and immediately erases the memory. *Stärker / als alle Sprache / der Tod*, this "death stronger than any language" transcends any Oedipal complication.

Antholz Mittertal, as its name states, is the centre of the valley, but it is also the last true village. Obertal, Anterselva di Sopra, is not a village, but rather a scattered handful of houses, lacking centre and unity; indeed it has neither church nor inn. Like a river as it flows towards its estuary, like all existences, individual and collective, a valley loses identity as it gradually approaches its end. A few cottages, haystacks, a woodshed, a chapel hidden away near the bridge, with a Madonna whose heart is pierced and who has many ex votos, the stream that shines brown.

Climb up to the lake and come down the pass, while the rifle shots of the skiers training for the world biathlon championships reverberate; the echo of one shot lingers in the woods, memory superimposes it on other echoes and when it fades it is already another year – this time

Irene hasn't come, the baby has chickenpox, for two years Francesco
has been promising to make it at least for New Year's Eve. Isabella
flies past coming down from Wildgall, the halo of her blonde hair in
the wind is an aurora of the snows, the ice yields under her skis and
regurgitates black mud onto the white, the years tumble down the hill.

The lake used to belong to Enrico Mattei, it was his favourite refuge.
Whenever he could he took the plane, landed at Dobbiaco and came
to the silent lake; he would stay for a long time, fishing, walking, gazing
at the water. His fishing stretch was the object of some contention
between Passler and the Bishop of Bressanone. The people here loved
him and still remember him happily and with respect. Heaven knows
what it was that would make Isidor Thaler, stumbling and drunk
already at ten in the morning but punctual and careful in his job at the
Wildgall ski-lift, go for a drink with the mighty captain of industry.
Mattei was privately incorruptible, but for his far-reaching ends he was
ready to stoop to corrupt methods; he faced off the world's leaders and
knew how to advance the goals of unassuming post-war Italy, giving
her a place on the political and economic world stage, but he had his
part in her moral decline and thus diminished her as well. Perhaps a
common aversion towards capitalism instinctively united the followers
of Andreas Hofer and the unscrupulous modernizer, who was soon to
be victim of a criminal sacrifice.

Near the place where his house was, now replaced by a hotel, and
where there is a bridge that rises with Japanese grace over the stream
and the reeds frozen in fantastic lacework, a holy painting recalls an
ancient tragedy on the lake – a boat sinks and people drown while from
the heavens the Madonna and the saints look on in impotent distress
like the people crowding on the shores. Above the image an inscription
asks the passer-by, *Mein Freund, wo gehst Du hin?*, "My friend, where
are you going?" It is difficult to reply the way another inscription does,
on a house: I live and know not for how long, I will die and know

not where and when, I go and know not where, and it's amazing how happy I feel.

The lake is a spectrum of colours. The snow is white, at certain moments it is gold, when the wind lifts it and drags it across the frozen surface it is a silver dust, where the shadow begins it is blue. On the sides of the mountain it is ivory, pink, pearl-grey; in the evening the blue becomes wine-red. Goethe hated Newton because of the colours. If white, as Newton explains, is the presence and mixture of all colours, then that means that all hues die there, the differences expire and this white, these years mixed and melded in the snow are only a muffled ending. If white were original light, as Goethe believed, then colours would still be latent, to begin and begin again – the azure of remoteness, the red of a flower and a mouth, the honey of a look, these things would all come back.

The lake changes colours, the green of the trees is black, white becomes gold, a bronzed gold that gets darker and is suddenly blue. The edges, quick to dissolve, are sharp; one looks at the lake and the snow is white, the strip along the bank is blue, the pines are a dark green, the world is there, it exists, irrefutable and solid like the snow-ball that Lucina throws at Hans. Goethe, Newton, Schopenhauer, Steiner, Wittgenstein have written about colours; poetry and philosophy are also branches of general chromatics, science of the glare that flashes for an instant in the sun, of cheeks burning red, rubbed with snow, of hair that is black and then is white.

Beppino is obsessed with chromotherapy – sanatoria with verandas where for hours patients contemplate the hues and their changing, following rigorous medical prescriptions. There are those who need blue, those who need grey, those who need bright colours and those who need more gentle hues; one person benefits from an hour's staring at an intense reflection, another has to be more careful, even the sea shimmering and twinkling at noon can result in a sadness at heart, or perhaps a happiness so intense that it is akin to melancholy and there-fore should be dispensed in measured doses. Chromotherapy has been fashionable for years, books and newspapers have dealt with it, but everyone can testify that Beppino first expounded its virtues even well before the first ceremony of the diploma of loyalty to the valley, which one receives solemnly at the Herberhof, at the end of each decade, from the *burghermeister* of Rasun.

Up to the Stalle pass. Here, so the maps say, runs the border between the Mediterranean and the central European climates. *Mitteleuropa* as meteorology, it has been suggested. It is cold, the *Oberland* wind, which comes from the east, is freezing, everything is still whiter; the world empties, a bell jar in which there is only sky and snow, a bottom-less bluish white, which sucks things into the void. The wind is strong, one resists it a bit walking head down against the gusts, but the wind is stronger, it drags and carries away, everything is suddenly left behind and moves away. It is to late to "redo", at the most one goes on to the end and next year back up to the pass again, to look down into the valley – the lake is a burning torch, but before we go down it will have turned grey. The sky is high, the dome of a glass ball shaken to start the snow falling; there is a flurry of snowflakes and we descend quickly, among the flakes and the hours that fall in the dark. The sun sets rapidly but it is still early and perhaps we can reach Antholz in time to get the car and go to Brunico, to Schönhuber's. We'll buy another four coffee cups and a milk jug, says Marisa, so the sixteen-piece set is complete, including all the extras; then Francesco and Paolo can split it and have an eight-piece set each, which is something.

Public Garden

No dogs, no bicycles, keep off the flowerbeds. A beginning is often accompanied by a prohibition, even the beginning of a walk in a park, in this case in the Public Garden in Trieste. The main entrance is guarded by a barrier of wrought-iron lances, black as the shadows that spread on high among the big trees – horse chestnuts, planes and firs, dark waters on which branches and leaves float and into which the birds disappear and sink like stones.

The dense shadow of the park is a foretaste of the evening; it falls a little earlier and is never completely absent, but lingers here and there, thickened in the foliage. Coming out of the Caffè San Marco and turning left up Via Battisti and Via Marconi, or crossing through the Garden, which runs parallel to the latter, to reach the church of the Sacred Heart, one finds oneself by the main entrance and the monument to Domenico Rossetti, wrapped in his cloak, hand on chest. The marks left by the pigeons have dribbled down his face, leaving him with noble rivulets of tears. Three massive, solemn women, draped in gowns, are arranged around the pedestal in a spiral ascension, proffering torches, codexes of ancient statutes, branches of oak.

Patriot, philologist, historiographer and antiquarian, Rossetti was a patrician nostalgic for the old small-town Trieste and he did not appreciate the new, tumultuous, cross-bred city born of the prosperity of the port. "In Rossetti's land nowt but Italian be spoken," sang the irredentists in homage to the learned custodian of the homeland's memory, apotheosis of all that is Italian cultivated under the centuries-old Hapsburg rule. While Rossetti, for his part, had also written dutiful verses celebrating Austria and its mighty leader too (who was saved by Trieste in the end), hoping that perchance that day will serve to remind generations to come, that Austria alone can warm our hearts.

Like some female silhouettes of a certain age, Rossetti's monument improves when looked at from behind, when one has gone past it and entered within the Garden; the rear parts have resisted the ravages of time a little longer. The only attractive thing in the entire statue is a foot belonging to one of the three women, which protrudes behind the base. It is perhaps a touch too robust, but is nevertheless a fine, semi-naked foot, kicking out imperiously, heralding incontestable orders, as lapidary as the inscription written in chalk just beyond the threshold of the Garden, between the ban on dogs and the keep out of the flowerbeds: "Elisa I love you."

A boy enters, holding a little bowl of water in which a goldfish wriggles. He sets off along the avenue leading to the lake, a name which the pond merits, despite its size, because of the bridge, the swans, the tiny mossy grottoes and the island among the lilies. The boy does not look at the foot, nor at the admonitory notices, perhaps because, judging by the anxious way he peers into the bowl, there must be something wrong with the swollen, bruised fish, something which keeps him from paying attention to anything else. But he, too, pushes on into the intricate order of the pathways, and enters into the wood of injunctions and prohibitions that jump out everywhere from behind the begonias, the pansies and the daisies.

One goes to the Garden for diversion, to sit in the sun or the shade (according to the season), to relax. Even when simply passing through it to get from one place to another, thus avoiding the traffic on the streets – for example going from the Caffè San Marco to the church of the Sacred Heart in Via del Ronco – the ties loosen, walking becomes a toboggan run. On some benches pensioners read the papers, on others the grand manoeuvres of a sentimental education are beginning, just over there mothers are pushing prams, children chase one another along the paths and among the bushes, disappearing into thickets, hiding in a hollow tree, laying ambushes in forests of the great North or on the dry savannahs, they push one another on the swings; beyond the wood a bus goes past along Via Giulia, but the wood is boundless. The swing flies high and the world falls into a bottomless well, sucked down like the blood from one's face; when it comes back there's nothing there any more, things have been blown away, swallowed up in a vortex. Even the leaves of the chestnut tree, brushed against just an instant earlier while falling up on high, have disappeared, blended into a shiny milky void.

But the oscillation of the swing obeys the laws of pendular motion; the whole Garden is an initiation into the law and the proliferation of its codicils – even Eros, another science of licences, prohibitions and infractions. In that vortex, that wild flowering, in that breathless running and those whispers in the dark, sections and subsections, meticulous regulations, lie nestling. To play is to obey; you cannot transgress in the way you can out there, where the cars go past, where men fight with no holds barred, anything goes and all the rules are fudged.

In the Garden, on the other hand, when you play at hide-and-seek, you have to count up to sixty or thirty, keeping your eyes tightly closed. The bottle top filled with wax, with Coppi's or Indurain's picture on it, has to go back to the start if it comes off the Giro d'Italia bicycle track drawn on the ground in chalk. Playing hopscotch you jump from one

square to another on one leg only, at flags you can run only when
your opponent has touched the handkerchief. The park keeper, with his
uniform, can be eluded, hoodwinked, but his authority and the order
towards which it is directed are never up for discussion. It is the gang
leader who decides whether or not to go and annoy the couple cuddling
near the drinking fountain. The open area with the bikes for hire, next to
the café space where there is a cinema on summer evenings, that is
the territory of another gang and you don't set foot in it, you don't go
beyond the border marked by an almost black cypress.

The shade of the Garden, with its multiform spaces enclosed within
limited perimeters, is an introduction to the law and its close relationship with mystery. There is a rigour, a dark mystery, an ancient wound
even in the law that makes the fish in the bowl lose its scales and gasp.
No one – not just the boy who only a few days previously won the fish
in the Sacred Heart parish lottery in Via del Ronco and happily took it
home – no one really knows why that fish, rather than enjoying the
water and life and its bread crumbs, has to be ill and perhaps has to die.

Everywhere in the Garden, Necessity reveals itself. Things are and
that's all there is to it. Elisa I love you, the virtues and the merits of
Elisa matter not. The chestnuts fall from the trees, the spiky shells split
with a dull crack, the season advances to the drumbeat of war; an old
tree leans on another, a wounded warrior who wants to die on his feet.
Even Antonio, his smile never changing and always arm-in-arm with
his mother, propounds an enigmatic and binding law, and the children,
as they come out of school generation after generation and go to play
along the pathways, soon learn to look upon him as if he were a warden
too, but a guard from a special corps, with secret duties to carry out.
And it is this way even if without his mother he would never be able
to find the exit from the Garden to return home and neither would he
be able to count the change needed to buy a drink.

Certainly, in the beginning the new arrivals do not realize, and they laugh behind his back, sometimes they even throw stones at him and, if his mother is distracted or just out of reach, they grab the little bunch of flowers that he always holds in his hand; but then other children, who initially had done the same things and then they too had learned in their turn from older children who no longer go to the Garden, they explain and the newcomers understand Antonio's mission once and for all. Even the listless, imperturbable way he lets them tear the flowers from him is a sign of authority. Towards evening when he leaves with his mother to return home, the beardless man with his thin, white hair disappears into the shadow of the pathways in the same way that Father Guido – in the church of the Sacred Heart, where the children are sometimes taken to Vespers as they prepare for Communion – leaves the altar after the blessing and disappears into the sacristy.

Immediately beyond the entrance, the Garden is straightaway a dark forest; among the tree trunks and the branches the roller-skating rink shines white, a remote frozen lake among the mountains – the skates glide and the smooth stone under the rollers slips away with a glitter of snow, the wind blows in one's face and, even if the circular rink is small and flat, the wind that comes from far away sends one careering into a long, dizzy descent. Sometimes it is as though one were falling on high, as on the swing; the blue beyond the tops of the trees is a dazzling dust cloud, the ground under the skates creaks like the ice on a lake as it breaks, the rink dilates into a bright clearing in the wood.

Some of the trees around are old; a big plane tree sprouts protuber-ances and warts, sagging breasts, knotty excrescences. Old age is a chaotic exuberance; life grows, destroying its form and dying from excess. Just twenty or so metres from the entrance, to the left, along the path that runs alongside Via Marconi, between a lime tree with its heart-shaped leaves and a young elm, there is a plane tree with an open, hollow trunk – the cavity makes a good hiding place during the games and skirmishes. The tree is diseased, but it is good to be in there, protected from the insidious immensity of the world. The walls inside are damp; it is pleasant to coat one's hands with that watery soil in the darkness of the hollow tree, like handling sand and mud in making castles or making shapes from moulds. Outside the leaves shimmer, the moisture drips like saliva along the channelled walls and ends up in a small puddle, the drips gather in a clear pool, a baptismal font hidden away in the wood; to touch that freshness with one's hand, to moisten one's hot forehead and cheeks is a relief, even some birds come in to quench their thirst and bathe in that font.

A little farther off, in front of the statue of a woman with an eagle on her shoulder, donated XX.3.MCMXXI by the Milanese Honour the Army Committee, there is a bench in a fine sunny position amidst tufts of verbena. This bench warrants attention in as much as it is occupied very nearly every morning during the fine season by Mr C. and his wife, as inseparable from the Garden as the statuary herms scattered along its avenues. The pause on that bench – effected especially, but not only on Sundays – is an interruption in the walk which, having begun relatively early, later on, towards midday, brings Mr and Mrs C. to the other side of the park, to the café in the open space. Here at that time it is certain that someone from the usual crowd will have arrived, and it is therefore possible to sit down without ordering anything and to accept the coffee offered by whoever is already drinking his. The usual company consists of some lawyer or pharmacist and a few ladies who, in their duels to decide the place and time of a dinner and in their comments on possible matrimonial candidates for Doctor Krainer, a recently widowed notary, display a thirst for domination no less rabid than Lady Macbeth's.

C.'s vocation for saving money, a result of the poverty of his childhood and of his having survived it so long ago, is a philosophical profession that transcends his persona, to the point where seeing others squander money depresses him; he would never order a second coffee at someone else's expense. In essence he would be happy if the others simply sat down on that bench with him, where money cannot be spent, and if he goes to join them at the café it is only because he thinks it necessary to frequent society and to maintain appearances, as he has always done. Even in his youth when he worked his fingers to the bone in a hundred different jobs, he would stand and read the newspaper from the copies on display in front of the newsagent's and deny himself a sandwich, even while buying polish for his shoes so that they shone like mirrors on Sundays and holidays.

At the café or earlier, on the bench, C. exchanges polite banalities with his acquaintances which exhaust his expressive and intellectual faculties: the requisite congratulations for a good school report, remarks regarding obvious meteorological facts or regret for the fine things of yesteryear that are no longer to be found – above all, he says, the porcelain chamber pots that have disappeared from people's homes, and those fine brass spittoons in offices which unfortunately have not been seen for some time. Every now and then he stops, blinks and looks dully at the verbena or listens to the others, assenting sweetly with the impartial decorum of a public authority during an official ceremony.

Whenever possible, C. tells the story of his party card. He worries not about repeating himself, because the colourless and innocent life that he loves is all repetition – sleeping, getting up, shaving, opening the window, doffing his hat when he meets someone. As an emigrant in America he worked in a factory in the outskirts of Chicago, far from the slum in which he lived and, to save money, he would get up almost in the middle of the night, catch the train without buying a ticket and pretend to have forgotten his wallet when the inspector caught him and made him get off at the next station. Here he would wait for the next train, a slow one that passed every hour and he repeated the same scene until, alighting and reboarding at the three or four intermediate stations, he reached his destination.

C. recounted all these details with indifferent bureaucratic precision, as if recounting someone else's business, or as if he were the inspector writing up a report on a methodically recidivist passenger, without ever making reference to hardships or exploitation or struggles, words that simply did not exist in his vocabulary, just like the Latin juridical terms with which Doctor Krainer, in the café, loved to flower his discourse.

Returning to Italy after the crash in 1929 and finding himself unemployed, he was told that to get work he needed a Fascist party membership card. He did not have the card for the simple reason that he had left before the advent of the regime, and so he rushed to apply for one, without suspecting – as he fails to suspect even when he tells the story – that the imposition of the membership card was an abuse of power. His acceptance of this situation grew out of a vague but unquestionable respect for all authority that he had held since childhood – perhaps transmitted to him by the Austro-Hungarian empire, which he had neither loved nor hated but had simply accepted as reality. For him this was something that did not exist for people to reflect upon, but was simply there and that was enough. Fascism governed and gave work and therefore it was right that a worker should be Fascist.

He explained his situation in the office concerned, meekly recounting his story in all its details, including the getting up before dawn, to an arrogant functionary and when he was criticized for not having applied for the Fascist Party card in one of the party's overseas offices he replied, probably with the same uncertain smile and the same blinking of eyelids with which in the Garden he recounts his reply: "Perhaps I haven't fully explained: I was over there for work, to work, and I worked, I got up at four o' clock every morning and in the winter, but in autumn too, it was so windy and so cold – how could anyone, getting up at four and working all day, go around thinking about stuff like Fascism or membership cards. . . ."

C. is still surprised that anyone could ask such questions and he does

not think for a minute that the term "stuff" might have sounded offensive for the Fascist party, which he respected sincerely and as a member
of which he was neither happy nor unhappy but thanks to which he had
anyway sorted himself out quite well – a modest, satisfactory career in
the civil service.

C. grows old on that bench or at that table in the Café, a conventional, magnanimous man, totally unaware of the fact that he is
ageing, totally unaware of anything. Around him the Garden withers,
loses its leaves, becomes green again and he continues to respect
all authority and to praise the government of the day. That pure,
quintessential conformism unwittingly takes the mystery out of any
conformism of broader scope that tries to pass itself off as something
loftier, in the same way as his desire to dress like a gentleman and
to frequent respectable society transforms him into an impersonal alle-
gory, into one of those solemn statues with their sightless eyes,spread
through the park.

Gardening is the art of harmonizing, of transforming Nature into
artifice, taming the chthonic powers into the symmetry of flowerbeds,
or into Nature running wild under control. The gardener trims the
hedges, a healthy tulip stands out from the green like the handkerchief
that C. tucks into his breast pocket. The violets near the bench are dark,
the shadows of the cypresses lengthen over those dark patches and
over those who walk at their borders, covering the leaves of grass with
a Lenten drape. Persephone gathers daffodils, those violet patches on
the grass are already the night into which she will soon disappear. But
C. sits, a smart, obtuse figure, next to the wife he married late in life,
a so-called pleasing woman who in her time, before the marriage, had
raised more than a few eyebrows, to the extent that some gossip-
mongers had expected C., whose passional initiatives as a bachelor had
been limited to hygienic encounters with the occasional prostitute, to
be unequal to the expert sloth of his attractive consort.

But the fact is they are always together and look perfectly replete, and his wife's beautiful pouting mouth is ever sweeter, ever kinder; she, too, has learned to bat her eyelids with that look of surprise, she likes to see people pass by and to exchange greetings without asking anything more of life. It's as if, after the racy tales that had all who knew her nudging and winking, she had learned to listen and to savour the rustle of shared time as it passes. If anyone at the café starts gossiping about failed marriages, marital incidents or new combinations of couples, they both keep quiet. C. is a firm supporter of the indissoluble bond of matrimony, above all because he finds it hard to keep up with the changes and the substitutions, to keep up to date with new pairings and to learn new names, to be careful not to put his foot in it.

C. contributes towards making the Garden reassuring, making one forget the cut flowers, all those shadows in that area. "What a fine gold-fish," he says benevolently to the boy passing by with his goldfish bowl. "Very nice, well done," without looking at the fish, which is almost belly up in the water, nor at the face of the boy, which gives nothing away.

Dominating the central flowerbed, whose circumference makes it suitable as a unit of measurement for long-distance races, (thirty laps, for example, constitute a considerable run), stands the bust of Muzio de Tommasini, leader and then mayor of Trieste until 1861. He was also the man behind the Paupers' Hospice and the Natural History Museum, not to mention his illustrious work as a botanist – he discovered more than thirty plants, and in 1854 he created the Public Garden. "In execution of a City Council resolution, and with intent to form a public garden, which is to be of use principally to youngsters of tender age, landowners are invited, if prepared to relinquish their ownership, to make offers of sale, indicating location and area in square Viennese *klafter*, asking price, and other relevant conditions. From the Civic Magistrate, Trieste, 25th day of September, 1852." At the land registry it was called "of the nuns", because it used to belong to the very reverend Benedictines.

Tommasini's statue, sculpted by Donato Barcaglia from Pavia, stands among the begonias, tufts of blue ageratum and daisies. In the midst of these plants hens, chicks and roosters scratch away in freedom, having come to prevail over the more prestigious species of birds, thus altering the traditional equilibrium of the Garden's fauna and maybe pointing towards a mutation of domestic animals, their slow return to the wild state that may well be a prelude to the similar regression of other families that have been laboriously domesticated and civilized. To the right of the flowerbed a plane tree of enormous dimensions, deformed by a gigantic protuberance, extends its branches horizontally to the point where they bend towards the ground; one branch which reaches out farther meets a branch from another plane, forming a triumphal arch opposite the gate leading onto Via Giulia.

When Tommasini negotiated the purchase of the land, Via Giulia was a stream in the midst of rows of mulberry trees; the Patok came down from San Giovanni and was much appreciated by the washerwomen who rinsed their linens on its banks. Patok, Staribrek, today Via dello Scoglio. The stream comes down from the small Slovene quarter and before one can wring out a shirt, at the level of the Garden it has already become an artery in a heart that beats for the Italy of Garibaldi and Mazzini. The water gurgles, carrying away the chatter of the washerwomen as it cracks the skin of their hands, fine robust, reddened hands that know what's to be squeezed and wrung; those hands deserve other games, but in that dirty freezing water they soon wear out, and yet the washerwomen chatter on and sing lustily, even though the song of the flowing water is always the same and everyone knows how it ends, *Why do you betray me? Why do you leave me? Before you loved me you weren't this way.* That water washes away the dust, the sweat, the effluence of the body in its slow dissolution. Life is deposit, oxidization, coagulated grease on plates and blackness under nails, yellow rings on underwear, the sad mark of Eros, and it requires detergent; even the rough soap those girls rub with will do.

The suds flow down, elongated in dribbling patches and disappear into a gutter at the edge of the Garden and in the meantime from San Giovanni a Vodopivec comes down or goes up into the city and becomes a Bevilacqua. The Patok flows from Slavia into the Mare Nostrum, Italy becomes a crucible for those who come from far away and soon these people feel themselves to be as Italian as those who bear a Venetian or a Friulian surname; the youths who in the Great War go off to be cut down on the Carso in order to unite Trieste with Italy have names like Slataper, Xidias, Brunner, Ananian, Suvich. But the hotch-potch thickens, elements are exchanged and balance one another; the frontier city is threaded and scored with frontiers that sunder it, scars that do not heal, invisible, ineluctable borders between one paving stone and the next, violence that calls forth violence. The water runs reddish in this gutter, history's menstruation; first my turn then yours, but in any case in that muddy water it is impossible to tell blood from blood.

The washerwomen see everything, but they are there only to wash, those Moirai with their peeling hands do not weave cloth, they only put it in to soak. They rub and rub at underwear and collars, and the fabric wears out with all the cleaning. The chattering drips as water chatters; from one bank of the Patok to the other it is all an echo of voices and blethering, Judgment Day gurgles in the drain. The stream has been covered since 1863 and now it is Via Giulia, the karstic river has descended into our veins. Giacomo enters the Garden from Via Giulia to play at cops and robbers, and years later to go and collect his children who are playing at cops and robbers. As a child he said his first words in Slovene, with his mother, at San Giovanni, but when he heard in 1945 that the Slavs had killed his father, an Italian, he became and was for many years a neo-Fascist, one of those who, had he been able to, would have forbidden his mother to speak her mother tongue. He loves his mother and she dotes on her grandchildren, and they in their turn know nothing of these stories, which in any case they would not be able to understand, stories which even for him are now lost in the past and almost beyond comprehension.

Let's play at being Indians, let us all take all the atavistic rancours, the arrogance of the majority, the resentment of the minority and throw it all in the stream like dirty washing. Gutters and canals lose themselves in the open sea, the ship weighs anchor and the wake is left behind for ever with the rubbish.

In the Garden it is the cats who hold pride of place. One could easily carry out a reliable census of them, because the feline population of the Garden is stable, intruders are rare and deserters rarer still. The generations are there for the studying, the destinies of the litters, the establishment of new families, the nexus of intermarriages. There is a central multi-branched dynasty founded by a large, black, one-eyed tomcat, who has no need to spit and hiss in order to defend his territory, together with a dull tabby, a scrawny, nervous creature, at odds with everyone. There are a few neurotic specimens around thanks to Luigino; whenever he sees one animal grab another by the scruff of her neck and hold her down miaowing, he thinks they are fighting and separates them just at the crucial moment with buckets of water.

The cat does nothing, he simply is, like a king. He sits, crouched, lying down. He knows the score, expects nothing, depends on nobody, he's sufficient to himself. The cat's time is perfect, it expands and contracts like his pupils, concentric and centripetal, no relentless anxieties to wear *him* down. His horizontal position has a metaphysical dignity that man has generally unlearned, for the most part. Man lies down to rest, to sleep, to make love, always to do something and he gets up again immediately after; the cat is there simply to be there, as one lies down by the sea simply to be there, in easy abandon. A god of time, indifferent, unreachable.

There are dormice and hedgehogs, with their homely friendliness. The birds, so many birds; in the evening their song begins suddenly, all of them together, a wind that rises among the leaves in a deafening rustle which after a while one no longer hears, like the rumble of a waterfall. The occasional gull, coming up from the sea, glides slowly, far from his usual territory. The owl, on that hollow plane tree again, is like an old aunt, a bore when she gets in touch but greatly missed when she keeps herself to herself. Most of all, however, there is the falcon. At least they say it's there, that it comes down from the Carso to look for prey. Actually they say it's a kestrel and that they've seen it with its bluish-grey head, its yellow breast spotted with black and its white-tipped tail. Someone saw it hanging motionless in the air, like the Holy Ghost, barely moving its wings, and Lucia says that near the lake she saw it dive on a worm so big and fat it looked like a grass snake; the bird tore it up with its beak and devoured it.

Actually sometimes Lucia says that that worm was eaten up by a fish, in the lake, sucking it up slowly like a piece of spaghetti. Perhaps both things are true, because there are worms enough for fish and birds of prey, even though nobody has ever seen such a big one. Birds of prey don't live in gardens, says Bruno, maybe just to annoy Lucia because after all what does it take for a falcon to come down here from the Carso? One swoop and that's it. And then if it really is a kestrel, perhaps it lives nearby, in some old house, or in the Sacred Heart belltower, a stone's throw away.

It comes down towards evening and they say it's the dormouse it's after. The dormouse is sweet and polite, he ought to be protected from predators. He could easily stick his head out; the kestrel, its sight so sharp, spots him and comes at once, but when you see it circling you throw a stone before it gets its talons on him. Towards evening you take up position. The sky is a deep blue, the sunset runs along the tree-trunks, bloody resin, and there's a bit of blood on your skinned knees too. A bat flies very close for an instant, while its shadow passes under the lamp that wavers in the avenue, it's huge, you feel its wing on your face, as big as the night. The night is high and looking up there gives you vertigo, the world is a word repeated until it loses all meaning.

The forest around you is already dark. A deep breath passes through the leaves, the wood is a den that welcomes and protects, inexhaustible, and it makes you feel that no one is more important and lasting than a rotting leaf or a trampled berry; that scratching, chirping, cracking is an impartial law and there is nothing to worry about if a cricket suddenly falls silent. The forest is all around, but you are not in the forest, invisible thresholds bar the way; there too, sitting in the tall grass under the pine and the elm challenging the ban, chewing and spitting out a bitter leaf that makes your mouth salivate, you are outside, excluded from the wood, which perhaps begins a metre farther on, but you cannot find the entrance that leads to all that gnawing and chattering.

Perhaps the kestrel is in there too. Nonsense, the kestrel lives up on high, not in the bushes. It's no wonder it doesn't come, with all that noise, people on the paths talking, the car horns blaring in Via Marconi, a little girl shouting. You'd have to prepare the ambush carefully, evacuate the Garden and close off the roads running alongside, hide and wait. That way the kestrel would come, big in the sky, you'd see it fly like the Holy Ghost for ages, just as the others have seen it. It's always other people who see things, all you can do is have them tell you about it and then tell others, until you believe you have seen them.

But the kestrel isn't big, it's small, perhaps it wouldn't even manage to get the dormouse; maybe it is here, but can't be seen in this fading light. But then it's not even the right time, the kestrel isn't a nocturnal bird of prey. The owl is though, and there is one of them and it goes "tu-whit, tu-whoo". It must be wonderful to hover motionless up there in the air, almost like managing to enter the wood, right into the thick of it. The hours, the minutes pass, the stars twinkle beyond the branches, candles on the Christmas fir tree, they fall into the black bottomless night. It's getting on for supper, and time to go home.

As in all self-respecting parks, the Garden has herms and busts dedicated to the city's illustrious men, and in a couple of cases their fame has gone beyond the city limits and has spread throughout the world. Scattered along the walks, underneath plane and chestnut trees, the solemn heads are a reaffirmation of *civitas*, noble cultural memory against the indistinct nature of the forest that envelops and entices, even in these reduced dimensions. It is above all the light that dilates space with the variety of its gradations, as though in coming into an open space from a path or coming out of thick vegetation, one crosses a time-band; where the leaves grow thicker it is already evening, while a clearing shines in the morning brightness and under a vault of branches the air is veiled in a glaucous underwater green. To leave the Garden, to emerge in the city, is to resurface out of deep water.

The busts are peaceful, reassuring; their teacher-like solemnity knows nothing of that suggestion of enigmatic melancholy which normally emanates from even the most commonplace statues in the solitude of parks. But in the Garden, dedicated as it is to childhood and the healthy education of children, there are no silent, awestruck goddesses, sirens of remoteness and the void; instead we have honest busts of worthy citizens, solid examples of virtue for children and adolescents. The marble heads carry a particular authority and dignity. The moustache of Riccardo Pitteri, poet, the hair of Riccardo Zampieri, journalist, the lyre and the laurels of Giuseppe Sinico, musician, these are the image of a paternal nineteenth-century decorum that keeps watch, ensuring that in this realm of childhood and adolescence, everything goes as it should. More recent and more soberly stylized, the bronze heads are even more discreet, they do not sit on an ideal podium to dominate things, but they hide themselves away, like Giotti's – a slender bird hidden among the leaves, worthy of one of his reticent poems.

Joyce is there too, with his pince-nez and hat, appropriately positioned behind the screen of the open-air summer cinema, appropriately because of his passion for the *cine*, acquired here in Trieste together with many others . . . a passion for the inns and for dialect, so fitting for the interior monologue and the ventriloquist's murmur of History. Years of Trieste and of *Ulysses*: the cafés, a mediocre city, impure and full of yearning like life itself, the English lessons given to clerks and merchants unaware that they were providing faces and gestures for a modern *Odyssey*, his family and the children, the urinal in Piazza delle Poste where the publication of *Chamber Music* was decided upon. A letter to Svevo of 5 January, 1921, in which he writes of the novel, "*Ulysses* – a Greek mother, a sea of a book", in a play on words which constitutes the best definition of the work that summarizes twentieth-century literature and which is in some way connected with the dubious honour of those enterprising women from the Greek colony of Trieste and of more or less all mothers and all seas, Greek or otherwise, promiscuous womb of myth, uterus of civilization from which are born the bastards who criticise one another's respective ancestry – even Maria Theresa, responsible for the fortune of the Adriatic port into which people of all types arrived to mix and rinse their origins, she too is a Great Mother.

"And Trieste, ah Trieste ate I my liver!" It is also a city that gnaws at one's liver, like Ireland, an unbearable and unforgettable Oedipal womb, dangling promises of happiness and disappointing immediately, and leading to the obsession of continually speaking ill of it, but of anyway continually speaking of it. For the English teacher who in the pub of an evening, merry or even rather more than that, says to hell with everything, even the Oedipus complex, Trieste is an anachronism and a *nebeneinander*, a beach littered with the detritus of History, in which everything and its opposite rub shoulders – Italian nationalism and Hapsburg loyalty, Italian patriotism and German and Slav surnames, Apollo and Mercury. In that cul-de-sac of the Adriatic, History is a tangled skein.

This contiguity of the seedy and the sublime is life's hybrid, which eats the liver but also warms the heart, and Joyce becomes the poet of this warm life, a classical and conservative writer – despite the verbal subversion – the heir to a tradition stretching over several centuries which confirms the values, the sacredness of the flesh and its withering, of the nuptial bed and procreation, of the home and the family. If other great bards of the twentieth century – like Svevo – narrate the disturbing odyssey of man as he alters his own thousand-year-old physiognomy, Joyce recounts that of man who remains equal to himself and who at the end of his day returns home, to his same identity. Joyce's individual words surprise the reader, but his story comforts, fulfils expectations, retells a story that he already knows and which he must listen to again. Even the dirty words of the dialect of Trieste can serve this end to perfection. At least, or rather above all on paper: when Svevo, as he talked, let himself go with some juicy expression, Joyce indignantly rebuked him, saying that such things may be written down, but never uttered.

Joyce's bust tips us a wink, probably in appreciation of the fact that the bust of Pietro Kandler, prestigious historian of Hapsburg Trieste, is sited opposite the urinals. Below Giani Stuparich is the inscription, "Gold Medal for Military Valour – Writer", while under Slataper, curiously, only the Gold Medal is mentioned. Slataper is the soul of Trieste, a soul that he discovered and invented; he dreamed a great aurora of the spirit for the city while it was on its way towards its sunset and he tore from this sunset the light and glow of a true dawning. He founded Trieste's culture while declaring that Trieste has no cultural tradition; the spiritual act of birth is a diagnosis of death and absence.

"Triesteness" was born with Slataper, and Triesteness is adolescence, senility and lack of assured maturity; utopia of real life and disenchantment because of the absence of real life, all combined under the dominion of a moral will that imposes a way of living as though the radical experience of civilization's discontents had never existed. To claim to live is megalomania, says Ibsen, and Slataper, who wrote the great book on Ibsen, decides to be a megalomaniac and dies. War is the future of these youthful lives who dream of life but sacrifice life to its dream and who are ready for sacrifice and self-sacrifice.

Triesteness – vitality and melancholy, nostalgia for purity that is perfectly aware of all the compromises but even when indulging them does not forget what they are and is not taken in by them. Adolescent need of the real life, senile awareness of the false life; all that's left is a binge in the pub.

Busts are not appropriate for Slataper and his generation, but they are the sad truth of that great generation that was burned out in its green youth. Theory is grey, says Mephistopheles, but the tree of life is green. Slataper's generation created Triesteness by denouncing the reassuring busts, the museum of traditional and systematic knowledge that makes for rigidity and eludes the drama of existence, inserting and neutralizing all phenomena in catalogues and classifications.

Trieste was even the site of a Nietzschean battle against fossilized culture with a European dimension. Triesteness is also (perhaps it is above all) this green vitality liberated, with all its adolescent bitterness and clumsiness, from the greyness of civilization. This generous, liberating impetuosity is fatal, because it tears from civilization's discontent the mask of noble decorum that allowed us not to look it in the face and thus discovers that real life – and once looked upon, one is no longer satisfied with the usual lies – real life is inaccessible. Whoever sees this bare truth dies. To come out from the comfortable stuffy atmosphere of the cafés and the libraries – full of smoke, of stale air, of chatter thick as a protective blanket – and to venture into the green, where one's lungs are not used to breathing, this is lethal.

The busts and the herms, in the Garden, are funerary statues. Slataper dies, and others with him. The companions who outlive him die in another way; to forget that unbearable revelation they become custodians of the knowledge, of the greyness that they had dreamed of destroying and which they are now trying to rebuild like a wall to protect them from the green. They become high-school principals, experts in classical studies, promoters of admirable and erudite local-history societies, frequenters of museums which tame the disorder of existence; the erstwhile haruspices of unease grow old dreaming of writing a great book about life, so as then to be able to start living, or covering up the debris of their dream with learned memoirs and bibliographies. Whoever reaches the green dies, like Daphne fleeing from Apollo; whoever manages to pull himself back in time is entrenched in the greyness he once held in contempt. In the meantime the boy, still holding his fish, has gone beyond the busts and is near the lake. The Garden is the promise, but is also the cemetery of real life.

One day the Garden is empty. The sirens sounded the alarm almost an hour ago and everyone ran into the air-raid shelters. They are bombing Trieste, though without trying too hard. Someone says that the British have had a tip-off from a spy, according to which the Germans have been doing experiments with heavy water at the observatory and they've sent the bombers over to stop them making the atomic bomb. But for the boy left alone in those deserted pathways, the only certain thing – although he has an imperfect awareness of it, the fact being as abstract as the pathways from which everything else seems to have been sucked up – is that his parents, from whom he slipped away while they were all going to the air-raid shelter, will be beside themselves as they look for him everywhere.

This emptiness is different from the one created gradually each evening, when everybody goes. No one has ever come in here, no one has ever seen those trees, those benches, those flowerbeds; an outer envelope has come unstuck from things, like the skin of a fruit or a layer of skin from a face, and those things are there, frozen, the landscape of a planet never seen before, not even with the aid of a telescope. The looks that land on things, like the hands that touch them, leave their mark, they crumple them and consume them, give them a little heat, just like clothes in being worn: they make them familiar, used, close at hand. Today that reassuring oxidization, which derives from the presence of humans, is not here; it has been scraped away and the Garden is naked. The flowers sit in their beds, stupid, dilated. The branches scratch the sky making black scars. Some conkers fall from the chestnut trees and explode, the air is a pane of glass that breaks because of some unbearable ultrasound, from the sky comes a rumble, the sun is white, wan.

Perhaps that vacuum means you have finally entered the Garden, through all those gates that usually bar the entrance to its secret heart. It is not possible to keep count of the laps as you run round the flowerbed, but you must run, run all the way round, forwards and backwards, masters of the Garden; you are master when you are alone, the only one, when there is no one left any more. A cat, in the bushes, looks on listlessly; the slit of its narrowing pupil is the strip of sun that disappears below the horizon. A livid wind beats piles of leaves, the statues have no arms and legs, a people of cripples and mutes. Very high walls surround the Garden and the sky too is a wall against which the branches stand out, cracks appear and spread out in many places, the walls begin to crumble, everything is silent, an enormous collapse.

It is so strange, little by little, to hear the usual noises once more, to recognize that that is a bench where many people have sat, to feel remorse and fear for the anxiety of his parents as they search for him. On the way home, even before crossing the gate, one feels that one is once again outside the Garden, that the immense vacuum has collapsed, contracted, has returned like the genie into the magic lamp and has disappeared, a berry buried in the thick of a bush.

The busts are exposed to the sun and the rain, as they are to the many birds of all kinds, pigeons especially, which leave more visible and lasting traces on them. The effect of this supplementary decoration varies from case to case. On the drawn face of Silvio Benco, in which the sculptor sought to express the fire of a troubled soul, the excremental marks that have rained from on high appear as spiteful vandalism, Nature's insult to the nobility of the spirit and old age. A few metres away similar signs of the birds' aerial passage seem less out of place on Umberto Saba's face, as it directs a lecherous, avid sidelong glance at some appetizing incarnation of the warm life that is presumably passing along the avenue at that moment.

Familiarity with all the vital bodily fluids, with the slime out of which life is formed and with which children are not afraid to dirty themselves in their games, is appropriate for the poet who had no qualms in expressing the age-old longing, the desire that goes beyond good and evil. Saba is the animal who has little acquaintance with the modesty and the regret of which he himself speaks in a great poem about old age, he is the predator that pounces on its prey, with a greed mingled with tenderness, love, lust, the will to power, and devours it without distinguishing a kiss from a bite. His poetry is great, of an intensity and a fullness that is rare in twentieth-century works, because of its sharp and ruthless transparency that reveals the dark underside of life and its impulses, its grace and its untameable cruelty.

In Saba there is also ancient pity, sagacity, lucid intelligence, simplicity, painful love of life that make up, in unity and harmony, the "voices vainly discordant" of life itself. That painful love is a relentless affirmation of the pleasure principle despite the inevitable victory, biological and historical, of the death instinct. Saba has the strength of innocence, an innocence at once clear and clouded, tender and cruel, like that of a boy who is enchanted by a flower but squashes an insect; it is the wild innocence of one who accepts life completely in its grace and in its feral nature. In this inextricable vortex of desire, never sublimated nor repressed, love and intimidation co-exist and often coincide, the clearest azure and the dirtiest mud; Eros as dedication and Eros as violence. In the absolute clarity of *Mediterranean* "reckless love" is painful passion and sordid profanation, moving nostalgia and calculated domination, torment, enchantment and abuse.

Those marks spurted out by the birds do not disfigure Saba's bust, which knows not disgust for any vital humour. Like children, Saba is capable of finding pleasure in covering oneself with any slime and extracting from it the purest of pearls. He is beyond that contradiction between green and grey, because he is beyond good and evil – he wallows in life, in its seduction and in its secretions. Unlike the other busts in the Garden, his bust, in its sagacity and lechery, is not a funerary monument.

The pigeons that besmirch the city's glory have not escaped the notice of the competent authorities. A city council resolution, distributed in the Eighties to the leaders of the local wards for their consideration as established by Article 17 of the code, suggested culling the local pigeons (*Columba livia*), given their worrying demographic increase. Making reference to the danger of contagion from infectious diseases transmitted by the pigeons, authoritatively described by a physician from the public hygiene office of New York, the council, "having ascertained . . .

beheld . . . noted . . . requested . . . all that is heretofore stated", provides for the capture of no fewer than two thousand pigeons and their transportation to outlying areas, naming the company to whom the job is to be entrusted.

The project receives support from the custodians of local history, upset by the insults heaped upon the busts of illustrious men by the pigeons as they streak through the air, prone as they are to dysentery. The war against the feathered tribe, greeted enthusiastically in the Garden, finds support elsewhere too, for example among the vendors and customers of the city's large fish market, where the pigeons have excellent nesting positions and love to swoop over the fresh fish stalls, with unpleasant consequences for the produce. Nevertheless, there is strong opposition to the project. Protests come from animal rights' associations, volunteers who distribute food to flocks of birds, both in the Garden and under the windows of the offices where the repressive initiative was born. Reports from police, their suspicions alerted by the extravagant abundance of the feed, which suggests considerable resources, reveal the existence of wills and donations made in favour of the pigeons.

The opposition is cock-a-hoop when the results of some bacteriological tests show that the pigeons carry no diseases dangerous for humans and when a University of Rome Professor of Infectious Diseases challenges the opinion of the physician from New York. Mediation between the two opposing groups is attempted, but with poor results; the Trieste section of the Animal Protection League agrees to the destruction of the pigeons' eggs, but the council is not able to organize a sufficiently large workforce to cover kilometres of roofs, gutters, cornices, dormer windows. In the fish market the application of a coating designed to repel the pigeons without harming them ends in disaster.

Providential aid then arrives from a town in Calabria, keen to establish a fraternal link with the city dearest to the heart of all Italians: the town asks for a few hundred pigeons to populate its squares and immediately it receives a few thousand, packed with all due care and sent by rail. Soon after, as the thank-you telegram states, and in the presence of the local dignitaries presiding over the ceremony, the pigeons take to the air in a radiant sky – symbol of an ideal twinning.

But Trieste still has too many pigeons, occasioning a variety of increasingly chaotic initiatives: furtive capture of the birds at dawn, loaded onto a truck and freed on an unidentified "mountain"; a suggestion to move them all to Alto Adige, perhaps in the unconscious and deplorable desire to see them fly over the spick-and-span little houses of the Schützen, leaving traces of their passage on the pretty window-boxes; the suspicious offer from a Piedmontese company to repopulate areas lacking in *Columba livia*, an initiative that is blocked because of rumours that the company was supplying pigeons to shooting clubs. Even during these phases there was no lack of enterprising underground warfare – automatic nets thrown in the Garden and elsewhere to trap the birds, commando groups to sabotage the nets.

The story culminates and ends when the council, taking advantage of the decline in the taboo surrounding the contraceptive pill, resolves after much debate to purchase massive stocks of corn treated with hormones for distribution among the feathered population; this despite reservations on the part of certain Public Health officers who fear terrible consequences for anyone who eats a pigeon that is on the pill. A Swiss company, ideally neutral in vexed questions of ethics, is invited to provide the medicated corn; this is duly sent to Trieste, where bureaucracy, with its combination of nit-picking and inefficiency, blocks everything. The product, having come from Switzerland, has to be taxed, but Customs do not know which category it belongs to, whether medicated food or alimentary medicine. The product never manages to clear Customs; thus a procedural quibble interrupts the

struggle against the pigeons' demographic exuberance and allows the
birds to continue flying in swarms targeting those below, even the
bronze and marble busts in the Garden, a small animal vendetta on the
majesty of History, which for the animal kind, even more so than for
mankind, is nothing more than a slaughterhouse.

The large plane tree that forms a triumphal arch opposite the entrance
on Via Giulia has a venerable majesty and brings to mind that other
ancient plane on whose branches Xerxes hung a precious necklace, in
homage to its age and its dignity. When defeated at Salamis, however,
the powerful king of the Persians had someone give the sea where he
lost the battle a good lashing.

General D., well read in the classics and therefore well acquainted
with those episodes, enjoys walking under those branches out of an
instinctive love for anything and everything that evokes glory; his gait is
haughty, worthy of an imperious sovereign, but he is more like the king
who has the sea whipped rather than the same king who bows before an
ancient tree. His carriage never varies, stiff and slow but upright, as
those who see him take his daily constitutional always in the same part
of the Garden can testify, but it is difficult to say for how much longer it
will continue this way. Neither the general nor the doctors know yet
with any precision, although the latter have communicated the ultimate
verdict directly, with no pretence, in a manner befitting an old soldier
who has never really given much weight to others' lives, nor to his
own, and it was anyway the manner in which he himself had asked to
be informed.

General D. learned to love the green, the shade of the trees, way
back in his childhood in the sunny Sicilian city in which he was born.
Since he retired to Trieste together with his wife, returning just once a
year to his lands in Sicily to dress down and browbeat a bailiff or two,
he goes to the Garden for his walk every day at the same time. For some

time now, in a departure from his usual itinerary, he has occasionally been sitting on a bench, writing on some sheets of paper in a large hand. He is polite, he responds to people's greetings, but he discourages any attempt at conversation. Even though he talks with almost no one, he is one of the most popular figures in the Garden – perhaps because he is so tall, so unusually haughty, absolutely a-Triestine, so Norman–Sicilian. They say he treated those of inferior rank with harshness and contempt. They also say that he was equally contemptuous of and offensive to the SS officer who came to arrest him in 1943, and who, in view of his response, sent him off to a concentration camp.

Since the doctors let him know about the cancer and its being at an incurable stage, General D. has not interrupted his walks and neither, for now, has he interrupted any other habits, but he has decided to spend the last months of his life preparing the answers to the condolences his wife will receive on his death, condolences from the highest-ranking officers on the general staff. He works as he walks; he thinks of names, jots down those who suddenly come to mind, carefully reconstructs the shared experiences with each of the future sympathizers, to prevent his wife from making any mistakes. "Your Excellency's grief at my husband's passing away – he always recalled the years you spent together at the Academy. . . . General, Sir, I am touched by your concern for my grief; just a few days before dying, my husband was telling me how during the African campaign your division . . . "

Rumour has it that there are already many letters, kept in stringent order, simply awaiting the moment when his wife will have to copy them; by hand, the General has said, and that's that, wives do not discuss but simply obey, like everyone else. Authority is the true form of goodness, as in this case where the husband, thoughtful beyond death, spares his consort the pain of thinking and composing.

General D. trusts no one; he wants to manage his own life and even his own death – anyone else would botch it, as usual. The General looks at the old plane tree, but he does not bow to it; he bows to no one, not even to God, who thinks He can frighten him with that inordinate multiplication of cells. He is used to fighting superior forces and he certainly never panics. For as long as he can he gives as good as he gets. That tree too, if he could, some time, he would have it felled. He fully understands those lashes of the whip with which Xerxes punished the sea; a good flogging is never a mistake. Those letters are his whiplashes, the gloves he slaps in God's and destiny's face, that way they'll learn just how a man can thwart all their battle-plans; he always did like Prometheus, who told Zeus where to get off.

Prometheus, too, he considers, had a bird of prey gnawing at his vitals, but that is no reason to offend him with one's pity. Just as he never had any pity for others during his lifetime, so now he does not even think of devoting any to himself. Nor indeed to that fish – he sees immediately, one glance is enough, that it's going to die, he has an eye for death – and certainly none at all for that boy, who sits for a moment on the bench near him, the bowl in his hands.

On 3 May, 1945 the New Zealanders were in that avenue. They had just arrived in Trieste and the city was drawing breath, although it was not to last long, following the fright of the violent irruption two days earlier of Tito's IX Corps. The New Zealanders in the Garden were driving about this road in jeeps, throwing oranges and chocolate to the people around them. A memory surfaces, almost certainly false and yet indelibly imprinted on the boy's mind: in the Garden a New Zealander throws an orange from his jeep and the boy catches it, as if it were a ball. It must be a story someone told him, perhaps one of his schoolmates later on, someone to whom it actually happened or maybe the school-friend had heard about it from someone else. Perhaps on that day his parents did not even let him go to the Garden, because of all the excitement and the tension out on the streets, and anyway he had never managed to catch a ball, not even when playing with his friends. And yet he sees the soldier's face, the place in the Garden where the event (never) took place, the reddish, spherical orange, a golden apple from the Hesperides. Perhaps we remember not so much the things we live through, as what we are told. It is always to other people that things happen. Memory is also a correction, adjusting the scales, justice giving each his deserts and therefore restoring to us whatever should have been ours by right.

The most unusual bust in the Garden belongs to Svevo, so fond of those benches and those paths, where Zeno walks with Carla and where Emilio, in *As a Man Grows Older*, meets Angiolina. Reality and chance display an inventiveness worthy of the great writer according to whom, as he was wont to say, life is original. Svevo is not far from Joyce and from Saba, near the little lake and the silt on its banks. On the marble base is the inscription, "Italo Svevo. Novelist. 1861–1928", but above the base there is no head, all that is there is the pin which is supposed to support the head, looking like a miniature neck.

The reason for this acephalous state is not clear. Anyway, it is the third time someone has deprived Svevo of his head: it happened in 1939 and again immediately after the war, when, so the story goes, Cesare Sofianopulo – painter, poet, translator of Baudelaire and devotee of shoreside sunsets, whose angled rays, he said, made women's dresses transparent – claimed: "This time it was not me." Whatever the motive behind the mutilation – theft, vandalism, fetishism, restoration – it is most likely that the competent authorities will immediately take steps to remedy the situation and reintroduce the park's visitors to Italo Svevo, glory of Triestine and universal literature, complete with head. In any case one cannot but admire the genius of chance that, out of all possible candidates, chose not to deprive Pitteri, Zampieri or

Cobolli, of their heads, but Svevo, the great, ironic narrator who once said that absence was his destiny.

That missing head seems to be one of the many misunderstandings, wrong turnings, failures and shocks that litter the life of Svevo, a writer who plumbed depths of ambiguity and emptiness, who grasped the extent to which things are not in order and yet continued to live as if they were, who revealed chaos and pretended he had not noticed it, who realized just how little there is to desire and love in life, and yet learned to desire it and love it intensely.

This genius dug down to reality's deepest roots, witnessed all identities changing and dissolving, and lived the life of a respectable upper middle-class family man and loving father – but he found things often going awry. He was a *schlemiel*, the character from Jewish tradition who always finds a spanner in his works; one of those irreducible unfortunates of whom it is said that if they were to set themselves up selling trousers, men would be born without legs, one of those clumsy and intrepid collectors of troubles who pick themselves up, quite unbowed, after each fall.

Svevo's story is woven through with tragi-comic incidents: there was the failure of the first novels, his family's benevolent disregard, for many years at least, for his literary endeavours, there was the card with which one of Trieste's leading citizens to whom he had sent a copy of *La Coscienza di Zeno* [*The Confessions of Zeno*], wrote to thank him for his wonderful novel *La coscienza di ferro* [*The Iron Conscience*]; and there were many other misunderstandings, failures to act, funny and sad mix-ups that became proverbial. His work and his existence orbit, without ever losing the capacity to love and to enjoy, around voids, around vertiginous absences concealed with a sphinx-like smile, around daily failures both comic and tragic, around the lack and the nullity of life, around the vanity of intelligence. The acephalous herm is therefore appropriate and it should be left as it is, a worthy monument to one of the great writers of the century, Italo Svevo, the bourgeois Triestine Jew Ettore Schmitz, of whom it is said that an old office colleague, on hearing that he had written some novels, exclaimed surprised, "Who? Not that jerk Schmitz?"

Scattered throughout the garden, the busts are especially concentrated around the lake. The vegetation is thick, tight-knit. Plane trees extend long branches that dip almost to the ground before leaping up again; sombre patches consisting of oak saplings and holm oaks mark the general brightness – a liquid gold that runs down from above the branches and flows into the opaque water. The lake is yellowish, greenish, covered with rust-coloured leaves and lilies, soft as jellyfish; it does not reflect the sky and the world in a mirror purer and more real than reality, as the romantics would have it, rather it tones down the images, clouds them. Muddy water of a childhood that has still not been separated from the womb of things, in which the boy does not yet look at himself and does not feel the pain, the awareness of being sundered from world.

Walking through the flowerbeds to reach the shore is not allowed, but the sign does not repress the temptation to play with that slimy soil on the banks, to model a tumbledown castle and to sail a paper boat. Big fat goldfish swim amidst the slimy grass and the reeds, a swan glides by regal and unresponsive, mud and sand make the brown water shallow and make it seem deep. Tiny grottoes covered with moss gurgle, trickles of streams flow down through rifts and gorges in miniature. One throws crumbs to the fish, some sticky worms even, and one tries to discover where the croaking of a frog comes from – it is constantly heard, but never seen. Hands linger in the water, yellow with sand and as tepid as milk fresh from the cow. Colour of urine and gold, the slime that creates life in all its warmth; that fluid is not so much different from the blood that absorbs the food digested by the gastric juices, reaches the heart and colours a love-struck face. The world floats on those waters like a spent leaf rich in larvae, sheltered from the storms, because here there is no wind, no swell.

The boy carrying the bowl has reached the lake. He walks into the flowerbed near the bridge, extends the bowl with the fish over the edge. Perhaps for the first time he is aware of his face reflected in the yellowish water, sees the tears gathering in his eyes. His fish, won in the parish raffle, is ill and it will die in the little water there is in the bowl, but perhaps, they say, it might get better in the lake. He tips the bowl over, his fish falls into the lake and descends towards the bottom, where one can just make out tufts of grass and pebbles, like the tesserae of a mosaic. The fish wriggles, red, twisting like a wounded, bleeding finger, a farewell is a knife that hurts and splits the world like an apple, the world that will never be whole again. The boy is here, on this side of the bridge, and the world is over there, on the further side, where his fish has disappeared, to live or to die. There's a fish in the church of the Sacred Heart, too, drawn on the floor, in a mosaic; it's swimming and has a name written with strange letters from a strange alphabet . . . something to do with Jesus and it means saviour, Father Guido explained it. But the other fish, the red one, is lost, for the boy at least; it has gone. A few tears run down his face, he wipes his slightly dirty cheek and spreads more dirt that ends up in his mouth and has a brackish taste.

In the main open area there is above all else the café and, in the fine season, the cinema. The man who runs the café, Benzini, also takes care of the exhibitions and the meetings of the Trieste Artistic Circle – and the regional grape show held every autumn – as well as the concert evenings, held in the winter in the Circle's headquarters and in the summer in a bandstand. Franz Lehár comes too, to conduct Smareglia's *Cavalcade of Fire* and the *Istrian Anthem*. In the summer, among all the various bands that come to play, there is one called the "Abandoned and Vagabond Youngsters".

The passage of time is marked too by the old cast-off material piled up behind the Circle's headquarters; among the grass and various old tools, faded rusty signs mention vague and in any case interminable works in progress. At the café mothers sit with their children in prams or on bicycles. The children are nice, but their mothers even more so, especially in the summer, with their arms exposed; the beautiful mouths drinking coffee or eating ice-cream are expert and satisfied. It is other people's mothers in particular who are beautiful. As a result of going to the Garden every day, throughout the course of a never-ending childhood, the Oedipus complex undergoes a small, precocious change at those tables out in the open. From the mother in the strict sense it is transferred to those additional mothers who sit every day at the same table, bestowing their caresses and confidences as generously on their friends' children as on their own.

They pick you up, stroke your face; the hand has long fingers, tender, strong, imperious, the red nails caress the cheek with a teasing threat full of flattery, the wide sleeve slides back from the naked forearm, all unaware. When they kiss a little boy, their mouth passes close to the lips before being planted on the cheek. Mrs Tauber has a pert nose and a slanting look; from the moment when she playfully perches her friend's son on her shapely thigh, as though he were on a rocking horse, the game's up, with long-term consequences.

Fathers and husbands are rarely to be seen, at the most they come to collect their family on their way home from the office at lunchtime. Every now and then some regular from the café comes to sit down, some rather elderly gentleman who savours that feminine fragrance or some slightly pathetic bachelor who gets into coversation with the ladies, trying to show off nonchalantly about some good book he has been reading. Nothing untoward happens in the Garden, no dangerous liaisons are formed, not even potential ones. Whether those things happen elsewhere, no one knows. The mothers are all for their children, especially for other people's children; the mothers are their harem and each boy is a sultan who passes as whim dictates from one woman to the next. Mrs Tauber is happy to make a present of a chocolate; she unwraps it with her pink nails, gives it a little bite and then puts it in the boy's mouth, pushing with her finger.

The adjacent open space cannot boast concerts with Franz Lehár nor other historical memories, but only a stand with bicycles for hire. This stand is very popular and indeed constitutes a sort of wayside station on the itinerary of a sentimental education, between the café's junior seraglio and the shadow of the bushes or the benches just a littler farther off, where, later, more decisive discoveries are to take place. Elena rides a bike; she has fine, strong, slender legs above her white bobby socks. Her nose is bold, her mouth, wearing a pout more often than not, is a rosebud – a rose with thorns; when you pluck up the courage to ask her to take a ride together on the bikes she will perhaps say yes, but then she turns her head, contemptuously, and sets off alone without another word, her small unripe breasts already hard beneath her blouse. It would be nice to be able to tell her about the fish, perhaps she would feel like crying too and that would be wonderful. But it's pointless chasing after her, she would get angry and besides, she's the faster rider.

Once she says yes, we can go round together, around the central flower bed, but she wants that little tin ring, copper-red, the one in the window of the trinket shop in Via Marconi, just as you come out of the side entrance to the Garden, the shopkeeper is an old man who always wears a beret. When the bicycle wheel gets blocked, she runs out of patience because you don't know how to mend it, she looks critically at all that vain fussing around the wheel and the hub and off she goes, leaving the bike too; the idea of holding her by the arm and telling her to carry on playing together, even without the bicycle, is too risky – she's capable even of scratching you.

She goes off and the bicycle is left there, it really is a disaster not being able to repair it, perhaps all it needs is a bit of oil; if you knew how to sort out that wheel everything would be different, you'd be riding round together and she wouldn't be disappearing down there, along that avenue. It's as though they should all stay there for ever, playing in the Garden – even Anna, her friend, a soft and flighty moon of a girl – and then instead they go, they both disappear so quickly and that's the last you see of them, all you can do is take the bicycle back to the man. Mohammed knows all about it, when he promises celestial pleasures and not only celestial with girls of one's own age; right from those first preludes girl playmates are the hardest to get through to, the hardest to keep, and their escape is the most painful to bear.

On summer evenings, in the main open space in front of the café, there is the open-air cinema, run by Mr Voliotis, who, after a few summers, has started running porno cinemas in other neighbourhoods of the city. Of course you have to buy a ticket, but you can also see the films from Via Volta, from just beyond the perimeter of the Garden. When they show *Mutiny on the Bounty* you can see the sailing ship on the high seas. The film is not in colour, but the immense black sea is blue, deep blue, and the white horses are brilliant white, a far-off smile like those remote islands. The mutineers disembark from the ship, the water breaks white on the sand, a strip of snow. Even though the film is in black and white, near those shores the sea – which farther away, down in the background is a sombre blue – is emerald green, the sea bed is a turquoise prairie marked with patches of indigo. There is no possible doubt, you hear those colours like a music, they arrive on a long breath of wind.

Even at Barcola – where you go in the morning, every day in the summer, to swim from the rocks – the sea has a deep breath, it is a great blue in which the sun's rays tremble and bend, spears that snap in the waves, but on that screen you feel the colours even more – the colours of things, of their proximity and their remoteness, of the tangible world that exists out there and benevolently reaches the cerebral cortex, red, blue, yellow, to let itself be seen touched, desired; like a flower, it dresses in loud hues to attract insects. The screen is large; with that ocean swell, waves running wildly into one another, it seems to dilate, to become larger than the Garden.

Before going home one has something in the café. Mr Voliotis would gladly stop longer, if he were not so busy with the other cinemas, especially the porno ones, which really are a worry because, unlike what you might think, very few people go to them. Anyway, one has to cater for all tastes and not only for the people who come to the cinema in the Garden. Mr Voliotis enjoys a chat; he is already thinking about Christmas and says he would like to spend it on the Nevoso with his children and grandchildren and attend Mass at Ilirska Bistrica, in the chapel at the foot of the mountain. The screen is extinguished, swallowing up the years that slip like a train into a tunnel, and one goes from the Caffè San Marco to the church of the Sacred Heart in Via del Ronco, passing through the Garden for a breath of fresh air, through forests, lagoons, cities, mountains, snows, seas, and it becomes clear that it was all there already, from the beginning, and if later, in some other place, one stopped in a clearing or noticed an effect of the light or a shore, it is because they were recognizable and had already been met with in the Garden.

From the open space, following the bend of the avenue that drags out like a wave, one goes down towards the side exit that leads on to Via Marconi, to the right for those who come from the café or from the bicycle shed. It's late, it's been a long time. Plane and chestnut trees – gradually on getting nearer the gate they become larger, towering arches, even the canes are thicker. Under that vault the boy returns home without his fish, and with nothing else in his hands.

The Vault

He wiped his hand over his face, felt it moist with sweat and mechanically dried it with his sleeve. It was hot, unusually so, because the Garden was always cool, even in the summer. A few drops slid onto his shirt and his neck, he lifted his head and realized that it was starting to rain. Big heavy drops from a sultry summer storm; they slapped onto the leaves of the plane tree and the horse chestnuts, exploding loudly near his ears and even the odd chestnut fell too, splitting open with a dull crack. Those blows resounded in his head, he felt the blood beating in his temples; it wasn't strange, with all that humidity, that he had developed a migraine. His father used to get them often too. The more time went on the more he resembled him, in ailments as well; the moment had come to do as he had done and to follow him, to go over his steps again quickly, yes, to shorten distances visibly.

He came out through the gate on Via Marconi, slipping on the wet ground and getting back up again. He had always gone through there when leaving the Garden – that was the exit. It was raining hard now, a rain that obscured the houses behind a grey beaded curtain, increasingly thick and dark. He headed towards the church of the Sacred Heart, to wait inside until the storm passed over.

Outside a small trinket and toy shop the water beat against the window violently and like a glass magnified a small tin ring on a stand, it shone big and golden, a gold the colour of flame. Behind the counter he saw the face of an old man, beret on his head, grinning and making a gesture of invitation, a slightly equivocal one. What an idiot, offering those children's trinkets to a grown man running soaked to the skin, chilled to the bone. But maybe not, perhaps it was basically just shelter and it would be worthwhile buying something to get out of the rain, that little tin ring, for example, which must cost next to nothing. But his feet were strangely faster than his thoughts, which choked up and remained behind, lost in the water flowing away along the gutter; he had already turned the corner and was in Via del Ronco, in front of the church. The massive, rough walnut door was ajar, the opening just wide enough to squeeze in sideways, with difficulty, and enter.

The church was dark, half empty, Mr Beniamino was lighting the candles. So he was still alive and did not even seem to have aged much. Perhaps that was because of the life the sacristan lived, a life he had always envied him; actually, maybe he was still young enough, if he sorted out all the other things, to become a sacristan. Freely, just like that, without making any claims and without anyone expecting that he himself should be devout, but simply willing to do all that was necessary for other people's devotions: preparing the altar, laying out the white cloth and putting water in the ampullae, lighting and putting out the candles, taking the collection and putting up parish notices on the door, and then a drink with someone in the café opposite and off home – what a full, regular, deep life.

He plunged his hand automatically into the holy water, almost as though washing off that sooty rain which must have gathered up the smog of the entire city as it travelled downwards, because his hands and his clothes were not just wet, but were dirty, blackened, as though spattered with mud. He went towards the lefthand side of the nave,

the women's side, being careful to step in such a way as to place a
foot, one after the other, in each square, alternately white and grey, of
the chequered floor. The floor was paved in Aurisina marble, the same,
he thought, as the family tomb in the cemetery in Sant'Anna. Each step
was a letter and the game was to find immediately a word with as
many letters as the number of squares to be crossed in order to reach
the wall of the nave.

The distance seemed considerable, he had not been in the church for
years and he didn't remember it being so big and he thought quickly
zitolo-zotolo, perhaps because just before he had seen a see-saw in
the corner of the Garden reserved for the smaller children, next to the
sandpit and the slide, its two extremities going up and down. But
he realised that the word was too long and so he tried to find a rule
that would establish a correspondence between letters and paving
stones, so as to allow him to reach the wall and the end of the word
simultaneously. For example three letters might correspond to one
square of the pavement or once three and once one, alternately, that
too was fair. He was disappointed in the end when faced with the
remaining squares, because the word had finished with the previous
one and he was left with a sense of disorder, of failure.

Perhaps it was because he was in the women's side of the nave and
he should have been on the other side, as on Sundays. The niche for
the baptismal font, sunk in the shadows, looked like a hollow tree, the
cavity of that great plane with its open and empty trunk in which you
can curl up and hide, protected by the dark. Outside the leaves rustled;
the big tree was diseased, but the water that gathered in the puddle was
clear, almost white in the obscurity, and its freshness eased the febrile
heat that parched his lips and his cheeks.

On the wall the border that delimited the lower band, decorated with
geometric figures nestling one into the other – rectangles within
diamonds in their turn within circles – was an undulating stripe, a sea

wave that flowed towards the altar at the end of the nave and rolled in a curl that fell and then started to flow once more, one wave after another moving and breaking at the foot of the image of the Virgin, protectress of sailors and star of the seas, high above the waters with her ultramarine mantle. He let himself go on that wave, sliding with it along the wall. Outside the storm must have become even more intense, because the noise was louder now, a prolonged and growing thunder roll, almost uninterrupted. Behind the apse windows, with their depictions of the saints, the sky was black; every now and then a livid, scarlet light illuminated one or another of the figures for an instant, and even the red colour in which the interior of the church was painted became darker, extinguished in a burning shadow.

That wave dragged him but he was also being pushed now by so many people; there was a whole crowd now, evidently they had all come seeking shelter from the storm. In particular there was a crush near the door because those arriving were frightened of being left behind and they pushed those in front of them. Some had brought in big bulky bags, as big as suitcases, and they sought to find room for them between pews or behind columns. In the press he found himself crushed and squeezed from all sides, almost suffocated but at the same time supported, because otherwise, with the weakness making his legs give way and his head spin, he would probably have fallen, just as had happened at the exit from the Garden.

He let himself be pushed and squeezed in the rolling crowd, closing his eyes. When he opened them again he found himself very close to a woman's face, a bitter and contemptuous face, the mouth beautiful and cruel, and the nose imperious; the eyes were looking elsewhere, ignoring him. The crowd pressed them, he felt her breast, hard and taut against him, a full, firm moon; the nipple pierced him like a lance, penetrating his flesh, and he let himself go, responding as strongly as he could to the pressure. Her hand, a fine hand with long fingers

ending in predatory nails, came up for a second to arrange her hair at
the back of her neck and he saw the copper-red tin ring on her ring
finger, and then it went back down and disappeared in the press.

As it disappeared he tried to follow the hand with his eyes, looking
down there in that fusion of bodies; the soft white foot stroking his
own foot belonged to another woman, the shapely leg rose up to a
provocative, soft bosom, to a vaguely familiar face that smiled at him
brazenly, while her half-moon eye winked invitingly to a man near
her. He would have liked to kiss that foot, he let himself be pushed
and crushed with shameful pleasure, he tried to get near those breasts
and to touch them, in the crush he suddenly had the impression that
the hand which had sunk into the tangle was squeezing his penis and
testicles.

But what am I doing, he said to himself, this is indecent, in church of
all places. The foot, the hand and the two faces had disappeared into
the blackness the people formed, the blackness that had pushed him in
front of the confessional, with its three wooden arches in walnut. The
old gold-coloured velvet curtains opened and he found himself face to
face with Father Guido, who stood up and stuck his head out of the
confessional. For the first time he noticed that he looked a little like
his father, on his face there was almost the same expression of justice
and respect. He was no longer ashamed now; he could say anything
to Father Guido without embarrassment or feelings of inferiority,
as though to an old tree, to that plane in the big open space in the
Garden, for example, where the bicycles were, and that little girl just a
moment ago, with the ring on her finger, she got on and pedalled with
her fine legs and her white ankle socks, then she got off and started
playing with a hoop, skilfully making it spin and roll, following the wave
painted on the walls, until it crashed into the tree. The plane tree was
big, enormous, its branches lengthened and extended beyond the
entrance to the Garden, in Via Marconi, the leaves trembled above him.

"Don't worry," Father Guido was saying to him, "this is what we're here for, there's no need to be afraid." "So it's not a sin? If at least we weren't in church . . . " "And where else could you be, if you're tired and you want to rest awhile? There's shade here, and bread and wine." Among the inlay work in the confessional a strange design stood out, reminding him of an inn sign. "Do not worry about what people think, it is holy oil that greases the axle of the wheel when something blocks it, like that time with the hub of the bicycle in the open space in the Garden. Rinse yourself in that spring," and he pointed to a mosaic below the altar, in which under a night-blue sky, which was also the background of a dark and familiar wood, two deer were bent over drinking the purest water from a small spring hidden in the forest, "but do not look down on the mud with which you have dirtied your hands making sandcastles, because it too is destined for humility and glory."

"Look up," and he looked up and saw on high, on the walls of the central nave, the large figures with their solemn gowns and imperturbable expressions, *Charitas Humilitas Iustitia Oratio Contritio*. "I have taught you to look things in the face, peer to peer, because no one, not even God, has the right to make you lower your eyes, least of all now. The mud of the lagoon flows and dissolves, and soon it is as pure as the sea. Do not be afraid."

The darkness of the church in that moment was a nocturnal sea that enveloped him sweet and fathomless, waters of brown eyes in which he had abandoned himself from the beginning and for ever, they shone in the dark above the Pannonic cheekbones and he was swimming confident and happy, not the brief fits of just before, but a strong overwhelming pleasure, peaceful, the love of a night, of a lifetime. The waters were dark but here and there they were clear too, there was a white beach and pebbles on the bottom that could be made out one by one, like the tesserae of a mosaic, and clear too was the fish drawn in the mosaic with the Greek letters on its belly, ιχθυς. A boy put out his hand towards the fish that was sinking through the water, then he started eating chocolate, dirtying his mouth and his face, but the tears that had come when the fish disappeared in the pond washed it all away.

He wanted to ask something else, but Father Guido shook his head. "Can't you see how many people are waiting for confession, do you think you're the only one and that the others have time to waste on your whims?" The queue was indeed long, and in continual disorder with other people breaking into it, people carrying blankets and some even had cooking stoves. Father Guido too came out of the confessional, took off his stole and started fussing around a camp bed for an old man who could no longer stand, brushing off those asking for confession with impatient gestures, as though saying that there were more urgent things. Quick, we're off, he seemed to say, as he distributed the people among the pews with the grand gestures of an orchestra conductor, as though leading a choir in the conviction that making music was just a question of moving one's arms up and down.

But he had no time to worry about the priest, so surprised and distracted was he by all those who had come to say goodbye. Everyone was there, school-mates, friends with children and relatives, the concierge from the building opposite, Antonio with the saliva dribbling from his chin at each convulsive jerk of his head. Outside the din increased, a crashing noise as though houses were collapsing, an incredibly strong wind made the church shake like a ship; the air that could just be made out through the windows and the stained glass had an acid colour, intolerable, as though rays of an unknown wavelength were reaching the retina with unbearable violence, announcing something that not even the herald angel, alongside the altar, could imagine. He felt a disgusting taste in his mouth and a weight on his stomach, he would have liked to spit out, even vomit the obscene images that came to him from the dark like bats, the flash of that cruel grimace on his parents' faces.

Throughout the church people were saying goodbye, shaking hands, some embracing. He squatted down, leaning on a column. He felt his hand being licked, a small tenderly rough tongue that passed over his skin with its salty taste. Buffetto squealed, he took him in his arms, glad that they hadn't left him outside, in the rain, or alone at home. It must have been Mother who remembered him, she never forgot anyone, maybe she'd run out and picked him up, in that hurricane, she was never afraid of anything. The guinea-pig cleaned its ears conscientiously with its paws, stretched out in a curve in his arms and started dozing, contentedly, oblivious to the chaos.

He was not surprised to see her alongside him, others too were settling down on the floor; he was not completely sure he had recognized her, it was her but not only her, and yet that tender and ironic sideways look, those pronounced cheekbones, that dress with its marine colours – there was no mistaking them. "Your trousers are all creased, I'll sort them out, I've even brought the iron with me," she told him. The photographs, too, she added and showed him an album, leafing through it in reverse, starting from the last page. "They've just taken this one, right now," and indeed the snapshot showed them there sitting on the floor, next to the column – her with her dress the colour of the sea at Miholaščica and him with Buffetto asleep – looking at the album. Then the hand leafed through the album ever more quickly, Christmas trees, diving from the rocks at Barcola, trips out on the Carso, the images flowed increasingly rapidly, mixed into an indistinct vortex, the speed superimposed and dissolved them, time rose to an uncertain trembling, perhaps it was the light of the candles flickering in the wind blowing through the church.

Go to sleep, she said, I'll wake you when it's time. He lay down. Above him the apse curved like the vault of the sky, a sky of flaming gold that darkened into a night blue. Many stars fell and sank into that blue blackness, they lit up and went out like the flowers drawn for a second by fireworks; up there or down here it was all a flowering, a feast, every single thing that fell into the abyss was the budding of a flower in the darkness, but he was afraid of falling, he held on to the column so as not to plummet. Where the golden sky finished and the blue one began, two large angels held on their outstretched arms two flaming hoops on which there was something written in Latin.

In order to dive into that sea, he was to jump through those hoops, and their tongues of flame. He didn't want to, he gripped the column, squeezed and crushed some wet leaves whose presence there on the floor was a mystery to him. Jump, they said to him, but he pulled back. "You'll see, there's nothing to it," but this was another voice, or rather two voices, almost identical to his own – his sons who had filled his house, his days, his life – and they told him not to be afraid. So everything is alright, he heard, we can jump, and he took her hand while Father Guido went up to the altar and started the evening service.